Out of Print

Newspapers, journalism and the business of news in the digital age

George Brock

KoganPage

LONDON   PHILADELPHIA   NEW DELHI

First published in Great Britain and the United States in 2013 by Kogan Page Limited

2nd Floor, 45 Gee Street	1518 Walnut Street, Suite 1100	4737/23 Ansari Road
London EC1V 3RS	Philadelphia PA 19102	Daryaganj
United Kingdom	USA	New Delhi 110002
www.koganpage.com		India

© George Brock, 2013

The right of George Brock to be identified as the author of this work has been asserted by him in accordance with the Copyright, Designs and Patents Act 1988.

ISBN   978 0 7494 6651 0
E-ISBN   978 0 7494 6652 7

British Library Cataloguing-in-Publication Data

A CIP record for this book is available from the British Library.

Library of Congress Cataloging-in-Publication Data

Brock, George, 1951-
    Out of print : newspapers, journalism and the business of news in the digital age / George Brock.
       pages cm
    ISBN 978-0-7494-6651-0 (pbk.) – ISBN 978-0-7494-6652-7 (ebook)   1. Newspaper publishing–Great Britain–Finance.   2. Newspaper publishing–United States–Finance.   3. Newspaper publishing–Economic aspects–Great Britain.   4. Newspaper publishing–Economic aspects–United States.   5. Online journalism–Economic aspects–Great Britain.   6. Online journalism–Economic aspects–United States.   7. Press–Economic aspects–Great Britain.   8. Press–Economic aspects–United States.   9. Digital media–Economic aspects–Great Britain.   10. Digital media–Economic aspects–United States.   I. Title.
    PN5114.F5B76 2013
    070.50942–dc23
                                                                                          2013020898

Typeset by Graphicraft Limited, Hong Kong
Print production managed by Jellyfish
Printed and bound in Great Britain by CPI Group (UK) Ltd, Croydon, CR0 4YY

To my father

CONTENTS

ABOUT THE AUTHOR

George Brock is Professor and Head of Journalism at City University London. He worked at *The Times* for many years, including as a correspondent, Foreign Editor, Saturday Editor and Managing Editor. Before that he worked as a reporter at *The Observer* and for the evening paper in York. He was President of the World Editors' Forum and is a member of the International Press Institute board. He broadcasts frequently and blogs at **www.georgebrock.net**

ACKNOWLEDGEMENTS

I owe thanks to countless people with whom I have discussed the business of news, in the broadest sense of the term, over many years. I am grateful to them all. I could not have found the freedom to write this book without the help of Lis Howell, my esteemed colleague at City University London. I thank Paul Hodges and Darrin Burgess, who read and commented on the manuscript, and Mi Zhang and Charlotte Rettie, who helped with research. None of the above are responsible for any of this book's judgements or errors. As ever, my greatest debt is to Kay, my most rigorous but most gentle critic.

Introduction:
from ink to link

The time is gone when one side of the (news) organization can practise determined ignorance of the other.

RICHARD GINGRAS, DIRECTOR OF NEWS, GOOGLE, 2012

I was chairing a lunchtime discussion on the prospects for the news media in Britain and the United States when the speaker, a business columnist, asked the audience in exasperation: 'I mean, who on *earth* would take advice on business from a journalism professor?' This book does not presume to hand out prescriptive advice to businessmen or women, but it does try to explain what is happening to journalism and the business of news and why it is happening. Many journalists would prefer to live in ignorance of the business inside which they operate and some succeed in doing so. But journalism is entangled with the business of news, like it or not.

News and journalism are in the midst of an upheaval. These changes, which have begun but are certainly not finished, force assumptions and practices to be rethought from first principles. Journalists find themselves at an inflection point. The internet is not simply a new publishing system, allowing faster, wider distribution of material assembled and edited as it has always been. The changes wrought by digital technology are transformative and not adaptive: they require journalism to be rethought. In different societies these changes will work through in different ways and at varying speeds. But the overall direction is plain: old habits of thought and behaviour have to be remade for new conditions.

This should hardly be a surprise: the ability to translate information into bits and thus to move it cheaply, quickly and in quantity over great distances reroutes much human communication and will have, however gradually, profound effects in democratic practice, books, money, law and social organization, to name only a few areas of life affected. Wireless technology and digitization profoundly alter the distribution of information of all kinds and how we learn what we know. Some of that is what we call 'news'. For anyone who reads, watches or listens to news, the questions posed touch basic assumptions: what we mean by 'news' – a flexible term that has taken on different meanings in different eras – may change again. If anyone can be a journalist thanks to cheap, simple electronic publishing technology, what is a journalist and can we define what they do? If we can identify what it is to be a journalist, exactly what value does it have in a wired society in which individuals can share information in such volumes with such ease?

Journalists in the 21st century rarely stop to recall that 'mainstream' journalism has only been a short period in the history of public information. The supply of information to democratic societies only matured as a mass-market industry in the 20th century, allowing journalism to be practised and controlled in more concentrated and organized ways. Journalism of an earlier era was smaller scale, more intimate, opinionated and much of it resembled the social networks now carried by the internet.

In theory, the disruption of journalism is a matter of urgent concern to democratic societies: is the free flow, integrity and independence of journalism not essential to citizens who vote? The luminaries who framed the American constitution thought so when they forbade any limitation on the freedom of 'the press' in the First Amendment to that document. But journalism – as an idea, as a business – is something that many busy people are not curious about. They take the media for granted; how journalists do what they do is studied regularly only by a small community of experts. Journalism and journalists may have been in the headlines about phone-hacking in Britain, but the kind of public inquiry triggered by that scandal is relatively rare across the world. Many journalists are defiantly uninterested in their own business. Many consider reflection on it to be a distracting waste of time and would not recognize, let alone endorse, the view that their work is being turned upside down. This book hopes to explain to as wide an audience as possible why the news media is undergoing such radical alteration and what the result ought to be and might be. However, 'ought' and 'might' may not turn out to be the same thing.

Having worked as a journalist, I have interests and a perspective to disclose at the start. I worked for newspapers for many years, beginning as a reporter at an evening paper in Yorkshire and I was on the staff of *The Times* from 1981 to 2009. I was a feature writer and editor, edited the paper's opinion page and was Foreign Editor. My last act as Foreign Editor was to post myself abroad in 1991 as the newspaper's correspondent in Brussels when the solid certainties of Western Europe's post-war life were dissolved by the collapse of the Soviet Empire to the east. I was later Saturday Editor and, from 1997, Managing Editor, a job that gave me an insight into the survival battles of printed media.

By the time I left, *The Times* was of course no longer only a newspaper but both a printed object and a constantly updated website. I now direct a university journalism school in London and enjoy the combined privilege of training the next generation of journalists and having the distance from daily journalism in order to reflect on what is happening to the work I once did. I have tried to put my experience into useful shape. If at any point I am critical of mistakes made by journalists (particularly in newspapers) in the past 30 years or so, you may take it as read that I have myself committed these same errors. My knowledge of what has gone wrong is derived from direct experience. A little of my time as an editor was spent in global journalism networks; I have tried to ensure that my analysis and argument here is not too Anglocentric or insular.

I was moved to write this book by taking part in many discussions about journalism's future. Many of these conversations were mournfully pessimistic. There was, and still is, much discouraging news to digest: many printed newspapers will never be profitable again or never as profitable as they once were. Most news websites, proclaiming themselves to be the future, struggle to survive. But I was gradually struck by how shaky were the assumptions underlying this pervasive gloom. The fact that journalism has changed and will change further is not the same as its ruin. While I may be pessimistic about parts of the business that support journalism, I'm optimistic about the robust survival of journalism in the long run. I want to show in this book that journalism in practice undergoes frequent change in which its prominent institutions come under threat. Change is the only constant in journalism's history. People in well-established newspapers or broadcast channels often identify journalism as themselves and their organizations. If their organization is threatened, they think that journalism itself must be in danger.

This is understandable but wrong. Journalism is an idea and a set of values. Ideas are worthless if they cannot be put into practice; in this, strong journalism institutions are important. But the idea of journalism is far stronger than the bodies pursuing it. Those bodies frequently fail to live up to their own values and are vulnerable to the winds and tides of change. Instead of asking what will happen to newspapers or broadcasters, we would do better to ask what will happen to the idea and ideals of journalism when they meet new conditions? Or how can we ensure that the best ideas and ideals of journalism are embedded in the new forms that journalism will now take? Ideas and debates about what journalism ought to be move in parallel to the economic fortunes of the organizations in which journalists work. Ideas and economics intertwine more closely than many journalists realize. The survival of journalism and the value it can provide rests in part on the existence of generative energy and ideas to renew the means of sustaining difficult, expensive and often controversial reporting and commentary. This book argues that the energy and ideas are gaining ground.

To understand where the many varieties of something known as journalism now stand, we need to look at the way in which the idea was born and developed in the later 19th and early 20th centuries. To see the significance of the digital disruption in the last decade of the 20th century, we need to look at the profusion of media right through the century: printed media's difficulties did not begin with the internet.

I make no apology for telling much of the story as one of business and technology. Both have been fundamental to the development of journalism everywhere. If journalism is to be independent of the state – as it should be – its economic self-sufficiency matters for its continuity and survival. That should matter to the consumers of news as well as its producers. If your favourite radio station, magazine, television or newspaper is threatened or you are simply fed up with the state of journalism locally, nationally or even internationally, you should take the opportunity provided by an unusual historical moment. Interactive media allow unprecedented freedom for commentary on what journalists, publishers and media owners do – and how they do it (they do not, of course, guarantee an audience for every commentator).

The provisional new business models for news publishing include philanthropic contributions large and small. Think tanks, blogs and campaigning organizations dedicated to monitoring the mainstream media are proliferating – and not just in Britain, where we have discovered that criminal behaviour by journalists went undetected. To say that today there are greater opportunities than ever to influence the conduct and creation of new news media is not to say that established media will welcome or allow participation in what they do. Plainly some will not. But the era in which technology, capital and self-confidence allowed journalists to operate as a club closed to outside inspection is over. That was true before Britain's Leveson Inquiry laid bare awkward truths about popular newspapers.

Journalists who think that the business which supports their activity is something done by others and nothing to do with them are deluding themselves. That might just be possible in a mature, large and rich news organization, but there are now few of those in Europe or North America. Journalists are now more likely than they have been for many years to be involved in the creation of new platforms, businesses, channels and start-ups. If those new creations are to be informed by best journalistic practice, journalists need to have the skills and interests to be present at the creation, even if they erect a wall to separate editorial from business activity. The necessary skills go wider than the skills of reporting or news production.

The future of journalism will be made by a combination of existing organizations that adapt and new entrants who can supply a demand better than legacy news media. Success or failure will be determined by the quantity and quality of experiments to find out what works. Journalism has grown and made itself useful through experimentation. Journalists must now experiment again in order to rebuild their role in a changing information system. That is the only reliable way of sustaining engagement with an audience, reader or user. Journalism should ask what people *need* to know, but it must also take account of what they *want* to know.

This book aims above all to be clear-eyed. To see where journalism now stands in rapidly altering conditions, we must separate the myths that journalists spin about what they do from fact. It should not be surprising that journalists are skilled at writing their own story in heroic terms. But they have no need to over-embellish a strong case. Being obliged to revisit basic principles can only help. Journalism can flourish in a new communications age. To preserve what's important, much has to change.

01

Communicating whatever we please

> **"**One way or another, self-governing societies must figure out the suitable commercial channels through which the information necessary for democratic decisions must be spread.

JAMES FALLOWS, *ATLANTIC MONTHLY*, 2003

Under a lead-coloured sky one October day in 2011, several dozen editors, lawyers, academics and pundits converged on a hulking grey conference centre that stands within shouting distance of the Houses of Parliament in London. They had been gathered to a preliminary debate by Lord Leveson, the judge who was to chair the inquiry hastily convened by the government after the newspaper phone-hacking scandal closed the *News of the World*. The inquiry's wide terms of reference made clear that it would range well beyond phone interception by journalists and look at the bigger questions of the relationship between the press, law, regulation and government.

Several speeches were heard, but one was better attended to than the rest. Paul Dacre, the editor-in-chief of the *Daily Mail*, is not a comfortable public speaker. A heavy-set man who looks angry before he has uttered a word, he read his speech as if incredulous that he had agreed to deliver anything as politely phrased as the sentences he was reading out. Inside his own newspaper office, Dacre's unprintable language to his subordinates is legendary.

His speech was both attack and defence. The inquiry's panel of experts might be 'distinguished people' but they did not have 'the faintest clue how mass-selling newspapers work'. The inquiry had been supported by politicians eager to exact revenge for the exposure of their 'greed and corruption' over parliamentary expenses. Worse, they wanted to over-regulate newspapers when the press was in a 'sick financial state'. He took a swipe at 'loss-making' papers, criticized the existing self-regulation system for the press and pointed at 'liberal hatred' of papers as popular as the *Mail*.

Much of this was hyperbole and Dacre would have known it: he casually minimized illegal intrusion and ignored the simple fact that the phone-hacking scandal itself had created the need to know more about how some popular newspapers, at least, had been working. But the speech contained two striking admissions. The first raised an issue with which the inquiry never truly grappled: the internet. Why consider tighter regulation, Dacre asked, when 'more and more of the information people want to read is being provided by an utterly unregulated and arguably anarchic internet'? This was an unusually frank admission that print was being outshone.

The second admission was implicit: by recommending a reformed system of press self-regulation, Dacre was conceding that the existing system had failed. The press, he said, could still regulate itself with prompter and more prominent corrections, more lay people to inspect it and an ombudsman to set standards and levy fines. At the end of the inquiry, 13 months later, Lord Leveson flatly disagreed with Dacre, concluding that newspapers could not be trusted to run their own regulation.

Dacre's defiant but defensive speech was an emblematic moment. Because he speaks rarely in public and represents a powerful force, he mesmerized his audience. The *Mail*'s circulation was in decline by the time he spoke, but had held up longer than most before slipping. Its online sister, enjoying the freedom of the utterly unregulated internet, was close to being measured as the most popular news sites on the planet. Like it or hate it, the *Mail* was the daily reading and voice of a section of the British population that politicians didn't dare ignore.

But some politicians had seen that a combination of the internet and the phone-hacking scandal was starting to weaken even the *Mail*. And that was what made Dacre's anger at the podium so memorable. Stripped of the vituperation, his speech amounted to a plea: in order to survive financially we must shame, intrude and sensationalize. Clamp down on that and we're finished.

Parts of the press had lost its moral compass and all of the press was losing income and influence. To see how these crises came to collide, we need to look into the past.

* * * * *

Human beings speak, write, sing, gossip, shout, broadcast, publish, whisper rumours, gossip and blog. They have done at least some of these things for thousands of years. This book is about only one kind of exchange of information: the activity that in the 19th century came to be called journalism. The account, analysis and argument of this book are not about all media or all communication but about a specialized activity inside those broad categories. Journalism is endlessly disputed: what it should be and how it should best be done. To see what is happening to journalism now, we need to look at how journalism has developed and the ideas and forces that have shaped it.

Journalism exists as an identifiable activity and it is not the same as storytelling, books, entertainment television, movies, letter writing, speech making or encyclopaedias. I would define journalism as the systematic, independent attempt to establish the truth of events and issues that matter to a society in a timely way. All societies argue about both the ends and means of journalism; they do not all reach the same conclusion. Different eras hold differing views about what is important. My definition describes the evolution of the idea today. When people first began playing with these ideas, 'truth' meant opinion and not fact. Independence as a desirable position for journalists only emerged gradually.

Journalism requires a community to work in and a means to circulate information and opinion. But there are two other basic elements common to all the very varied activities that go under the heading of journalism. First, those who publish and those who receive information assume that there is a public value and importance in circulating facts and views, even if the community is small or specialized. Take that assumption away and the communication is of a quite different, often private, kind. Second, journalists separated their activities from those of the authorities, both the government and the church. In Europe, the conditions for those assumptions to be made were created by the arrival of printing in the late 15th century and the slow subsequent growth of literacy. Printers, once they and their new readers had freed themselves from the idea that written text could only be about religious subjects, began to seek out the subjects that people wanted to know. They began to experiment to find communities linked by common interest. The sharing of information became more dynamic and the possibilities of using the new technology became clear. There were many different motives for wanting to publish.

Messy, unethical and opinionated origins

Before the 20th century, news was circulated only in print. The first 'news-papers' illustrate as well as any succeeding phase a simple truth. Any publication that establishes a connection between the provider and consumer of news becomes a platform on which a number of different motives, aims and purposes jostle for space. Early newspapers, just as much as their successors, were platforms on which different designs were projected. Each one was an empirical experiment. Printing technology offered new ways of reproducing information: news was created by using that opportunity to supply a need.

Written information travelled along Europe's trade routes before the invention of printing. Markets and traders needed prices and quantities to be able to work. The printing of bibles was expensive for printers and very tightly controlled; mistakes were not tolerated and the business was inherently risky. By the late 16th century, printers all over Europe looking for quicker returns began to discover that packages of news and advertisements, while carrying legal risks, improved their precarious cash flow. Copying newsletters by hand was slow; printing was quick. Early journalism was, as one historian puts it, an 'appendage' to a printer's business.[1] Early postal systems helped. France was among the earliest, having set up a postal system as early as the 1480s; England and Denmark did not follow suit until the 1620s (in England this was due to the fact that the country was late building a national road system). One of the most impressive postal networks was built by the Holy Roman Emperor Maximilian I in the early 16th century, which competed with city and national systems. Its couriers could cover the distance between Augsburg and Venice (more than 200 miles) in six days, which was faster than any rival.

Augsburg and Venice were among the most active and prosperous trading centres on the continent in that era. Commercial intelligence depended on speed. One strand of information carried in early news publications was a spin-off from the trade information and gossip that merchants had long employed agents to gather on their behalf. A banker in Augsburg, a major trade centre with access to the Alpine passes, needed to know which ships had docked in Venice, when and with what cargo and at what value. This data was what present-day business reporters call 'market moving' news: up-to-date information improved the odds of striking a good price.

Very early newspapers often took the form of books; news wasn't yet disposable and was an improvised mixture of history and almanac. Before 1600, there was little expectation that publication would be regular or even frequent. A printer would collect together a saleable mixture of details about battles fought abroad, merchant's letters, sensational trials and executions, natural catastrophes and sea monsters, and publish enough pages to make it worth his while. These might appear annually or every six months; the odd one was written in rhyme. Truly valuable recent information from reliable agents was not printed and still travelled down private networks. For publishers hoping to sell to the literate public, whether the information was recent or not was of lesser importance. Publishers of newsbooks and their agents would wander an area of London such as St Paul's, or the Rialto in Venice, to hoover up titbits that could be accumulated and printed. Some items they borrowed or stole; no intellectual property rights existed. Intellectuals were duly annoyed by the misuse of what they considered their property. 'If he get any Coppy into his power likely to be vendible,' wrote one George Wither in *Schollers Purgatory* of around 1625, 'whether the Author be willing or no, he will publish it... which is the reason so many Bookes come forth imperfect, and with foolish titles.'

Around 1625 foolishness was not confined to book titles. Printing, by extending the distribution of written material previously copied by hand, helped to enforce a distinction between myth and fact, but it was a slow process. Just as people now complain of being unable to tell what is reliable online, people in the 17th century found that the new way of spreading information outran efforts to assess its accuracy. An English pamphlet appeared in 1609 under the title 'A true relacon of the birth of Three Monsters in the Citty of Namen in Flanders'. A German periodical in 1654 reported a Catalonian monster with a goat's legs and seven heads. Sensational facts that were more reliable were almost as good. In 1624 a newsbook reported on the trial of three men and a woman who were convicted of murdering and dismembering a Somerset curate called Trat. The details of the butchery (pieces of his body were boiled and salted) were considerably more lurid than any court report from the trial of multiple murderer Fred West in Britain in 1995.

In the first few decades of the 17th century, the occasional and marginal business of printing 'news' grew and accelerated in frequency. In England between 1591 and 1594, nearly one-quarter of all registered publications were on current affairs. A printed version of Christopher Columbus's own account (first circulated handwritten then in a printed version) was a bestseller in Spain in 1493. Single-story publications gave way to 'corantos' (from the French *courante*), which ran a series of unconnected items into a single publication. This variant began in Germany where the *Mercurius Gallobelgicus* began publication in Cologne in 1594 and appeared twice a year in Latin until it closed in 1635.[2] Its contents covered central Europe and it was mainly distributed at trade fairs. It was read in England: the poet John Donne disapproved of its inaccuracy and dishonesty.

Select and noteworthy happenings

The energy that quickened the rate of publication across Europe came from Germany and the Netherlands. The Dutch regime for control of printing was relatively liberal for the time; German cities and trade were growing rapidly. There was a steady trickle of sporadic publications that usually called themselves *Anzeiger* ('advertising') and sought a readership only of those who wanted to buy, sell or rent; but even these publications gradually incorporated short news items to leaven the advertisements, often births, marriages and deaths. The Dutch economy was seaborne and the Habsburg connection with Spain meant that printers had access to large transcontinental networks. In both Germany and the Netherlands – and elsewhere – religious tensions were becoming political ones, generating both passion and curiosity. A printer on Lake Constance switched from an annual publication to monthly in the last years of the 16th century; in Strasbourg a 'relation of select and noteworthy happenings' began to appear at the same monthly frequency in 1609 from a local bookseller.[3] An Antwerp printer, Abraham Verhoeven, produced *Nieuwe Tydinghe*, occasionally at first then weekly in 1617 and, in the 1620s, it was coming out three times a week.

As demand grew, starting a regular publication became a more attractive business proposition. Material was appearing in greater profusion and could be plundered if the readers were interested. Between 1600 and 1620, regular publications began in Augsburg, Basel, Frankfurt, Vienna, Hamburg, Berlin and Amsterdam. By 1619, Amsterdam was publishing two weekly corantos and by the next year sending others to England and France. In Leipzig in 1650, the first daily appeared, the *Einkommende Zeitung*, followed a decade later by another in which news was better sourced and recency had begun to count: its title was *Latest News of Wars and World Affairs*.[4] By 1626, there were 140 news publications in Dutch. An early version of the same kind of publication in Spain (reporting on France, Flanders and Germany) used the Dutch formula. The first regular news published in Copenhagen was produced by two Germans: a bookseller and a printer.

While some characteristics of later newspapers were present in outline form, many were not. Almost none of the corantos were presented with anything resembling editing: there was little or no attempt to shape or select the material. If claims to reliability and accuracy were made, they were not believed. There was little reporting, as it would now be understood: almost all of the material was copied from other publications. The term 'news-monger' was not used as a compliment – the playwright Ben Jonson, in fact, accused British coranto printers of degrading the work of a writer. Most of the material was foreign to the country in which it was published, not because early demand was for international news, but because accounts of foreign wars were less likely to attract the interest of the authorities. English translations of Dutch publications appeared with the British stories cut out. The print runs in England are estimated to have been 400–500 copies. They sold for 2*d*, a price that guaranteed they would only be seen by an elite audience of noblemen, gentry and some professional men.

The twin authorities of the church and the monarch supervised and licensed what appeared. The printers operated independently of the author-ities and could try to dismantle and move their small, flatbed presses if they had warning that they had gone too far. But in England before the Civil War, these cat-and-mouse games for printers seem to have been rare and weighted in favour of the authorities. For someone who wanted to use words for a subversive purpose, print was not the ideal method of evading censorship.

Handwritten newsletters were at least as influential as printed material until at least 1650. In many ways, they more closely resembled newspapers than the corantos. By the end of the 16th century, what had begun as letters for merchants was becoming institutionalized as a small industry, much of it developed in the great trading centre of Venice. Because of their origins in the transmission of facts whose accuracy mattered, their authors cared more than coranto printers about whether what they were reporting had actually happened. By gradual degrees, what had once been a private infor-mation supply was spreading to a larger readership as letters were copied and distributed. Those readers had access to more than one account and could contrast and compare. Cities arranged reciprocal exchanges with others. The municipal archives of Frankfurt contain three versions of the same battle in the 1540s by different authors.

Newsletters written and copied by hand held significant advantages over printed newsbooks. The authors and distributors could more easily control who saw them. The more regular of these newsletters had what might very roughly be called a 'news agenda' and their compilers did some eye-witness reporting. One contemporary description says that they were men who 'rambled from coffee-room to coffee-room collecting reports, squeezed into... the Old Bailey if there was an interesting trial... obtained permission to the gallery of Whitehall and noticed how the King and Duke looked'.[5] Newsletters had editorial personality – often more than their printed equivalents – but no details of the people behind them have been passed down to us. Open authorship was too dangerous.

For the most part, newsletters were not sold: that avoided any action liable to be levelled by the authorities that the 'publisher' was putting dangerous thinking in the hands of just anyone. No European monarchy or its official servants or the aristocracy in 1600 would have subscribed to the idea that any person in the kingdom had an enforceable right to read anything at all. The authorities no longer expected to hold a monopoly on words, but words were a risk and risks were to be controlled. During the 17th century, newsletters declined as printed news took over, but any clampdown on print saw a resurgence in handwritten newsletters. After the Restoration in 1660, a new official called the 'Surveyor of the Press' took the monopoly of printed news. Newsletters written and sent by hand once again became the vehicle for uncensored news.

The system of control in England on the eve of the Civil War was three-cornered. The Archbishop of Canterbury, along with the Bishop of London, held the right to nominate master-printers. So nominated, the printers were obliged to work under the rules of the Stationers' Company, to whom the secular and ecclesiastical authorities had outsourced the supervision of print. The company registered every work and had the right to search any printer's premises. It held the exclusive right to these procedures in exchange for ensuring that what was printed obeyed the rules and the law.

The pervasive and mostly effective controls created fear that limited the accuracy of what was available. A French scholar lists almost 120 surviving reports on battles printed in France between 1498 and 1559. None report the heavy French defeat at Pavia in 1525 when the French king was taken prisoner.[6] No publication marked the death in 1601 of the Earl of Essex in terms favourable to the earl – or at least none did so until two years later, after the death of Queen Elizabeth I, who had the earl executed. The Crown encouraged as well as discouraged. The scientific philosopher Francis Bacon, keen to advance his political career, is thought to have been the author of a pamphlet on the alleged conspiracy led by Essex and to have been handsomely paid for writing it.

The inanities of popular writers and ballad makers were condemned by intellectuals. Governments not only suppressed publications of which they disapproved, they subsidized sympathetic coverage. Publishers had begun to get a sense of demand, of what would sell and what might not. But the idea that information, in order to be useful, should be as accurate as possible was a long way off. In *The Winter's Tale*, Shakespeare satirizes ballad makers and the credulousness of their customers: a composer of ballads attempts to sell a shepherdess verses composed by a fish. At the end of the play, there is a hint of the jostling competition that was beginning to seize the attention of readers or listeners. The king has been reconciled with his lost daughter and a character is asked for 'the news'. 'Such a deal of wonder is broken out this hour,' he replies, 'that ballad makers cannot be able to express it.'

Crude news platforms now existed and many ideas scrambled to use them. They ranged from subtle state propaganda to eye-witness reporting to sensational, supernatural fantasy to strong opinion. The restraints that had held back the development of fuller flows of information were about to be broken.

An explosion of opinion

A small patchwork of elite audiences across Europe expected to be able to satisfy their curiosity for news in ways that went beyond face-to-face conversation. But the news they read was irregular, haphazard and mostly about foreign states, battles and the occasional sea monster. The demand for news could hardly be described as strong or focused. The 'public sphere', if it could be said to exist at all, was small and the news consumed in it did not give a complete picture of anything. In 1641, events changed that for good. The conflict between king and Parliament that led to the English Civil War, the execution of King Charles I and the six-year Protectorate under Oliver Cromwell suspended the controls and inhibitions on the press. The opening was brief, but long enough to reveal new possibilities.

After years of inconclusive struggle over the rights of Parliament to control the monarch's spending and law-enforcement, events were beyond the king's control in late 1641. Parliament, itself often secretive and conceal-ing its deliberations from the king, was debating a 'Grand Remonstrance' listing its grievances. In November, a bookseller called John Thomas pub-lished a small weekly, written by Samuel Pecke, with an elaborate title typical of the time: *The Heads of Severall Proceedings in this Present Parliament*. Pecke and Thomas knew that they and others sensed the enor-mous importance of recording what was happening and that people would want to know. The style was dry and straight but, as often, a low-key factual account released sensational information. They got away with it. By mid-December, a second weekly appeared, doing just the same. At the end of

December a third began and, seven weeks after Pecke's breakthrough, five weeklies reported on Parliament. Pecke's judgement about the demand for this news had been right. For the next eight years, including years of civil war, no political force was powerful enough to reimpose controls.

In a rush, modern newspapers took early shape. An early version of shorthand allowed speeches to be taken down at almost the speed at which they were spoken. Pecke, unlike coranto publishers, went out to report news that he witnessed. One paper used a woman reporter, nicknamed the 'she intelligencer'. In the years of warfare, journalism and espionage were hard to distinguish. Interest in foreign news slumped; a paper aimed at merchants and carrying foreign commercial news failed quickly. 'Wee talke of nothing else but what is done in England,' one journalist wrote at the time, 'and perhaps once a fortnight we hearken after newes sent out of Scotland.' This news was national and mostly political: local news was passed by word of mouth. Facts were bolstered by writing that would now be called 'colour'. *A Perfect Diurnall* claimed to reproduce the poignant conversation between Charles I and his executioner on the scaffold.

Facts were also put to the service of invective, which predominated as the armed struggle for control of the country grew more bitter. Information was passed by newsletters and newsbooks, sometimes in the form of strip cartoons distributed by newsboys, writers and editors who were backstreet fugitives if their cause was failing. Newsbooks may initially have strained for a dry style, but their information was largely an extension of politics; most supported the parliamentary cause. The power vacuum and resulting chaos of ideas swiftly generated new factions and parties. A limited kind of 'public opinion' was now something worth persuading. Factions supplied money and intelligence to sympathetic writers and editors.

Newsbooks carried debates on rights and laws, freedom and order. But that was plainly not as much fun as insult, abuse, espionage and intrigue. One propagandist described another as 'the quibbling prick louse... an underling pimp to the whore of Babylon and thy conscience an arrant prostitute for base ends'. Both men were, of course, working for political forces that would expect to reimpose legal controls on newspapers (and particularly on unfriendly ones) if only they could establish a firm enough grip to do so. Marchamont Nedham's *Mercurius Britanicus* was informally licensed and vetted by an official of Parliament. Nedham delighted in evading these controls, but he frequently failed. In the 20 years after 1640, 30,000 books, pamphlets and sheets were published, mostly carrying pungently strong opinions to small readerships at high risk of imprisonment or worse. Fencing with opponents and authority left a long-standing imprint.

'The tribulations of journalists during the Civil War provided the infant traumas which shaped the personality of English journalism', writes one historian.[7]

As Cromwell gained ascendancy, not only over the Royalists but over other parliamentary factions, censorship was rebuilt. In 1649 Parliament passed the 'Act against Unlicensed and Scandalous Books and Pamphlets'. That was promptly overtaken in 1655 by a ban on all newsbooks, except two that were licensed by what became a military dictatorship.

The Restoration under Charles II was no better. Press control came into the hands of Sir Roger L'Estrange, who recommended to the new king that the system of control for news needed an overhaul and that he was the man to do it. L'Estrange knew that his problem was not merely one of fashioning an efficient control system, for he faced the timeless conservative dilemma: did he ignore subversive opinion-makers or fight them with their own weapons? The Chinese Communist Party of the early 21st century wrestles with precisely the same problem in a country where the circulation of unofficial news and information has been accelerated by the internet.

L'Estrange thought that news 'makes the multitude too familiar with the actions and counsels of their superiors, too pragmatical, too censorious'. John Dryden incorporated L'Estrange into his poem *Absalom and Achitophel*:

In vain seditious scribes with libels strive
T'enflame the Crowd, while He with Watchful eye
Observes and shoots the Treasons as they fly:
Their weekly frauds his keen replies detect;
He undeceives more fast than they infect.

Dryden's image of a body politics vulnerable to infection by fraudulent reporting captured the contemporary view inside the educated elite of news and its publication, more than any modern assumption that sunlight, in the form of reporting, makes power accountable. But that view was changing.

Playing with fire

In the late years of the 17th century, the English governing class began to change its mind about information. The pressures of change were not confined to England, although they went further in England than anywhere in Europe except the Netherlands. The Civil War had propelled more people into the business of political and religious argument; they had discovered that print was an effective means of prosecuting a point of view, that gossip and novelty helped the argument go down with a larger readership, and that some printers and writers were better at this than others. The gradual spread of Protestant ideas, centred on the individual conscience and autonomy, encouraged thinking about the right to hold and distribute political opinions. At a more basic level, Protestantism encouraged literacy, even if only for the purpose of reading the Bible.

Above all, England was convalescing after a traumatic war and men were reflecting on what they had learnt about truth and lies told amidst and about events in which people died. Lies had a tendency to multiply and were hard to suppress with the force of law. The Chief Justice of England might say in 1702 that 'if people should not be called to account for possessing the people with an ill opinion of the government, no government can subsist. For it is very necessary for all governments that the people should have a good opinion of it.' But the exchange of opinions and the idea that truth will prevail over falsehood was undermining the hold of the belief asserted by the Chief Justice. An appeal to reason and fact, contrasted with faction and fiction, gained ground. The first issue of Daniel Defoe's *Weekly Review* proclaimed that it was 'purged from the Errors and Partiality of News-writers and Petty Statesmen of all Sides'. Defoe had a poor claim to the high ground for he was for a period paid in secret by the government of the day. But he believed in eye-witness, first-hand reporting and stressed its value.

The opportunity to experiment with new platforms and forms of journalism came with the peaceful revolution of 1688. The received idea of the divine right of kings was under increasingly aggressive attack and the accountability of governments was debated. The accession of a foreign Protestant monarch and a new constitutional settlement eased the political and religious strains of the decades after the Civil War. In 1695, the Licensing Act was repealed, not least because of the accumulated hostility to the monopoly held by the Stationers' Company. There was regular discussion of new press controls but nothing was enacted until the first Stamp Act in 1712 imposed new costs on publishers. The lifting of controls was decisive: many writers and printers were waiting to exploit the opportunity.

Laws against blasphemy, obscenity and seditious libel still stood but the freedom to publish in England was then strikingly different from most of the rest of Europe. 'Looked at from Paris, Milan or Frankfurt,' one historian writes, 'the English authorities appeared to be playing with fire.'[8] The English authorities almost certainly did not know what they were doing, because they were relying on the law of seditious libel to control printing. Parliament promptly made that harder to do.

But the sparks that flew did not start a fire. This was in part because the journalists of the new age were anxious to be read but not to divide. There was plenty of argument, but it stayed clear of what many recalled as the excesses of the years from the Civil War to the Restoration. For many years afterwards, journalists shuddered to recall the vituperative and scabrous writing that had appeared between Cromwell's death and the accession of Charles II.

In the decades after 1695, many newspapers and periodicals laid heavy stress on their independence from, and lack of interest in, party and faction. The most successful of all, *The Spectator*, wrote ceaselessly about politics and political ideas but always claimed, however implausibly, that it rose above mere faction. 'There cannot a greater judgement befall a country than such a dreadful spirit of division that rends a government into two distinct people... A furious Party spirit, when it rages in its full Violence, exerts itself in civil war and bloodshed,' wrote *The Spectator*'s editor Joseph Addison, who boasted that his paper carried 'not in it a single word of news... nor a stroke of party' and did not allow 'no obscene ideas, no satyres upon priesthood, marriage, and the like popular topicks of ridicule.' A glimpse of the dreadful reality of civil war made printers, editors, writers and publishers very reluctant to court the charge that they were encouraging it.

That did not stand in the way of an explosion of printed news and opinions. In 1663, the diarist Samuel Pepys had been trying to buy insurance on an overdue ship when he dropped into a coffee house. He was in luck: 'There by great accident (I) hear that a letter is come that our ship is safe come to Newcastle.' Personal communication was now giving way to publics linked by print. By 1708 a writer is referring to the century just begun as 'this century of newspapers'. In 1702, the first daily paper in London, the *Daily Courant*, began publishing. Its founder Samuel Buckley was a bookseller with a good trade in French and Dutch journals, so his supply of foreign news was good. He was concerned to establish superior new standards, writing that the *Courant* would always name its sources and give no 'comments or conjectures' of its own.

Until 1695, the licensing and censorship systems had effectively confined printing to London, York, Oxford and Cambridge; now presses popped up all over the country. There was plenty of material for news. From 1694, elections were held every three years: opportunities for the creation of political parties and party argument expanded. Commercial intelligence was in as much demand as ever and England's trade was expanding rapidly as the new century began. The end of the monarch's absolute power and

the peaceful revolution of 1688 generated speculation on the accountability of those who ruled. John Locke's 'Two Treatises of Government',
which discussed the legitimacy of power and rights of resistance, appeared
in 1690. A succession of near-crises in politics, an infusion of new ideas
(often brought by political refugees from the Continent), the rising popularity
of Protestantism and patriotism – all contributed to a more open political
culture and a growing demand for news and opinion. Only the Dutch
could claim to outdo England in printing and distribution of both, and their
freedom was to publish what was happening in countries other than their
own United Provinces.

The way was open for printers and publishers to experiment with new
ways of matching demand with supply. By 1715, there were 70 printers in
London; 40 years later the number had doubled. Samuel Richardson, the
novelist and bookseller, employed 20 compositors at a press that turned
out two weekly papers and at least one daily, all in the normal four-page
format.[9] By 1750, London had five daily papers, six appearing three times
per week and five weeklies. The number of titles of all kinds and frequencies
appearing in England in the 1620s was 6,000; in the 1710s that number
had risen to 21,000 and to 56,000 by the 1790s. The annual total sale of
newspapers in 1713 was around 2.5 million. By 1801, when London had 13
daily and 10 tri-weekly papers, the figure had climbed to 16 million.[10]

This surge in activity brought forth a new figure, the editor.[11] In an emerging industry of public culture, a periodical could no longer rely on the first
account of a battle, a ship come safely home or a misshapen monster.
An editorial personality and a philosophy were required to stake out and
defend a circulation territory. A master narrative was needed to give coher-
ence to the jigsaw of material. This was the key to the first publication to be
the talk of the town and to create its own large, faithful following. *The
Spectator*, which appeared first in 1711, was the product of a partnership
between Joseph Addison and Richard Steele. It had a snarky mocking style,
original ideas, a modernizing editorial philosophy and accessibility. It was a
hit and gave people something to talk about. '*The Spectator* is in everyone's
hands,' wrote the Revd John Gay, 'and a constant topic for our morning
conversation at the tables and coffee houses.' *The Spectator*'s writers often
wrote as if seated in the corner of a coffee house, and they frequently were.
Coffee houses were very popular as trading places for gossip, for hearing
newspapers read out and for political intrigue, to the point that more than
one politician tried, and failed, to shut them down. A journal founded in
Leipzig in 1698 took the name *The Curious Coffeehouse in Venice*. A

mid-18th-century Italian journal that played an important role in spreading Enlightenment ideas between Rome, Florence and other cities was simply called *Il Caffè*.

The Spectator derided ignorance, stupidity and divisiveness, praising courtesy and good taste. Life was a theatre and their readers were spectators at a fashionable play. The modern English governing class was holding a new and self-confident conversation with itself. *The Spectator*, astutely spotting a cultural market gap, positioned itself as the style police for the new elite. The key, then as now, was to mix levity and seriousness in exactly the right amounts. Its editors aimed, they said, 'to enliven morality with wit and to temper wit with morality'. In effect, the paper was writing the rules for a new metropolitan public sphere, which linked 'Scholars, Citizens, Courtiers, Gentlemen of the Town or of Country, and all Beaux, Rakes, Smarts, Prudes, Coquets, Housewives and all sorts of Wits... who have ever made Thinking a Part of their Business or Diversion' in a rolling conversation. *The Spectator* claimed a circulation of 3,000 – enormous for the time – and assumed that 20 people saw each copy.

The demands of a large and heterogeneous readership affected editing and writing style. Daniel Defoe wrote: 'If any man were to ask me what I would suppose to be a perfect style of language, I would answer that in which a man speaking to five hundred people all of common and various capacities... should be understood by them all.' Defoe and Jonathan Swift were among the polemicists who drove circulations, infuriated their political enemies and gave rise to calls for the reintroduction of licensing. Gossip and scandal were proliferating in print. The *Female Tatler*, edited by a woman whose nom de plume was 'Mrs Crakenthorpe, a Lady that knows everything', was launched in 1709. She was nicknamed 'Scandalosissima Scoundrelia' by her rivals.

Under the guidance of the politician Robert Harley, the government accepted that it could not reverse the tide and that it needed to control its unbridled force. Taxation would raise money, damp down the overall noise level and make papers depend on subsidy and bribery. In 1712, the first of the Stamp Acts was passed, taxing publications per page. This system, which lasted for more than a century, slowed down the development of large readerships and the development of content in England. As the historian Paul Starr puts it: 'While the early modern public sphere represented a shift away from political secrecy, it was still socially exclusive, subject to the mundane influences of money and status, and routinely manipulated by those in power.'[12] The next important moments in the evolution of journalism occurred in America and France.

'Bible, ax and newspapers'

Even with the new burden of the stamp taxes, England's press in the middle of the 18th century was still unusual. England had experienced its revolution and counter-revolution early and was to enjoy a long period of stability while other societies underwent convulsions. The political systems would settle into a two-party system, the communications system and banking systems were growing. These laid the foundations for a relatively confident national press. 'Nothing is more apt to surprise a foreigner, than the extreme liberty which we enjoy in this country,' wrote David Hume, 'of communicating whatever we please to the public, and of openly censuring every measure entered into by the king or his ministers.'

Across most of the rest of the world, the idea of freely circulating discussion of the government, its personalities and policies was still regarded as fissile, dangerous material. Chinese emperors and their officials had no truck with the idea. No shift in attitudes took place in Japan until the second half of the 19th century. In Germany and Italy, information was published on a local scale only since nation states had not yet come into existence in either place. France and Spain saw publishing increase but it was efficiently controlled and censored. In the pre-revolutionary years in France, pamphlets and periodicals from the Netherlands and Switzerland were smuggled along covert networks. In Britain's American colony, the stamp taxes did not apply but the colonial authorities were well aware of the risks posed by schooling and instruction in reading. They frowned on policies to found more schools in the infant Commonwealth of Massachusetts. 'I thank God, there are no free schools, nor printing,' William Berkeley, the governor of Virginia, wrote to London of his own area in 1671, 'and I hope we shall not have those (for a) hundred years. For learning has brought disobedience, and heresy, and sects into the world, and printing has divulged them, and libels against the best government. God keep us from both.'[13]

Even before the political polarization and warfare of America's independence struggle, conditions favoured the development of a well-read, discursive press. Colonial laws imitated those in England but there was no machinery of licensing or censorship. Literacy grew rapidly and newly colonized regions were being farmed by well-educated Bible readers. Alexis de Tocqueville, visiting Michigan early in the 1800s, found a man in an isolated cabin and was surprised by his learning: 'A very civilized man, prepared for a time to face life in the forest, plunging into the wilderness of the New World with his Bible, ax and newspapers.' Even in the middle of the 17th century when the Civil War was being fought in England, the risk of prose-cution for publishing what the authorities disliked was falling. It was not wholly free expression but it was not severe censorship either. By the start of the 17th century, newspapers were competing. Boston, a town of 15,000 people had two newspapers in 1719 and five by 1735.

The small and vocal American political elite was beginning to divide into its own factions; after independence, plural, competing newspapers would be critical in defining new parties. Political tensions between colonists and governed rose. Campaigns demand ammunition in the form of arguments and evidence. The smells and sounds of debate blew over the sea from London and writers were not slow to connect freedom to print with the opportunity to criticize and organize. Arguing successfully for the acquittal of a German-born printer on charges of seditious libel in 1735, Andrew Hamilton spoke for 'the liberty both of exposing and opposing arbitrary power... by speaking (and) writing truth'. Two English radical Whigs, John Trenchard and Thomas Gordon, had in 1720 argued a defence of a free press in 'Cato's Letters', published in *London Journal* and then as a book. the *Boston Gazette* reprinted the free-speech essay seven times in the quarter century after 1755. 'We talk the language we have always heard you speak,' Samuel Adams wrote to a friend in London in 1767.

Small American communities were well equipped for news even if it was not all printed. In 1798 the town of Michigan refused to wait for federal help for printing or postal services and started a local spoken newspaper with a town crier. The role was later taken over by a priest and the arrange-ment continued until a printer arrived in the town in 1809. The average circulation of newspapers in 1775 seems to have been around 600 copies each.[14] Communities circulated letters by means of 'committees of corre-spondence'. What all these improvised social networks had in common was linkage and then mobilization of people who saw themselves and their destiny differently. News was political glue.

Alexis de Tocqueville saw this when he visited the new republic a few years later. He wrote: 'A newspaper takes up the notion or the feeling that had occurred simultaneously, but singly, to each of them. All are then im-mediately guided towards this beacon; and these wandering minds at length meet and unite'. He continued: 'The newspaper brought them together, and the newspaper is necessary to keep them united.' Isolated communities and separate colonies began to see themselves as a distinct nation with shared opinions. Several centuries later, people were to make almost identical observations about a new wave of discoveries of communities of shared interests, thanks to the arrival of the internet.

Newspapers writing in opposition to colonial power were discovering that if a readership is primed to want strong opinion, the strongest voice will capture the largest number. When Britain attempted to impose the Stamp Act in 1765 or the import of Indian tea in 1773, the newspapers had the causes with which to attack the British and their American supporters without restraint. Shall Britain enslave America, which is 99 times bigger and capable of supporting 'hundreds of millions of people', asked the prescient *Massachusetts Spy* in 1773. In America, supporters of Britain were labelled as 'diabolical Tools of Tyrants'. Imported tea was reported to be a 'slow poison' that would cause horrible diseases. Suspiciously undetailed accounts of bad behaviour by British soldiers filled the columns of American newspapers, which were happy to encourage mob attacks on 'loyalist' presses. Accuracy may not have been paramount, but style reflected the need to unify a large readership. The exiled English activist Tom Paine's pamphlet *Common Sense* was printed in 150,000 copies over years, exerting a powerful influence. Paine said that he had set out to 'avoid every literary ornament and put it in language as plain as the alphabet'.

Against this background, it is hardly surprising that the framers of the American constitution wanted to make sure that the press was protected. When the Constitution was drafted and its First Amendment was written to protect both freedom of religion and the press, no country in the world had any form of law shielding freedom of publication. The freedoms that had emerged in England were the absence of what would now be known as 'prior restraint'. The authorities or complainants could only act after publication, and not before; American politicians came quickly to disagree about what exactly press freedom meant. Thomas Jefferson advised James Madison to insert qualifying wording allowing the punishment of 'false facts' and many state constitutions prohibited 'abuse'. But the First Amendment was passed without qualification and became part of developing ideas about popular sovereignty. The specific local circumstances that had made newspapers and newsletters so important in the anti-British agitation converted into a principle of government accountability. It is in the nature of republican government, James Madison said in 1794, that 'censorial power is in the hands of the people over the government' and not the other way round.

A brief flowering

These ideas were causing an attack of nerves in the European political classes, not because of events in America, but because of the French

Revolution. Again, new space for publishing was created by conflict. Unlike the American case, the freedoms enjoyed were temporary and promptly snuffed out when the revolutionary era, which began in 1789, ended 10 years later with Napoleon's constitution. But in both the American and French cases, two public spheres had developed, side by side but largely separate. In both cases, the officially approved publications and their patrons in government failed to realize that the unofficial media were completely outstripping them. A similar blindness to the outcome of an uneven competition between bland, official media and more exciting and informative new social media networks contributed to the fall of governments in Tunisia and Egypt in 2011.[15]

Royal control of print in France was extensive – King Louis XVI had 130 censors working for him on the eve of the fall of the Bastille – but inefficient. Dutch newspapers and newsbooks were the major source of news from abroad, although they also filtered in from Cologne, Swtizerland and from what is now Belgium. The most influential was the *Gazette de Leyde*, edited by French Huguenots, which is estimated to have had a sizeable circulation of 4,000 by the 18th century. That newspaper published, in full, documents issued by the growing movement opposing royal absolutism; the two officially licensed papers in Paris never mentioned such matters.

The French king's ministers paid the unofficial publishers the compliment of planting leaked stories in their periodicals, because they were considered better informed. The print explosion of the French Revolution's early years was preceded by an increase in the almost-open sale of *libelles* during the last decade of the Bourbon monarchy. These were, in the words of one historian, 'an indiscriminate jumble of pornographic libels, vitriolic satire and radical political theory'.[16] Marie Antoinette had been impregnated by a cardinal; the king's mistress, Mme Dubarry, had ascended 'directly from the brothel' to the throne. Even Voltaire complained about the 'absurd calumny' and 'poison' published. A riot began in 1750 when a rumour spread that working-class children were being kidnapped in order to supply blood in which a prince could bathe.

'The Parisians had more of a propensity to believe the malicious rumours and *libelles* that circulated clandestinely than the facts printed and published by order or with the permission of the government,' mourned Louis XVI's police chief.[17] The official *Gazette de France* did not report the fall of the Bastille. The march on the Bastille itself was triggered by a mistaken belief that royal troops had killed citizens elsewhere in Paris. The publications that began to appear in colossal volume after the disintegration of the government kept up the tradition: they provided the fuel for the factional debates that rapidly divided the revolutionary Assembly.

Before the Terror began in 1793, papers and periodicals – both revolutionary and royalist – were printing a total circulation estimated at 300,000 copies a day. By 1792 there were almost 500 newspapers in Paris. The *Feuille Villageoise* took the news of the capital to the provinces; schoolmasters would read it to assemblies of villagers. Events were moving too fast for books or pamphlets; at least 250 newspapers were founded in the last six months of 1789. The printed press was by now interchangeable with radical agitation. The French revolutionaries had watched the Irish use the press in England, had seen the suppression of the brief independence of the city of Geneva, the patriotic uprising in the Netherlands in 1785 and some had been in America when the revolution broke out at home.

Three years of open and prolific publishing came to an end with new definitions of sedition and libel in 1792. In 1797, the press was put under police control; 44 Paris newspapers were proscribed and stamp tax hiked the price of all newspapers. Napoleon, in the years after his coup, set up a complete control system for publishing and did not merely require newspapers to avoid doing wrong, but to do good. The system was extended to countries under French influence. In German states occupied by France, newspaper titles appeared in French-language versions.

The world's great informer

The American Revolution and the traumatic events in France left their imprint on European political cultures and on what people wanted to know. People were newly curious about constitutions. The extraordinary turbulence in Paris drove newspapers to worry about the timeliness of their reporting of events that had implications for all of France's neighbours. By 1803, the newspaper begun in 1785 as the *Daily Universal Register*,[18] and soon renamed *The Times*, was switching from relaying news selected and copied from other publications to sending its own reporters to events.

The turbulence in France made governments everywhere nervous of agitation. Attitudes to the press in Britain, France and America began to diverge according to the reactions inside the governing class to the events of an age in which print was so closely identified with radicalism and the risk of disorder. 'I have lent myself willingly as the subject of a great experiment,' Thomas Jefferson reflected in 1807, 'to demonstrate the falsehood of the pretext that freedom of the press is incompatible with orderly government.'

The freedom of which Jefferson wrote was not then so much freedom to report, but to express opinion. Vituperative hyperbole and insult were the standard weapons of the battle of ideas after the American War of Independence between the Federalists and anti-Federalists. The country's second president, John Adams, attacked the work of anti-Federalist editors as 'terrorism'.[19] War with France led Congress to bring in the Alien and Sedition Acts of 1798 and editors were convicted of 'false, scandalous and malicious writing'. Matthew Lyon, a senator known as the 'roaring Lyon of Vermont', was jailed for insulting Adams and re-elected with an enlarged majority while in prison. Jefferson, who succeeded Adams, let the Acts lapse.

In England, wary governments taxed newspapers, tightened laws on seditious and criminal libel, and made new laws to stop workers associating for political purposes. But newspapers and magazines continued to grow just the same. Educated people felt empowered to hold views about the government, authorities and even constitutional arrangements, which could be formed by comparing rival printed opinions. Inhibitions and the most direct controls used by the states were gone and would not return. The demand thus created for news and opinion led printers and publishers to adjust their agendas to appeal to growing readerships, beginning to grasp that 'public opinion' was coming into existence.

Political discussion and education were being gradually expanded by newspapers and periodicals as well as by books. Postal services, road networks, new schools and rising prosperity all contributed. English writers envied the Dutch Republic their freedoms; French writers looked to England. Samuel Johnson observed of newspapers that: 'Their cheapness brings them into universal use... their variety adapts them to everyone's taste.' The proliferation of printed material for sale began to create specialist workforces. Critics of books, operas and plays were in demand. Local newspapers flourished, shaping their own public spheres and helping to create civic identity. The *Salisbury Journal*, founded in 1731, recorded sales of 4,000 copies by 1800, which was larger than most newspapers in Paris at that time. The first owner died leaving a fortune of £100,000; the paper's income was from advertisements, many of which were for newly established schools. By 1760, some 35 provincial newspapers were selling a total of around 200,000 copies per week. By 1800, that sales figure had doubled.

Newspapers were edging towards higher moral ground. In the 18th century, newspapers often took payment to insert unsigned political attacks or puffs. A character in a farce written in 1793 says: 'If you are inclined to blacken, by a couple of lines, the reputations of a neighbour whose character neither you nor his life can possibly restore; you may do it for two shillings in one paper.' James Perry, the editor of *Morning Chronicle*, refused what were coyly known as 'insertion and correction fees'. He stopped taking free theatre tickets. *The Times* and *Morning Chronicle* competed to improve the reporting of parliamentary debates. In 1810, of the 23 reporters working in Parliament, 18 had university degrees.

But James Perry was prosecuted more than once when he was an editor. The limits of what the law or the government would tolerate had to be discovered by experiment and challenge. Henry Bate may have been the first journalist to be given a peerage (he became Lord Dudley when his political allies were in office) but he was also a priest, a magistrate and a playwright. A quarrelsome temperament, boastful self-promotion and sharp writing style made him a minor celebrity; he was nicknamed the 'Fighting Parson', was friendly with David Garrick and was known to Samuel Johnson, who disapproved of him. He had been an editor at the *Morning Post* but fell out with his colleagues and started the liberal *Morning Herald*. In 1781 Bate was jailed for 12 months for a libel on the Duke of Richmond; he was only able to serve the sentence when the prison had been rebuilt after a riot. His comic operas included *The Flitch of Bacon*. Towards the end of his life he helped to suppress riots by farm labourers protesting at enclosures in East Anglia. Bate's career illustrates the provisional, part-time and polemical nature of journalism in that era of popular disturbances and edgy governments. Many 21st-century bloggers are provisional, part-time and polemical.

Every species of intelligence

The development of journalism and ideas about what it should be were pushed and stimulated by new commercial possibilities. Editors such as Bate were giving way to men like John Walter II, who took over *The Times* in 1803. Walter's father had looked coldly on his son's plan to make the newspaper the printing firm's principal work. Walter Senior had defined a wide role for news, writing that papers should 'record every species of intelligence' and connect 'commercial intercourse between the different parts of the community'.[20] His son sharpened the newspaper, stopped the practice of taking bribes from ministers, successfully fought the Post Office over their expensive monopoly of translation of foreign papers and began exercising the influence that elite papers could wield in that century. *The Times* published details of the attempts by the Post Office to intercept mail from the newspaper's correspondents abroad; the interference stopped.[21] Walter was imprisoned for libel against two dukes but that did not stop him imagining and pursuing broader and higher ambitions. Journalists had to rely on their own resources and judgements. These astute strategies ensured that *The Times* achieved circulation dominance at the upper end of the market until it was overtaken by the *Daily Telegraph* in the middle of the 19th century.

But the breadth of this readership diluted political passion. *The Times* was perhaps the first newspaper to taste the pressures that came with a large readership. In 1823 William Hazlitt was one of the first to acknowledge the paper's agenda-setting power, describing it as 'the greatest engine of temporary opinion in the world... the origin of the mercantile interest'. But this was not quite the same as leadership of opinion: 'It takes up no falling causes; fights no uphill battle, advocates no great principle.'

The stamp tax on newspapers, which lifted their retail price by around one-third, was supposed to ensure that strong opinion did not circulate too freely beyond the educated elite. Like most such measures imposed in a society hungry for news and opinion to which it feels entitled, small new public spheres were created by the newspapers and magazines that did not pay the tax. These radical papers made early connections that built working-class associations, which became more influential as the Industrial Revolution gathered pace. They also helped to inspire the popular press. The 'unstampeds' saw two peaks of activity in the early 1820s and late 1830s. They began to disappear when the duty on Sunday newspapers was cut back in 1836. Copies were smuggled all over England in carts, coffins and by people dressed as Quakers; street sales relied on teams of dedicated sellers prepared to run risks. Titles ranged from *Knowledge Is Power* to the comic *Figaro in London* and the anti-clerical *Slap At the Church*. One of the most significant was simply called *Destructive*. One publisher tried to avoid the tax by printing on calico and calling it the *Political Handkerchief*. The readerships of the unstampeds were, for a relatively short period, large. William Cobbett's *Political Register* sold at 2*d* and at its peak sold more than 40,000 copies per week, probably more than all other stamped papers put together (and each copy would have been read by several people). When Cobbett began to pay the stamp tax, his sales fell to 400 per week. By 1836, the government estimated that the sales of the unstampeds exceeded those of the taxed papers.[22]

Alongside the political unstampeds were cheap, popular newspapers relying on improved and more systematic reporting of what was coming to be called 'police intelligence'. Raw material provided by crime and the courts could be trusted to help circulation; the establishment of police forces expanded the works of the criminal courts. Serious papers with smaller readerships were being taken more seriously by the political class; others were experimenting with new selections of material and presentation. No self-respecting newspaper would now do as the *Gloucester Journal* did back in 1720 and apologize for news being scarce, offering poems instead. The jumbled form of many newspaper stories, with facts and happenings piled in on top of each other, even if inconsistent, was giving way to better-marshalled narrative. A more systematic handling of sensation was also beginning to show. The violence was worse than in 21st-century news-papers, but sex was referred to in the most oblique terms. The first editor (and owner) of the *Daily Telegraph*, Joseph Moses Levy, insisted on what he called 'the human note' in his paper.[23] He was well ahead of his time and, by 1861, was selling twice as many copies as *The Times*.

The press had won much of its struggle to be free of government control. They had expanded their ideas of what they could be in a parlia-mentary democracy. They were about to enter mass markets and industrial publishing.

Notes

1   Smith, A (1979) *The Newspaper: An International History*, Thames and Hudson, London.

2   Williams, K (2010) *Read All About It: A History of the British Newspaper*, Routledge, London.

3   Smith. *The Newspaper: An International History*.

4   Smith, *The Newspaper: An International History*.

5   Williams, *Read All About It*.

6   Stephens, M (2007) *A History of News*, 3rd edn, Oxford University Press, New York.

7   Smith, *The Newspaper: An International History*.

8   Smith, *The Newspaper: An International History*.

9   Smith, *The Newspaper: An International History*.

10 Porter, R (2000) *Enlightenment: Britain and the Creation of the Modern World*, Allen Lane, London.

11 One of the first uses of the word listed by the *Oxford English Dictionary* is for 1712.

12 Starr, P (2004) *The Creation of the Media: Political Origins of Modern Communications*, Basic Books, New York.

13 Starr, *The Creation of the Media*.

14 Starr, *The Creation of the Media*.

15 See Chapter 5.

16 Schama, S (2004) *Citizens: A Chronicle of the French Revolution*, Penguin, London.

17 Stephens, *A History of News*.

18 Today, the name is still used for a single page of miscellaneous information in *The Times*.

19 Adams to Jefferson, 30 June 1813, quoted in Stephens, *A History of News*.

20 From the newspaper's editorial on its first day of publication, 1 January 1785.

21 Smith, *The Newspaper: An International History*.

22 Curran, J and Seaton, J (2010) *Power Without Responsibility: Press, Broadcasting and the Internet in Britain*, Routledge, London.

23 Marr, A (2004) *My Trade: A Short History of British Journalism*, Pan, London.

Furnishing the world with a new set of nerves

02

"A magazine or a newspaper is a shop. Each is an experiment and represents a new focus, a new ratio between commerce and intellect.

JOHN JAY CHAPMAN, *PRACTICAL AGITATION*, 1898

From the middle of the 19th century, the printed press went through a series of transformative upheavals. In what became the world's leading industrial economies, newspapers shed their origins as newsletters circulated among the politically and intellectually curious and began fighting to divide a mass market. The principal arguments about the media's influence today were defined in the last decades of the 19th century.

Shifts in technology and economics changed the value placed on journalism by its consumers and producers. Small-circulation publications, often driven by moral and political motives, were pushed to the margins by newspapers – and later by broadcasting channels – which had a more complicated relationship with their readers because they had more of them. Political, moral and commercial aims competed on larger editorial platforms, which shifted and reinvented their editorial personality and outlook accordingly. Newspapers also carried a wider range of content and coverage of societies, which were changing quickly.

Great institutions have grown from small beginnings, and periods of accelerated growth and opportunities see more new creations. The stress on politics, or what was often then called 'political economy', was diluting as papers grew to bigger businesses and depended more on advertising. In America, Britain and the major European states, the 19th century was a time of steadily expanding freedom and opportunity for the middle classes, best placed to benefit from parliamentary democracies whose franchise was cautiously expanded. The state's opportunities to control or manipulate were gradually shrunk. But this progress was ambiguous: there were prices to be paid for progress. Separated from subsidy, economic competition for survival became the driving imperative for any news business. This sets up the most basic tension present in one form or another in most newsrooms, the resolution of the tension between commercial and editorial objectives. Seizing and holding the attention and allegiance of a large readership was often the key to survival. Amid enormous economic and social changes in the developed world, the public sphere once dominated by monarchs and governments was being divided between public and private voices.

A great moral organ

The entrepreneurial boom in news that was to take place in the industrial societies in the second half of the 19th century can be captured by the foundation of four newspapers in New York in the space of 18 years. The four men who started them represented the range and mixture of motives that drove people to start newspapers. It was an era when founding a news-paper in that rapidly growing city was not too hard: competition had not yet driven start-up costs to discouraging levels.

The first newspaper in this quartet was *The Sun* ('It Shines For All'), founded in 1833 by a young businessman, Benjamin Day, who wanted to expand his printing business. 'The object of this paper,' the new publisher wrote, 'is to lay before the public... all the news of the day, and at the same time offer an advantageous medium for advertisements.' Advertising was the rising tide of income that was floating new publications, although many did not survive for long. American newspapers by this time were already devoting a majority of their space to advertisements and were relying on them more heavily than their British equivalents.[1] At a cover price of 1 penny per copy, Day's business model was to win advertising on the back of a high circulation. Day was promising broad coverage, but he was not pro-mising accuracy: two years later *The Sun* featured a sensational story that British astronomers had discovered life on the Moon. By that time, Day had driven *The Sun* to sales of 20,000 copies per day; the city's total newspaper circulation when he started had been 26,500, with the largest selling 4,500.

Success of that kind breeds imitators. The most remarkable of these was James Gordon Bennett, who established the New York *Herald* in 1835, which was to become the largest-selling paper in the world. This success was almost entirely due to Bennett's extraordinary talents as a showman. He was three times head of the New York Yacht Club and liked to be known as 'the Commodore'. He was independently wealthy and a bombastic, volatile bully with an inventive mind and a popular touch. The *Herald* was the first newspaper to cover the stock market. Bennett thought big and travelled incessantly: his yacht carried a crew of 100, a Turkish bath and an Alderney cow. His reporters did not have to wait for news to happen. The Commodore would start a stunt, an event, a competition, as one employee reminisced, 'that should find an echo in popular imagination and stimulate demand for more'.[2] His greatest coup was to send Henry Morton Stanley to find Dr Livingstone in Africa. He reached the magic sales number of 20,000 in a year, doubled the *Herald*'s price and saw the circulation reach 60,000 by 1860.

Horace Greeley started New York's twelfth newspaper, the *Tribune* in 1841. He made a point of saying that the paper would hope to be self-sufficient in news. That is to say, it would not rely on curation, picking up and repeating material from other publications or scraps of unverified information that reached it. The *Tribune* would have its own correspondents, and not just in the United States but all over the world; Karl Marx contributed articles from Europe, many of them actually written by Friedrich Engels. This new form of editorial organization, Greeley assured his readers, would make the newspaper a 'Great Moral Organ'. In his editorial organization and research, Greeley was ahead of his time.

A decade later another newspaper began life in the same city, founded by Henry Raymond and called the *New York Times*. Raymond's mission statement was more nuanced and less bold. 'We do not believe,' he wrote, 'that everything in society is either exactly right or exactly wrong; what is good we desire to improve; what is evil to exterminate and reform.' In a society still profoundly influenced at all levels by religion, the urge to moral improvement was still present. But it is tempered in the *New York Times* editorial by an early stress on the importance of balance, of taking into account many possible points of view and trying to appeal to them all simultaneously. From this instinct a wholly new professional sense of identity began to slowly take hold. Journalism was no longer being seen as truth and falsehood grappling in a battle of ideas, but something produced by professionals using means defined by consistent rules and scientific self-discipline. Truth began to be associated with the idea of objectivity and the neutral viewpoint.

Many newspapers 'scaled' – as we would say now – very rapidly, growing fast in conditions favourable to forming communities based on shared curiosity. The technology was different, but the effort to establish new editorial identities and reader loyalties is not so different to the search by today's online start-ups for market share and a workable business model. A connection with a community of readers is the building block on which all other ambitions have to be built, whether the ambition is serious or frivolous, or a combination of both. In the 1860s, manufacturers who had become wealthy from cotton or steel financed new publications. In the early 21st century, the investors in news are dotcom millionaires or venture capitalists. In both cases, the dividing line between commercial, political and social aims can be hard to see.

The true Church of England

Britain in the years before 1832 was dominated by the struggles over parliamentary reform, the battle of ideas sharpened by the knowledge of the bloodshed and terror that had recently gripped France. The English political class grasped the French lesson that suppression of radical political movements and the information and networks on which any such movement depends would not merely fail if attempted, but might actually light the fire of violent revolution that they so feared. That calculation both encouraged the radicals and tempered aristocratic and Tory dislike of the press. If the choice lay between burning workshops or hayricks on the one hand and insulting, provocative editorials in unstamped papers on the other, enough of the landowners who dominated the voting rolls knew that vituperation in print was the better price to pay. They might not have agreed with the radical paper *Yellow Dwarf*, but they were nervous of entirely suppressing opinions such as this: 'Public opinion can never exist as a power in the State, unless there exist also persons who expose to hatred and contempt those Ministers and those laws which they conceive to be detrimental to the interests of the community.'[3]

And so ideas about the accountability and transparency of monarchy and aristocracy, about representation and social justice circulated more freely. Taxation ensured that newspapers, stamped or unstamped, did not circulate very widely. Newspaper readership in France began to overtake that of Britain and the number of new papers in America grew both in established centres of population and newly built ones.[4] But even in the limited communities linked in print, every reader was getting used to the feeling that they all knew about the same ideas. Not everyone sharing the ideas was a reader: until at least the middle of the 19th century, newspapers were still regularly read aloud in clubs, marketplaces and – later – public libraries.

The circulation and publishing of information – or attempts to suppress that freedom – has been pivotal to insurrections in history. That has been true of the English Civil War (1642–49); also of revolutions: American (1775), French (1789), Italian (1848–70), central European (1989), Russian (1917 and 1991) and Arab (2011–12). Many people in the governing and middle classes feared that Britain in the early 19th century was in a pre-revolutionary state. But they were at least as fearful of ill-considered attempts to suppress or disrupt agitation.

Most newspapers reported news at second or third hand, 'curating' or 'aggregating', as we say now, or simply borrowing stories printed elsewhere. Direct eye-witness reporting was rare but not unknown. In 1819, Thomas Barnes, the editor of *The Times*, sent John Tyas to report an outdoor meeting on parliamentary reform on St Peter's Fields in Manchester. Competition to report speeches, accurately and at length, was warming up. Tyas was helped up on to the speakers' wagon by Henry Hunt, one of the meeting's organizers. From this vantage point, Tyas had a clear view of the bloodshed in what became known as the 'Peterloo massacre'.[5] The Manchester Yeomanry charged into the crowd, killing 12 men and wounding more than 400. Tyas's stubborn insistence on the simple fact that the crowd had been unarmed helped to demolish official disinformation that the mounted soldiers were in danger. *The Times* was keen to underline that Tyas had no connection with the meeting's organizers, making a distinction that would have been irrelevant to most newspapers. It stated: 'The individual who furnishes this report... had never previously spoken to' Hunt or any other organizer. *The Times* was starting to see that its influence rested on being seen as independent of the actors in the political drama. To many people, there was an edge of danger in tolerating press freedoms, but they were beginning to relax and see these freedoms as helpful and not dangerous. They began to think of newspapers as a natural part of an industrializing urban world.

Around 1830 the term 'journalist' began to be used in England to describe people who were beginning to earn a living from working on newspapers. One of the first people to revel in this change had been an influential French revolutionary, Camille Desmoulins. 'Here I am a journalist,' he wrote, 'and it is rather a fine role. No longer is it a wretched mercenary profession, enslaved by the government. Today in France it is the journalist who holds the tablets, the album of the censor, and who inspects the senate, the consuls and the dictator himself.'[6] The freedom and prestige that Desmoulins had so briefly enjoyed soon evaporated,[7] but the memory of what was possible remained and seeped slowly into Europe's consciousness.

It is only a short step from Desmoulins to the historian of the French Revolution, Thomas Carlyle, indulging in hyperbole in 1829 over the moral and political influence of English newspapers and particularly of *The Times*, then near the peak of its influence: 'The true Church of England at this moment lies in the editors of its newspapers. These preach to the people daily, weekly, admonishing kings themselves, advising peace or war with an authority which only the first reformers, and a long-past class of popes were possessed of.'[8]

The Steam Intellect Society

The scene was set for a steady expansion of media power and reach from the middle of the 19th century onwards and it occurred, with important local variations, in Britain, America and France. Similar developments did not occur in Germany and Japan until later in the century.

In Britain, the growth was gradual because the debates that prompted the abolition of the Stamp Acts lasted decades. The forces eroding the laws that kept newspaper prices artificially high were a rich mix of varied motives very typical of their times. Some, but by no means all, of the arguments that eventually prevailed were claims for the democratic importance of press freedom of the kind that would be heard today. But more common and more effective were the appeal of wider education, political literacy and the promotion of moral and religious ideas. The debates over the constitution driven by the revolutions in America and France had expanded newspaper readerships, but also convinced some commentators that the small scale of the readerships was itself a problem. If a newspaper could be used to mobilize a segment of society, could this power not be harnessed to a less partisan purpose and contribute to wider social harmony? The killings at Peterloo saw a number of angry new radical newspapers created in Manchester; the *Manchester Guardian* (now *The Guardian*) was founded by cotton manufacturers who wanted a more reasonable publication to squeeze radical rivals out of business, which they succeeded in doing. If social improvement was an important aim, more readers needed to be drawn in. For that to happen they had to be educated. That would not be achieved in schools alone, but by making journalism reach further.

The expansion of the readership for print began with educational and moral aims more easily achieved by capital and machinery, which made news publishing more profitable and enabled innovation and experiment. Victorian journalists did not feel in the least self-conscious about seeing their work as 'improving' or 'lifting' readers out of ignorance or poverty, or both. The novelist Wilkie Collins found himself curious about whether people who did not read the long, grey columns of broadsheet newspapers read something else and, if so, what that might be. He embarked on an anthropological expedition to find out. He published his results in *Household Words* and called his discovery 'The Unknown Public'. He wrote: 'Do the customers at publishing houses, the members of book-clubs and circulating libraries, and the purchasers and borrowers of newspapers and reviews, compose altogether the great bulk of the reading public of England?... The public just mentioned represents nothing more than the minority.'

Collins found the same in 'the deserts of West Cornwall', in Whitechapel and in a 'dreary little lost town at the north of Scotland'. People who did not read newspapers and 'reviews' read illustrated 'penny-novel-journals', which mixed fiction with problem pages. These journals were interchangeable and their readers 'unfathomable', but the readers probably numbered in the millions. He noticed that, apart from stories, each of these magazines carried non-fiction in the form of 'Answers to Correspondents'. The editors replied to queries about cures for warts or knock knees, protocol on flirting with the opposite sex and whether you could sell lemonade without a licence. In noticing the consistent demand for this kind of information Collins was making an early observation of one of the most consistently neglected aspects of newspaper and magazine publishing then and now: guidance about the problems of daily life has always been a faster route to a mass readership than essays about political economy.

We are all learning to move together

From the abolition of the last of the 'taxes on knowledge' between 1853 and 1861, all the significant trends pushed the publishing of news to become, for the first time, a sizeable commercial industry. Britain enjoyed an unprecedented economic acceleration. The average annual per head growth rate between 1830 and 1870 was between three and four times that of 1760–1800. In 1850, just over one-fifth of the British population was active in farming, at a time when the figure on the Continent would have been closer to 50 per cent. By 1910 only 1 in 11 Britons worked on the land.[9] Cities grew in proportion and millions of consumers joined manufacturing economies. Newspapers explored and expressed embryonic urban and civic identities. Real incomes grew and leisure time increased for many. Kerosene lamps enabled people to read in the hours of darkness at lower cost than candles. Literacy grew steadily and its growth accelerated after the Education Act of 1870 made school compulsory for children aged between 5 and 13. The voting franchise was extended at intervals,[10] creating a wider pool of potential readers who could be persuaded to read about politics. Political parties remade themselves as they adjusted to marketing their policies for votes and competed to create friendly publications.

In the United States, a rooted opposition to stamp taxes ensured that newspapers were never priced artificially high to protect stability and a ruling class. By 1850, 3 million American children were in primary school and in 1852 a law allowed newspapers very cheap prepaid postage, a development subsidy of great importance. Railways in many countries allowed newspapers to be sold at increasingly long distances from wherever they were printed.

Capital was available to adopt technical innovations quickly. In the 1820s the discovery by the Fourdrinier brothers of a process to make newsprint from vegetable and animal fibres in rags allowed the price of paper to fall by between one-quarter and one-half. By 1860, printing was routinely on rolls and not single sheets of paper. From the 1830s and 1840s, the fall in the price of books and newspapers were especially steep in America and both were markedly cheaper than they were in Britain at the time. American newspapers, untaxed, could be sold at 1d per copy in the 1830s, anticipating prices not achieved in Britain until the 1860s. Although not simultaneous, price changes in Europe and America were all in the same direction. It was not a sudden or uniform change, but cumulatively it amounted to a revolution in availability and useability of information. In democratic societies, the increase in information in storage and in circulation has continued to grow ever since.

The greatest changes came in successive waves of innovation in printing machinery on both sides of the Atlantic. *The Times* had first installed a steam-powered press in 1814, which greatly speeded up the 250 copies per hour produced by hand presses. In 1846, the American Richard Hoe developed a fast rotary press and sold it to a Parisian newspaper. With refinements, these presses could print 20,000 copies per hour. The technique of 'stereotyping' allowed moulds to be taken from type and put on presses; the precious type could then be reused. Print runs could be better adjusted to demand.[11] The economics of publishing grew more attractive as urban retail advertising markets – which, among other things are information networks – spread and grew richer.

The repeal of three specific taxes completed the removal of the British government's restrictions on news publishing: advertising duty ended in

1853, stamp duty in 1855 and paper duty in 1861. Reformers had argued that if newspapers could be sold more cheaply then society's differences would be settled by calm, better-informed discussion. Walter Bagehot defended the influence of the 'propertied class' on the press because 'its weight is always in favour of order and decency without which political life soon becomes a mad strife of factions'. Charles Dickens, launching the *Daily News* in 1846, said that its aims were to press for 'principles of progress and improvement... the bodily comfort, mental elevation and general contentment of the British people'. The journalists who dominated public commentary saw the extension of the franchise as a careful rebalancing of the constitutional contract between elite and voters. Charles Knight, proprietor of the *Penny Magazine* and campaigner against taxes on knowledge, wrote: 'It is not only necessary that the people should feel their rights, but that they should exercise them wisely and temperately.' Radical journalists, not surprisingly, felt that promotion of the press's educational mission was nothing but a subtler form of social control. Knight was one of the founders of the Society for the Diffusion of Useful Knowledge (nicknamed 'the Steam Intellect Society') whose earnest publications the radicals dismissed as ineffectual.

The drive was to increase knowledge rather than to monitor or hold accountable the government or the state. The government could only function with the consent of those able to vote and it required watching; criticism could be, and was, uninhibited. But editors also felt that they held a responsibility for the quality of public debate. The state was, in that era, a very much smaller organization than it became in the 20th century and, as such, it had very much less direct effect on most peoples' lives. Writers who observed and debated the expansion of both the franchise and newspaper circulations were, with few exceptions, optimists. Society and its governance, science and economics were growing more complex and required explanation and popularization. Strong political opinion was normal inside limited confines of the political class, but a wide readership needed a broader approach. A wide range of experiments could now take place. They were enabled by relatively low investment costs, technical innovation and the fall of prices kept high by tax. A search began for better ways to anticipate readers' tastes and more ingenious ways to satisfy them.

The *Daily News*, edited by Dickens, had been designed by its backers as a challenger to *The Times*. Dickens abandoned the editorship after only a few weeks, finding the job demandingly incompatible with his wish to write novels, conduct a gregarious social life and travel abroad when he felt like it. The newspaper survived his departure but never made a dent in the position of *The Times*. Dickens fared better with another start-up, the weekly *Household Words*, which mixed social reporting (for example, against child prostitution and in favour of better public health action against cholera) with fiction. Besides the easier weekly publication schedule, Dickens had taken the precaution of making sure that he appointed a capable editor to get the publication out. One of Dickens's earliest hires was the novelist Elizabeth Gaskell, with whom he was by turns both exasperated and flirtatious. Gaskell first published both the Cranford series and *North and South* in *Household Words*.[12] Fiction and non-fiction were both part of the press's educative endeavour.

Well before the truly mass audiences for broadcasting in the 20th century, the new scale of publishing reshaped ideas about how people were connected. Reflecting on many changes in communications, personal and public, the periodical *Scientific Siftings* noted in 1892 how 'we are all learning to move together, act together, achieve in vast companies'.[13] Newspapers and their pivotal role in embryonic political organizations had been responsible for raising voter turnout in America,[14] and elsewhere. Now dawned the realization that newspapers could mobilize, galvanize and influence on a very large scale indeed – and that this power might trump influence and prestige among a small, elite readership. But this required the trick of mixing serious news with entertainment in exactly the right quantities. Experiments in this new chemistry began.

Popular and cheap magazines and books had grown in reach as literacy and leisure grew. American popular newspapers had been growing fast and English journalists began to import their techniques. In 1845, two American journalists had founded the solidly named *National Police Gazette*, which flourished for more than a century on sex, crime and violence. Edward Lloyd, a Chartist who started out selling books and newspapers, launched a *Penny Sunday Times and People's Police Gazette*. He trumped these two years later with a better-judged mix in *Lloyd's Illustrated Sunday Newspaper*, which was renamed *Lloyd's Weekly* and became the first paper to sell 1 million copies. Lloyd had raised his capital from the sale of Old Parr's Laxative Pills.[15]

Flourishing Sunday papers had been founded in Britain in the 1840s, the three largest from radical origins and selling strongly in the smokestack industrial areas sympathetic to the Chartist movement: Yorkshire, Lancashire, the Midlands, South Wales and lowland Scotland. The first edition of the *News of the World* in 1843 carried a headline that set the tone for the whole of the newspaper's 168-year history:[16] 'Extraordinary case of drugging and violation'. In 1856, *Reynold's News* was one of the first Sundays to reach a circulation of 100,000, which probably meant an actual readership of half a million. These figures were not to be overtaken by daily papers until the *Star* reached 200,000 in the 1880s and the *Daily Mail* close to 1 million in 1900. At least until the 1880s, *Reynold's News* devoted one-fifth of its coverage to politics.

A vast agora

Motives are rarely unmixed and purposes usually multiple. Economic opportunity and the degree of political and legal freedom allowed a very broad range of opportunity for trial and error. Publishers aimed at new demographic groups, imported new techniques and ideas from abroad and drove technical innovation in searching for a competitive edge. The Second and Third Reform Acts (1867 and 1884) doubled the size of the British electorate, taking it from 1.5 million men to 5 million. Politically partisan newspapers ran alongside popular, non-partisan papers. Newspapers rose in circulation, others began; editorial identities changed or were reinvented. What were often known on both sides of the Atlantic as 'penny papers' began as entrepreneurial experiments to pursue circulation and advertising income but their editors and publishers quickly saw that a sustainable business could wield independent political influence – and shifted their coverage to do so. Newspapers brokered of a new relationship between the middle and upper classes. Their editors and publishers experimented energetically at the intersection of politics, education and market choice.

Journalists grew to realize that their larger influence meant both more controversy and more prestige. The telegraph and faster printing presses, wrote the editor W T Stead, 'have converted Britain into a vast agora, or assembly of the whole community, in which the discussion of the affairs of State is carried on from day to day in the hearing of the whole people'. Some journalists seemed to think that they were responsible for the shining glory of Britain's freedoms and empire. Charles Pebody, writing in 1882 when he became editor of the *Yorkshire Post*, thought that the English press had 'purified the public service; raised the tone of our public life'.

Affluence and fiercer competition changed the work of reporters. Foreign and war correspondents gradually escaped from wholesale manipulation and control of governments and wielded new power as a result. William Howard Russell of *The Times*, in his frankly critical reporting of the incompetence of the Crimean war generals both on the field of battle and behind the lines, carved a new path by being both vividly personal and, as a result, influential. Russell was benefitting from a readership that was more prepared to read reporting, which was no longer written in a style dominated by the impersonal, deferential memorandum. Eye-witness reporting in detail was being used in a newspaper that had come slowly to this new style of writing. Russell was untypical among war correspondents in that he was interested in – and good at talking to – ordinary soldiers as well as to generals.

The battles between *The Times* and the government had a delayed effect not fully visible until the reporting of the Franco-Prussian war of 1870–71. The star reporter in that war was Archibald Forbes, who argued against censored despatches: 'Independent war correspondence has become necessary to the contentment of the nation. It placates the just uneasiness that is occasioned by meagre, unexhaustive and not always wholly candid communications from official sources.' The phrase 'just uneasiness' catches exactly the equilibrium point for the wary attitude of the Victorian newspaper reader towards government: neither monitory in the suspicious, sceptical sense of the 20th century but not entirely deferential and trusting either. They wanted a strong state but they wanted to be able to watch what it was doing.

Competition for fast news in the Franco-Prussian war had been speeded up by the arrival of better rotary presses (both *The Times* and the *Daily Telegraph* bought them in the 1860s[17]) and the wide adoption of the telegraph. Before the war, summaries of news had been sent by telegram and a correspondent had followed that with a longer narrative sent by post. The *Daily News* now told its correspondents to telegraph all their reporting; the paper tripled its sales during the war.[18]

British reporters, adopting a practice begun in American newspapers, not only interviewed people but began quoting what they said directly – and this was seen as an extraordinary degree of informality when it began in the 1880s. Advertising income was beginning to give newspaper owners a sense of permanent political independence and leverage. Journalists began to think in terms of careers in newspapers, rather than switching between literature, news and politics. A National Association of Journalists met for the first time in Birmingham in 1886.[19] In America, from the beginning of the 20th century, journalists were being professionally trained in university-based schools.[20]

An American visitor noted with approval in 1888 that *The Times* had broken with the sordid employment practices of the past and made its offices 'a comfortable club'. Other newspapers demonstrated by the breadth of their activities that they were grand institutions of permanent status. *La Prensa* of Buenos Aires, by the early 20th century, maintained a gym, hospital and restaurant for its employees; the newspaper's offices dispensed free advice to the public on law, medicine and agriculture and laid on concerts, lectures and other events.[21] All of this reflected a conviction driven by the development of the press that the issue for the society it served was not simply the accuracy of facts gathered and transmitted but the quality of the selection and the interpretation of those facts. Scrappy start-ups were becoming institutions.

The driving force behind these shifts in attitude and social position was the steady expansion of supply and demand. Between 1837 and 1887, the number of English provincial newspapers grew from 264 to 1,366, more than a fivefold increase. London-based newspapers grew twelvefold over the same period: from 56 to 680. These figures are for newspapers of all kinds: daily papers went from 43 in the capital in 1868 to 139 in 1886. By 1900, the number had risen to 172.[22]

Newspaper publishing, no longer an add-on to the printing industry, was becoming capital-intensive, but it was also profitable if the formula was right. To start Dickens's *Daily News* a sum of £100,000 had to be raised, and around the same amount was spent over a decade before it broke even. *The Times* made £30,000 in 1845; the *Manchester Guardian* made nearly £7,000 per year. A provincial daily could make £3,000 per year.[23] But by the late 1890s, the attractions of profit and influence had lifted the barriers to entry. The start-up investment for the *Daily Mail* in 1896 was £500,000 and the equivalent cost in the United States at the time reckoned at $1 million.[24]

People with no previous access to regular printed information now had greater information at their disposal than ever before. Sudden expansions of available information have long effects in successive waves of change, some of them delayed. The explosion of internet-borne information in the 21st century will be felt equally gradually. The exploitation of the new opportunities for publishing news in the 19th century was pragmatic and opportunistic: zig-zag progress directed by trial and error. The 21st century will not be different.

I order five virgins

Almost every significant press trend of the last years of the 19th century was present in the emblematic career of the peculiar W T Stead, best known as the editor of the *Pall Mall Gazette*. Stead created one of the great news sensations of his day, experimented with new publications and readerships, and considered himself a moral campaigner. He held fierce religious views, even if he expressed them in unusual terms: he called God the 'Senior Partner'. He campaigned against the exploitation of women, particularly as child prostitutes, while being a flirtatious predator towards attractive young women, whom he hired to his staff in large numbers. He understood the use of sensation better than anyone of his era, but allowed himself wide licence with the facts. He was gifted at dramatizing issues, the confidant of ministers, far-sighted and a hero to many women who appreciated his campaigning on their behalf. He was also inconsistent, dictatorial, dishonest, grandiose and shipwrecked one publication he had founded by campaigning, insistently but in vain, on behalf of spiritualism.[25] He can certainly be described as radical and a maverick. Stead's career also illustrates the power and risk of sensation.

Stead saw no distinction between journalism and activism. He argued at one point in his career that 'government by journalism' was preferable to being governed by Parliament, filled as it was by less-well-informed and more passive men. The reportage and campaign in 1885 with which Stead is most famously associated did succeed in strengthening the momentum for a change in the law on child prostitutes. The legal age of consent was raised from 13 to 16. In much the same way, Stead had created a climate of concern about housing conditions, which saw the creation of a Royal Commission. The newspaper, Stead wrote, is 'the great court in which all grievances are heard'.

The *Pall Mall Gazette*'s story in which Stead 'bought' a 13-year-old girl to take her to a brothel, ran for seven days and temporarily took the staid, clubland evening newspaper's circulation from 12,000 to almost 10 times that number. Reprints of the series, selling for 2*d*, were read by 1.5 million people.[26] The overall title was 'The Maiden Tribute of Modern Babylon' and Stead, who had pioneered the more audacious use of pictures and 'cross-heads' (subsidiary headings in the text designed to make long articles more appealing to read), went to town. Using techniques already common in the penny press and the popular Sunday papers, Stead served up material not before dealt with in a respectable newspaper, under lines such as 'Strapping Girls Down', 'The Forcing of Unwilling Maids' and 'I Order Five Virgins'.

Child prostitution was one of the most appalling aspects of Victorian cities. But the sensation generated by Stead's story has created a myth so strong that the drawbacks of his 'reporting' are rarely looked at. Stead was not founding but was introducing to mainstream journalism a hypocrisy that continues to this day and that suits many readers: complaining indignantly about a scandal while reporting the details in full and with relish. He was not solely responsible for the reform that raised the age of consent: his complaint was that MPs had been discussing the change for too long. In procuring the girl, Stead had broken the law and, for this, served three months in prison; this additional drama was, of course, very welcome publicity both for him and for the campaign. But the central difficulty of the story lies in the impossibility of working out how much of it was actually true. As Stead's most recent biographer says, 'it is impossible to distill fact from fiction: there is simply too much of the reformer's zeal mixed in with the impartial observer's commentary to get a firm hold on reality'.[27] Huge as the temporary increase had been to the *Pall Mall Gazette*'s circulation, it returned to its usual modest levels when the fuss had died down.

The question that Stead posed with the 'Maiden Tribute' stories was one that he himself considered foolish: 'Sensationalism in journalism,' he wrote, 'is justifiable up to the point that it is necessary to arrest the eye of the public and compel them to admit the necessity of the action.' Much great journalism, disclosing facts not known, or concealed, has relied on being entertaining and selective as well as true. Important revelations rely on sources that cannot be disclosed. But at least some of what Stead wrote was probably untrue or embroidered; there is – and was at the time – simply no way of knowing for certain. Stead acknowledged no obligation to account for how he knew what he had discovered; much of what he wrote was not verifiable by anyone else. But he had forced powerful people to confront an issue that they had preferred to forget about. It was a powerful piece of emotive reportage. It was also a sloppily reported stunt that provided an example for later imitations, with less notable results.

The few dozen lines of drivel

Affluence, a widening voting franchise and school education, accelerated communications technology; a lack of any restraining legislation allowed mass-circulation daily papers to become permanent features of society and politics in Britain – and on a truly national scale. These conditions were rare in the rest of Europe in the late 19th century: many states were small or had less developed communications infrastructure across the whole country. With the tapping of new readerships in Britain, new commercial imperatives set more of the context for journalism. The foundations were laid for the press barons of the 20th century.

But the power of popular newspapers, becoming evident just before the beginning of radio broadcasting in the 1920s, also inaugurated a heated debate over the responsibilities of journalists, editors and publishers, which continues to this day. These arguments began to connect the idea of editorial autonomy with professional quality, which began to be seen as associated with objectivity, impartiality and detachment. The First World War played a large part in this change of mind. In Britain, a strong current of opinion after the war criticized newspapers and writers who had been censored, or had censored themselves in the war years by helping to conceal the grim truth of the war. Mistrust of the state, and of field marshalls and generals in particular, had deepened. British correspondents covering the Irish revolt immediately after the First World War showed a marked reluctance to see through military eyes what was happening, or to rely on their readers believing in the authority of official versions.[28]

The rapid rise of the popular newspapers can be measured by their prices. In 1889, there were 42 1*d* and 10 halfpenny morning papers in England. By 1913, the proportions had been reversed: there were 19 halfpenny morning papers and 10 1*d* papers.[29] In 1888, T P O'Connor launched the *Star*, a radical halfpenny paper that had backers with traditional political motives. O'Connor, much influenced by the uninhibited techniques of the newer American papers, blended anti-elite radical feeling with plenty of non-political coverage. O'Connor lasted only two years as editor but his attitude and innovations outlasted him. The *Star* ran a gossip column and a sports section and began using 'Stop Press'. Long-winded writing and 'obsolete journalism' would be left behind: the paper promised to be 'animated, readable and stirring'. Reporting for the first time an event usually treated as one of importance in the political calendar, the newspaper referred casually to 'the few dozen lines of drivel known as the Queen's Speech'. By the time O'Connor left the editor's chair, circulation had reached 140,000.[30]

The progress of popular newspapers was slower in France, and briefly went into reverse. The attempted revolutions of 1848 were followed by reaction that brought with it laws to suppress news and comment, which were not lifted until 1877. A 'law of hate'[31] was proposed in the Assembly in 1850. The seconder of the motion said: 'We must finish with journalism as we have finished with barricades.' The practice of reporting, as opposed to commentary, came relatively slowly to French newspapers; relatively few had foreign correspondents posted abroad before the turn of the century. Meanwhile, in the United States, American newspapers growing in a geographically dispersed society enjoyed a postal distribution subsidy that weighted the odds in favour of starting a new paper. There were 9,810 newspapers of all kinds in the United States in 1880, 16,948 in 1890 and 21,272 in 1900.

American newspapers were starting to rely on national and international news relayed by 'wire' from a new cooperative, the Associated Press, which had been started by the larger publishers. Wholesaling news as a commodity to many different outlets meant strict guidelines and rules keeping reporters to a neutral viewpoint.

The pace at which news had to be published had been quickened by the use of the telegraph. One writer just before the First World War captured the extent to which newspaper culture coloured popular consciousness, by saying that it was 'furnishing the world with a new set of nerves'.[32] Once a reliable network reached far enough – a cable connected London to India in 1863 and London to New York in 1866 – it proved a boost to the newly created Reuters agency, which could dispense with the services of pigeons. Reuters, aiming to sell their service all over the globe, also required their reporters to omit comment and opinion and to record the facts. In more serious newspapers, the balance shifted between fact and comment, although at different rates in different countries. Reporters were not just competing against rival newspapers but with news agencies, which gave their editors back home a benchmark for speed and accuracy. New technological possibilities had emerged and in due course a new journalistic template was created.

Press development in Germany and Japan was relatively slow and the attitudes of authority did not soften before 1880. Japanese governments of the Edo period saw the governance of the media as an issue of public order;[33] new laws were not published in papers so as to inhibit public discussion. Later in the century, matters improved when the publication of news was treated as public education. The foundation of what is now one of the largest daily newspaper markets in the world probably began with compulsory education and a national school system in 1871. Italy's newspapers, despite being boosted by the Risorgimento and national unification, suffered from a low literacy rate: two out of three Italians could not read or write in 1875. Imperial authorities in the empires that then coloured the map also saw news, particularly in local languages, as a matter of public order. The Indian Mutiny of 1857 saw severe controls imposed and the Vernacular Press Act in India in 1878 consolidated them. English language newspapers were, because they were less restricted, important in creating political momentum for detaching India from Britain. The Australian province of New South Wales saw a bitter struggle waged by Edward Smith Hall, who founded the *Sydney Monitor* as early as 1826, against the British colonial authorities who regularly put the editor in jail. The authorities lost: by the time of Hall's death in 1861, there were 50 independent newspapers in the province.

In Britain, the steady growth of circulation, advertising and profits in the last part of the 19th century laid one foundation stone that had profoundly important consequences in the future: by experiment, using the latest print-ing and distribution techniques and taking advantage of the fact that Britain is a small, densely populated island, the major newspaper owners built 'national' newspapers. The difference between this market structure and the norm in most other countries of the world is often not noticed. British national papers both enjoyed, and became dependent on, a nationwide readership and advertising market. By the middle of the 20th century this had become ferociously competitive, because the keenness to access the power and influence that went with national newspapers meant that there were always more newspapers than the market could sustain. A national newspaper market provides huge profits in good times and big risks in bad times.[34] A national market structure also tends to create a high concentra-tion of ownership of large circulations. Decentralized newspaper markets, which occur in many more places such as America, France and Germany, are harder to dominate even in the current era of remote printing.

A press typhoon

The principal beneficiary of the rising appetite for cheap newspapers in Britain was Alfred Harmsworth, later Lord Northcliffe, and deservedly best known for being, in 1896, the founding proprietor of the *Daily Mail*. By the early 1920s, the Harmsworth brothers controlled newspapers with a total circulation of 6 million copies – assumed to be the largest circulation under one company anywhere in the world. The creation of the *Daily Mail* and its rivals changed the balance of power in politics. Newspapers had already freed themselves from constraining laws and now built real economic autonomy. That success generated a quantity and kind of power that could intimidate whole governments. As the 20th century opened, newspapers were commanding readerships large enough to claim to represent huge con-stituencies. If they were claiming to represent opinions to the government, they wielded enough influence to do so without much fear that the govern-ment could retaliate.

There were limits to the exercise of this power. The press lords who enjoyed such power for a brief period in the first half of the century could goad, threaten, provoke and stimulate. But they could not guarantee how readers would react. They could spread, amplify and intensify feelings but only if they connected to widespread instincts and beliefs. If a newspaper's personality or views decoupled from those basic feelings, its influence and reach shrank. Decades of research have not settled the question of the extent

– if any – to which mass media create or instil basic opinions or instincts. Much reflection on this, from academic analysis to journalists' instant evaluations, tends to look for journalism's direct effect. Can it be said that a certain story or series of stories caused a particular result? Very rarely can this neat cause and effect be established. As research has more often indicated, the news media's influence lies more in defining the agenda of what is important or in marginalizing either debates or opinions. It is for that reason that plurality of voices and ownership became, in early 20th-century Britain, a contested discussion for the first time. If one editor or publisher can exclude or minimize an issue as being uninteresting to the public, are there enough alternatives who can test that conclusion? These issues came to a head with Lord Northcliffe and the *Daily Mail*.

Northcliffe's original formula had nothing to do with reporting news or public affairs at all. He had worked for George Newnes, founder of *Tit-Bits*, a weekly magazine that curated short paragraphs of amusing information from magazines all over the world. Newnes had no pretensions to be doing journalism that 'directs the affairs of nations'; he published 'wholesome and harmless entertainment' and had an enviable circulation of 700,000. Northcliffe saw that Newnes was sitting on a formula that had still greater possibilities. 'The man who produced this *Tit-Bits* has got hold of a bigger thing than he imagines,' Northcliffe wrote. He started his own rival, *Answer to Correspondents*, and rescued it from early death by running a competition for readers to guess how much gold there would be in the Bank of England on a named date. He added other titles: *Comic Cuts*, *Chips* (with the first strip cartoon), *Forget-Me-Not* and *Home Sweet Home*.

Northcliffe, joined by his brother who ran the powerfully effective and innovative business operation, launched the *Daily Mail*, majoring on brevity. It was the 'Busy Man's Daily Journal' and, in a signed editorial on the newspaper's first anniversary, Northcliffe pointed out to his rivals that their weak spot had been their 'verbosity'. Readers didn't want it and had taught him so. This did not stop Northcliffe wanting to teach once he had a daily paper under his hand – the 'Chief'[35] sent dozens of instructions to his editors every day, and the Mail alone had nearly 1 million readers. He published half the newspapers read in London in 1914, including the *Daily Mirror*, *The Times* and *The Observer*. By 1948, the three largest press groups owned 43 per cent of all circulation. Northcliffe had instincts both radical and conservative and pushed his opinions ranging from politics and war to the attractions of wholemeal bread and sweet peas. He conspired with Lloyd George to bring about the downfall of Herbert Asquith and to install Lloyd George in Downing Street. Lloyd George handed out 23 high honours to men connected to the press at the end of the First World War.

But Northcliffe's power was reduced by the war, which through the scale of the slaughter and the disillusion it generated, altered the climate of public life. Northcliffe's dictatorial obsessions grew worse and he died mad. The role of the most prominent, powerful and resented press magnate was taken over by the Canadian-born Lord Beaverbrook, who took over the *Daily Express* in 1916 and drove it to catch up with the *Daily Mail* in 1945. Beaverbrook's preoccupations were empire and political manipulation. He was shrewd enough to see that good newspaper editors needed latitude to make good papers. But there were limits. Asked by the post-war Royal Commission on the Press what happened if his editors took divergent views on empire, Beaverbrook replied: 'I talked them out of it.'

The journalistic establishment of the time was ambivalent about tycoons like Northcliffe and Beaverbrook. They disliked the tone of the newspapers, their aggression, their inconsistency and distortion of agendas. But they had a sneaking admiration for the efficiency, verve and flair with which the papers went about competing. But the wholesale commercialization of the printed press created an equal and opposite reaction among at least some journalists. They began reflecting on what could be done. In the high days of Victorian confidence, journalists had crowed that the press was 'indispensable to civilisation'.[36] No one disputed that newspapers were part of society's nervous system, but the system was unhealthy. What exactly had gone wrong and how could it be put right?

The waning power of the harlot

The debate was not confined to the power of press tycoons. Arguments over Soviet Russia and Germany, as it came under Hitler's control in the 1930s, sharpened the debates that had begun in the wake of World War One. There was much criticism of the fact that newspapers were controlled by ever larger, conglomerate businesses. Ten years before Prime Minister Stanley Baldwin made the phrase well known, a commentator accused Northcliffe of wanting 'power without responsibility'. Another writer said that he had shown 'an infamous servitude to the changing passions of the hour'. Hugh Massingham, a prominent pundit, called popular journalism a 'masked power', a monopoly power and a 'non-moral power'.[37] Politicians such as Baldwin were, of course, complaining that newspapers and their owners were no longer buyable or biddable. But many voices believed that while owners such as Northcliffe might be a malignant one-off, there was a systemic problem with preponderant publishing power squeezing out too many relevant facts and opinions.

In America, pundits such as the columnist Walter Lippmann argued that if newspapers (and he extended his argument to early radio broadcasters) could manipulate opinion on a large scale and do so on a whim, then the policies of government should be made by a disinterested elite of public servants who could be insulated from these influences. The battle of ideas was too anarchic, Lippmann thought, to produce the best government. In 1923, the American Society of Newspaper Editors produced the 'Canons of Journalism', which said that reporters should be free of bias and be obliged to report all points of view fairly and accurately. Partisanship in newsrooms was slackening with larger editorial staffs in which views were more mixed. The dominance of advertising in print tended also to dampen partisanship in the quality press: advertisers didn't like to appear in shrill, outspoken papers.

The concerns about bias, advertising, chain ownership and reporting standards were put on hold due to the Second World War. Under Britain's post-war Labour Government and at the urging of the National Union of Journalists, a Royal Commission sat in 1947–49 to ponder these claims. One striking conclusion of the evidence they gathered was that the golden age of print might already have ended. This had relatively little to do with the start of radio broadcasting in the 1920s. It had much more to do with the tendency of firms to try to dominate markets, to the now-high costs of entering and surviving in newspaper publishing. Incentives to innovate and experiment had shrunk. In June 1933, the four key popular newspapers were estimated to be spending a total of between £50,000 and £60,000 per week between them on promotions and competitions to 'buy' readers.[38] Periods of expansion in news media stop when a market is saturated; the intensity of the competition between papers such as the *Daily Mail* and *Daily Express* had strained all their rivals. The efficiency of such distribution operations had gradually hurt many provincial papers. The Royal Commission could not have known it but, when they deliberated, a historic moment was passing. The total circulation of all British national papers was very close to its peak.

The Royal Commission was looking at the paradox that institutions supposed to be critical to the functioning of democracy are attached to fast-moving businesses that are fallible, unstable and at the mercy of new trends in technology, society or economics. They concluded that the anxieties expressed before the Second World War were either groundless or the results of conditions so unusual that they were unlikely to be replicated in the future. With the advantage of hindsight, we can see clearly that the members of the commission had no sense that they were analysing the beginning of a long financial decline in print. The commission conscientiously recorded that from 1921 to 1948, the number of general daily papers in England, Wales and Scotland had fallen from 169 to 128. Three new national Sunday newspapers had started in that period; seven had disappeared. Only one national daily had opened in that time and that was the *Daily Worker*, which was supported by the Communist Party and ran at a loss.[39] The age in which ambitious editors sought out men with capital to start new papers and magazines had finished.

But the Royal Commission did see that the headlong expansion, which had driven so much change, had come to a stop. The golden age of popular newspapers dominating news would turn out to have been brief. Economic conditions were tough and the post-war era was to see a succession of new technologies that put print's dominance under increasing pressure and strain. The Royal Commission worried long and hard about monopolistic tendencies in print. But for the newest mass communications technology, even print commentators in Britain thought that a monopoly was right. And that monopoly belonged to the British Broadcasting Corporation.

Notes

1 Starr, P (2004) *The Creation of the Media: Political Origins of Modern Communications*, Basic Books, New York.

2 Maxwell Hamilton, J (2009) *Journalism's Roving Eye: A History of American Foreign Reporting*, Louisiana University Press, Louisiana.

3 1818, quoted in Wilson, B (2005) *The Laughter of Triumph: William Hone and the Fight for the Free Press*, Faber, London.

4 America became home to more newspapers than anywhere else in 1825. Stephens, M (2007) *A History of News*, 3rd edn, Oxford University Press, New York.

5 The name was an ironic conflation of St Peter's Fields and the battle of Waterloo, fought a few years before.

6 Desmoulins, C (1789) *Les Révolutions de France et de Brabant*, 2nd edition.

7 Desmoulins was guillotined by rival revolutionaries in 1794.

8 Carlyle, T (June 1829) 'Signs of The Times', Edinburgh Review, 49.

9   Ferguson, N (2012) *Civilization: The Six Killer Apps of Western Power*, Penguin, London.

10   By parliamentary reform Acts in 1867, 1884, 1885, 1918 and 1928.

11   Starr, *The Creation of the Media*.

12   Tomalin, C (2011) *Charles Dickens – A Life*, Viking, London.

13   Quoted in Briggs, A and Burke, P (2009) *A Social History of the Media: From Gutenberg to the Internet*, Polity, London.

14   Starr, *The Creation of the Media*. From 27 per cent in 1824 to 78 per cent in 1840.

15   Briggs and Burke, *A Social History of the Media*.

16   The newspaper was abruptly closed in July 2011 after a series of damaging revelations about phone hacking.

17   Williams, K (2010) *Read All About It: A History of the British Newspaper*, Routledge, London.

18   Brown, L (1977) *The Treatment of News in Mid-Victorian Newspapers*, TRHS 5th series 27.

19   Later, the Institute of Journalists.

20   The first US university journalism school began at the University of Missouri in 1908, the Columbia Journalism School in New York in 1912.

21   Maynard Salmon, L (1976) *The Newspaper and the Historian*, Octagon, New York.

22   Chalaby, J K (1998) *The Invention of Journalism*, Macmillan, London.

23   Smith, A (1979) *The Newspaper: An International History*, Thames and Hudson, London.

24   Chapman, J (2005) *Comparative Media History*, Polity, Cambridge.

25   Sydney Robinson, W (2012) *Muckraker: The Scandalous Life and Times of W T Stead*, Robson, London.

26   Chalaby, *The Invention of Journalism*.

27   Sydney Robinson, *Muckraker*.

28   Walsh, M (2011) *The News from Ireland: Foreign Correspondents and the Irish Revolution*, I B Tauris, London.

29   Chalaby, *The Invention of Journalism*.

30   Williams, *Read All About It*.

31   It also became known as the *Loi Tinguy*, after the Marquis de Tinguy who proposed it.

32   Walsh, *The News from Ireland*.

33   Also known as the Tokugawa shogunate 1600–1868.

34 Unless the market is informally rigged so as to remove some of the risk: Japan is the only other major developed economy with national newspapers, but informal agreements fix the market shares, which change only very slowly.

35 He was also nicknamed 'Northoleon'.

36 *The Economist*, 1852.

37 Hampton, M (2004) *Visions of the Press in Britain 1850–1950*, University of Illinois, Illinois.

38 Royal Commission on the Press 1947–49, Cmd. 7700, HMSO 1949, London.

39 Royal Commission on the Press 1947–49, Cmd. 7700, HMSO 1949, London.

The gilded age

03

> 'Th' newspapers have got to print what happens,' said Mr Hennessy.
> 'No,' said Mr Dooley, 'they've got to print what's different.'
> **F P DUNNE, *OBSERVATIONS BY MR DOOLEY*, 1902**

In 1966, the *Daily Mirror*'s chairman, Cecil King, gave a lecture on the future of the press. King, educated at Winchester College and Oxford, was at the time the cerebral prince of popular papers. Newspapers had faults, he conceded, and people were right to be worried about concentration of ownership. But papers were still 'the voice of the people' and the only check on the inherent tendencies of all governments to 'conceal their blunders'. King went on: '"Let us hope", they say, "that the Press doesn't get hold of this." Fortunately the Press often does. Without a fearless, probing, exposing, independent and uncorrupt Press, we should be far worse governed than we are.'[1]

Apart from King's lofty indifference to broadcast journalists, his view was widely held and fair. But this crusading story that print journalists told themselves was already being undermined by the slow decline of the platform on which they worked. The 1960s saw a revolt against deferential and formulaic journalism, but another change, the start of long-term financial decline, went barely noticed.

The 'gilded age' title to this chapter is ironic. The second half of the 20th century, a period seen by many journalists as an era of heroic achievement and stability, was also a long decline for newspapers, which contended with a host of new competitors. The period saw both great and bad journalism, but the commercial foundations of print journalism were being eaten away. By the time the truly disruptive force of the internet arrived at the end of the century, print was a much weakened force. If the post-war era was a golden age for anyone, it was one for broadcasters. However, television went through its own upheaval with the proliferation of channels and deregulation in the 1980s in many Western countries.

Television and radio remade news media again, mixing inherited ideas with new solutions for new technology. Radio had become immensely powerful in a short space of time, the change accelerated by war. Television changed daily life, experience and entertainment to an even greater degree. Other technological innovations allowed broadcast platforms and channels to multiply. The change in the hardware again altered the journalism and brought crushing economic pressures to bear on print media, well before digital media and the internet changed the way we capture and distribute information. Print journalists and their managements, in enjoying a long and apparently stable period of prosperity, created cultures and practices that became fixed – to the point where they took their readers for granted.

A fluid mass

When radio broadcasts began in the 1920s, the full significance of the popular press worried the political class. A mass readership for news, including both middle-class and working-class readers and owned by a handful of companies, created a quite new political landscape. Politicians fretted about the shift in the balance of power in favour of the press and against them. Their anxieties were assuaged not by policy or legal changes but by new technologies of radio and television. A political class frightened by ruthless and whimsical press tycoons knew that it could not restore the old system of politicians setting the agenda and having it debated by deferential but opinionated newspapers: agenda-setting power was now more widely dispersed. A state-created broadcaster became an attractive idea because it would be a standard by which journalism could be measured.

Winston Churchill wrote wistfully in 1930 that 'before the liquefaction of the British political system set in, we had a real political democracy led by a hierarchy of statesmen, and not a fluid mass led by newspapers'.[2] The then Alfred Harmsworth[3] had made the same point from a quite different angle in 1903: 'Every extension of the franchise renders more powerful the newspaper and less powerful the politician.'[4] The first instinct of politicians, as always, was to build weapons to fire back at what they saw as a hostile and – much worse – unpredictable and uncontrollable press. A parallel debate was under way in the United States, where Joseph Pulitzer had pithily expressed the formula for turning popular newspapers into power: 'Circulation means advertising, and advertisements mean money, and money means independence.' The total revenue of US newspapers had tripled between 1915 and 1929.[5] That rate of growth was never matched again.

The *Daily Mail* was suspected by some commentators on the Left of having started both the Boer War and the First World War. Faith in a self-correcting free market in ideas was battered. H G Wells told a Liberal Party summer school in 1932 that those opposed to the press lords should take the gloves off by using the methods of the Counter-Reformation, Nazis and Communists: 'I suggest that you study the reinvigoration of Catholicism by Loyola... I am asking for Liberal Fascisti, for enlightened Nazis.'[6] Later in the century this same kind of idea, less eccentrically expressed, would emerge as proposals for the foundation of left-wing newspapers, which rarely flourished.

Worries about the new and alarming power of public opinion also began to create pressures for the regulation of newspapers and helped to ensure strong media controls during the Second World War. Debates about both government propaganda and the influence of press owners generated pressure to take decisions out of the hands of both politicians and press magnates. In Britain, this took the form of 'boards' composed of supposedly non-partisan men (women were rare) who could plan rationally and act from a disinterested position and with detachment from the short-term currents of opinion. This argument took its most memorable form in America in two books by Walter Lippmann, the young star of the comment pages: look at the disaster created by the sleepwalking politicians who allowed the war to happen, Lippmann argued. A firebreak was needed so that people who made important decisions could be insulated from volatile public opinion and to give them accurate information on which to base their decisions. That information wasn't likely to come from newspapers in their current form. A British variant of this kind of thinking underpinned the founding of the British Broadcasting Corporation (BBC).

The brute force of monopoly

Considering how fiercely newspapers had always fought for their individual autonomy, there is an enjoyable irony in their early opinions about how the new broadcasting medium should be controlled. The very first body overseeing radio broadcasting in 1922 was the BBC, the name perhaps suggesting that radio might be owned by private companies, as was the case at the time in America. But the BBC's first head, John Reith, argued for a different BBC mission, name and governance. Reith, an immensely tall, forbidding and relentless Calvinist engineer, harked back to a Victorian ideal of communications media being vehicles for education and improvement;

he despised politics and politicians. Winston Churchill nicknamed him 'Wuthering Heights'.

When Reith had been interviewed for the job of running the embryo BBC he had, he told his diary, not 'the remotest idea as to what broadcasting was'. He was a quick learner. Reith grasped faster than anyone the depth of the social change that broadcasting would make. In his manifesto for what would become the BBC, he wrote:

> Till the advent of this universal and extraordinary cheap medium of communication a very large proportion of the people were shut off from first-hand knowledge of the events which make history. They did not share in the interests and diversions of those with fortune's twin gifts – leisure and money... Today all this has changed.[7]

Reith advocated what he later called a 'brute' monopoly to preserve standards and received support not only from ministers but from editorial writers. Broadcasting, said the *Manchester Guardian*, is 'clearly marked out for monopoly'; *The Times* agreed that a single organization 'with an independent monopoly' would be right, with 'public service as its primary motive'. Most governments, the British and American included, had taken stringent legal measures to control news media during wartime.[8] New media such as radio were fascinating but also terrifying. But the idea that clever, disinterested people could keep the government at one remove created the BBC's almost unique relationship with the state: the BBC was, and remains, dependent on politicians for its income and charter but is not under direct political influence.

This formula was imitated elsewhere in the British Empire of the time and those public broadcasters survive today in recognizable form in Australia and Canada. Many countries shattered by political demagoguery and war in the 1930s and 1940s made public service broadcasting a symbol of change and a vehicle for social cohesion. France's new post-war constitution nationalized broadcasting with wide public support at the time; the problems of manipulation by the state and government did not emerge until years later. Japan's NHK was loosely based on the BBC model. In both Japan and Britain television acted as a powerful leveller of pronounced local differences. Germany adopted a public broadcasting system that distributed informal influence among the major political parties. In post-war France, the reaction against pro-Nazi press owners of the previous age extended to reforms of the written press. New laws restricted each owner to having only one newspaper, state aid was given to newspapers (which continues today) and the Agence France Presse was set up to act as a national press agency to set a benchmark for impartiality standards.

But in the United States, the ideal of detached experts supervising broad-casting gained no purchase at all. The government preferred to persuade rather than to legislate and the geography of the United States made govern-ment control harder to contemplate. Lawmakers had the precedent of the telegraph, railroads, electricity and telephones all in private hands. By 1938, 90 per cent of American urban households, and 70 per cent of rural ones, had radios.[9] Radio was at first a lucrative monopoly, developing into a lightly regulated competition between interlocking local and national chains. National Public Radio, established in 1971 and publicly funded, produces a respected output but even today reaches only 2 per cent of the population.

In Britain between the world wars, very few people other than John Reith betrayed any grasp that each developed society's system for informing itself was about to be radically reorganized. Printed media would now have to compete with rival platforms of unprecedented power. A new series of experiments had begun. The first head of the BBC's infant news section explicitly contrasted the internal rules for BBC news with what he derided as the habits of newspapers. In his first guidance for his colleagues, he wrote that their aim would be to 'avoid the errors into which journalists, as such, seem inevitably to fall' and defined these as sensationalism, inaccuracy, partiality and overstatement.[10] With the growth of broadcast journalism alongside print, Britain was acquiring a mixed economy of editorial styles and controls. New media rarely substitute for the old: much more often they are added as new layers on top of earlier platforms.

The competition to be trusted and believed had changed. Radio redefined the way that reality was seen and how perceptions of it were exchanged. Radio was not immediately regarded as trustworthy, not least because of what was seen by some as the BBC's pro-government stance in the General Strike of 1926. 'There surely cannot be any sane man or woman who would argue that the Ministry of Information, or its near relation the BBC, have so far offered a serious alternative to the newspapers in conveying informa-tion?' asked the editor of *Picture Post* in 1940.[11] But the number of people who would say just that was growing, boosted by the wartime need for reliable information. By the end of August 1939, a Mass Observation Poll recorded that three-quarters of their respondents thought that the BBC was more reliable than newspapers.[12]

Radio's immediacy gave it authenticity that made it intuitively believable by comparison with the methods of newspapers, which could be made to look occult and impersonal. A BBC Home Service talk in 1941 sniffed that newspaper stories might come from 'a report from a Mexican correspond-ent of a Portuguese journal quoted in a Roman paper'.[13] H G Wells, excited by anything that would hasten the demise of the press lords, prophesied in a broadcast talk in 1943 that newspapers would soon be 'dead as mutton'. Ideas would be spread by pamphlets and summaries of news from 'the last two or three hours' could be got from a service on the telephone. London commuters with their heads down and pecking at the news on their iPhones and Blackberrys 70 years later might not have surprised Wells.

'In all the history of inventing,' said a breathless *Outlook* magazine writer in 1924, 'nothing has approached the rise of radio from obscurity to power.' Nothing, that is, until the equally sudden arrival of television shortly afterwards. The very idea that a medium could arrive and grow huge, apparently almost instantaneously, was new. The radio audience rapidly grew to become the closest thing to a single 'public' in Britain, but it did not hold this position for long. The BBC launched a public television channel in 1936 and rapidly consolidated its hold in a richer post-war society. Competition in TV news did not arrive until the foundation of Independent Television News in 1955. Even that competition was limited to a single channel.

A few newspaper executives, having watched the radio audience grow at speed, saw that television would be at least as influential. In the late 1950s, the foundations of the long circulation supremacy of the *Sunday Times* were being laid by its editor, Denis Hamilton. Displaying foresight that many of his rivals lacked, Hamilton reckoned that the best way for print to adapt to television was to 'analyse and amplify the news and what lay behind it'.[14] Popular newspapers could no longer mix information and entertainment in the old accustomed ratios. Entertainment had the upper hand. Cecil King, in a note to one of his editors in 1943 on the implications of radio, advised that popular newspapers would now have to concentrate on 'the simply human' story. 'I am not arguing that instruction should not be given,' King wrote, 'but that our main function is, and is likely to remain, entertainment.'[15] That became yet more true in the television age, but few editors of popular newspapers were ready to admit it. Popular newspapers began to edge away from mixing politics with pleasure and to concentrate on pleasure.

Sorrow, sorrow, ever more

Newspaper editors and their critics continued to debate media issues in language drawn from the arguments of the 19th century. The playwright Arthur Miller may have described a newspaper as a nation talking to itself, but television became the most widely shared experience of news and current affairs. From the 1960s journalists at the BBC explored slowly, and widened gradually, the limits of what governments and the public would tolerate. They enjoyed the advantage of social and cultural changes that the broadcasters amplified but did not create. The moral authority of institutions such as the churches, universities and politicians shrank. The intricate social, corporate, school and university links that had bound the press to the political and administrative elite in London weakened. In the words of one historian, journalists now 'stood midway between a public which had lost its awe of the natural governing class and the forces of authority'.[16]

The earlier fashion for organizing society from the top went into reverse. Freedom and choice became a dominant theme of politics and culture in the increasingly affluent developed economies, ideas common to both the liberalization of the 1960s and the swing to free-market ideas of the 1980s. This anti-authority, anti-elitist mood gave an edge to the disputes of the 1960s between the press and politicians, civil servants and judges. A number of reports, starting with the Royal Commission of 1947–49, recommended regulatory bodies for newspapers, starting with the Press Council. Newspapers had loosened or removed most of the council's teeth by the time it began to operate, and popular newspapers did not need to take much notice of its strictures. Twenty years went by before newspapers agreed any kind of conduct code for journalists.

The tone of melancholy condescension adopted by the press lords of the day towards the first of many such post-war inquiries was caught by a message left by Lord Beaverbrook for one of his underlings inquiring about the Royal Commission, which had just been announced. He would be glad to know more, Beaverbrook said, for it sounded to him like yet another government agency engaged in 'the persecution of newspapers. Sorrow, sorrow ever more. There is nothing I can say about it except to bow my head in misery.'

A well-conducted press

The government became a source of information and opinion and just one among many. Politicians complained that they were powerless before ungovernable newspapers and the magnetic pull of television. They were adapting to two shifts that have turned out to be of long-term importance and have permanently altered thinking about what journalism is for and how political information circulates. Society was becoming steadily less deferential to the political class and the idea that it should set the public agenda. Developed societies changed in the 1960s and the news media changed with them. Deference to social class faded and, to a lesser extent, to authority. Mistrust of political and cultural elites quickened. Many factors drove these shifts: rising affluence, wider access to public education (radically improved in Britain by the 1947 Education Act), opposition to the American war in Vietnam and the accumulated effects of political elites being discredited and exhausted by two world wars in 30 years.

The quantity of news was growing and it would not stop increasing. Radio and television grew channels and outlets; politicians were required to learn new tricks in order to perform and persuade. They faced a media that became hungry to monitor an ever-larger range of subjects, institutions and activities.

The rules to govern that monitoring role were a matter of permanently unresolved negotiation between a changing cast of actors. The balance in journalism between partisanship and impartiality is never stable or fixed. Post-war debates over journalism in Britain and the United States make an instructive comparison and contrast. Both countries had growing media, coming to be dominated by television. Radio had already demonstrated that broadcasting demanded more informal skills from both journalists and politicians. Newspapers, despite no longer dominating public information, nevertheless continued to produce the stories that set the television news agenda for the evening. They had depth that neither broadcasting platform could match.

In both the United States and Britain, there was a rebellion in the 1960s against deference and too intimate a relationship with power in general, and politicians in particular. American newspapers were disappearing rapidly between 1950 and 1975 as television sucked the advertising out of local city markets; many cities were left with only one or two newspapers. The early part of that period, between the end of the Second World War and the spread of network television in the early 1960s, might be called the high modern peak of US newspapers. Washington was the most powerful Western capital in a world divided by the new cold war. Journalism's mission was, as many US practitioners saw it, lifted by their country's new and significant role in the world. Newspaper journalists were close to their political sources but enjoying a prestige and influence that they had never before enjoyed. In many cases they were too close: one of the most powerful brokers in the Republican Party in California was Kyle Palmer, a political reporter for the *Los Angeles Times*.

This is David Halberstam's portrait of Washington's leading political journalist of the 1950s, James Reston:

He used the telephone brilliantly but his voice was never demanding. There were long pauses between the words. His voice showed that he was never in very much of a hurry. That meant he was trustworthy. He had become... the journalist that all the young reporters in America admired and wanted to work for, a symbol not of a journalism past, but of journalism to be fair, civilized, intelligent and internationalist.[17]

But journalism, because it is open to every current of change in an open society, rarely institutionalizes for very long. The prestige of men (women were still very rare exceptions) like Reston did not last for long. The arrival of television as the medium that politicians needed and wanted, and the turbulent divisions then carved by America's war in Vietnam, destroyed this comfortable world. The picture of the world painted by columnists such as Reston quickly seemed stuffy, insiderish, formal and limited. In contrast, writers such as Tom Wolfe used whimsy, personality and atmospheric detail as regular tools of their trade. There was an explosion of 'alternative' written journalism, ranging from periodicals that faded to a few, such as *Rolling Stone*, which lasted. But the revolt against journalistic deference in the United States had limits because the countervailing force of neutrality and objectivity was so strong. Television journalism quite soon avoided outright opinion in news programmes, both because the companies were worried about regulatory disapproval and because they were trying to build very broad constituencies in a diverse nation.

One of the most famous television news broadcasts of the time, Edward Murrow's demolition of the rabidly anti-communist Senator Joseph R McCarthy, was called at the time television's 'finest half hour' and likely to 'rewrite the definition of journalism'. It did no such thing. The *See It Now* programme had been late to the small chorus that criticized McCarthy, and its arguments rested on patient hard work by print journalists who took apart McCarthy's smears detail by detail. But that did stop the programme becoming a totemic piece of journalism.[18] The judgemental style Murrow adopted did not set a trend. Television was adopting balance as its guiding principle. On that occasion Murrow had abandoned it.[19]

Very similar forces were felt at newspapers. To command larger and diverse readerships, city papers needed a justification rooted in a professional ethic. The most obvious expression of this was the separation of news and comment. Papers such as the *Washington Post* had an editor in charge of editorials and the op-ed page, who reported separately to the publisher and not to the managing editor for news.

British print journalism had always been highly opinionated. Newspapers bore the imprint of their origins as political opinion sheets. Ferocious competition between newspapers on a national playing field required fervent opinion to maintain distinctiveness. This had not been effaced in Britain, as it was in the United States, by a later professional doctrine of objectivity. National newspapers differentiated themselves, to varying degrees, by their political stances. A few made a point of stressing their independence of political opinions held by owners.[20] Broadcast journalists were prohibited from expressing explicit opinions and, where they voiced them at all, did so obliquely in their selections of stories, voices and faces.

'So will it be goodbye to Fleet Street?'

Post-war consumer spending and leisure time grew; electronic devices shrank to ever-smaller and more portable sizes. Economic growth in the developed world generated advertising. That revenue turned out to be enough in most countries to sustain television advertising when the number of channels was restricted to a handful. It was not enough from the 1980s onwards, when technology and deregulation allowed the channels to multiply. Print advertising was enough to sustain the illusion that all was well with newspapers, whose economic decline was everywhere slow. But the slide was also irreversible.

Total sales of British national papers, boosted by war, peaked between 1950 and 1955 (see Figure 3.1).[21] The number of newspapers read per 1,000 people declined in Britain from 534 in 1950 (the earliest point at which this figure was measured) to 351 in 2010. American newspaper total circulation peaked in 1984 before falling steadily. But the US figure is deceptive if population increase – common to most developed countries in the post-war era – is not taken into account. In 1950, American daily newspaper circulation was 58.83 million copies and 48.59 million in 2008. But expressed as sales per 1,000 people, the fall over 58 years is 353 to 160, or 55 per cent.[22] Dependence on advertising varied from country to country and paper to paper but, the larger the advertising market, the more likely it was that newspapers relied on advertising for more than half – and as much as three-quarters – of their income.

Advertising was an attractive business model, providing that two conditions were fulfilled: the economy needed to be growing and the number of outlets for advertising limited. Recessions were felt first and painfully in newspapers, as businesses turned off advertising as a cost that could be cut quickly. But until the proliferation of television channels in the 1980s and the start of online advertising in the 1990s, print advertising prices could be

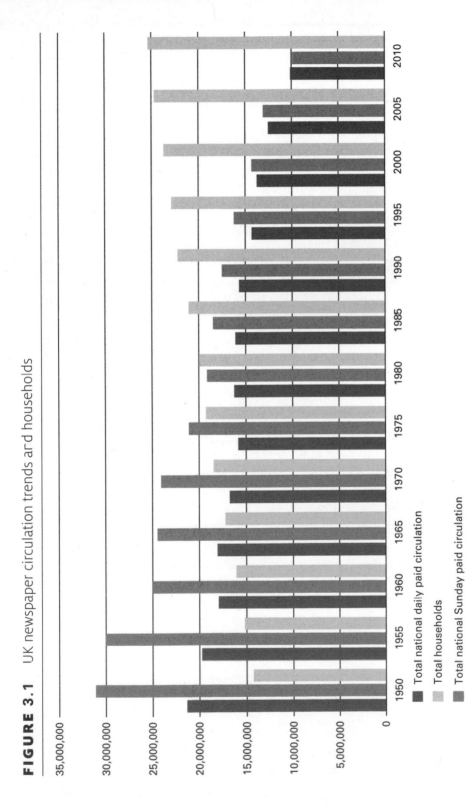

FIGURE 3.1 UK newspaper circulation trends and households

SOURCE: Sixty years of daily circulation trends, Communications Management Inc, May 2011

Legend:
- Total national daily paid circulation
- Total households
- Total national Sunday paid circulation

kept high by rationing the supply of space in a limited platform. Where either circulation was as high as it would go, or where there was no more advertising income to be squeezed, competition took the form of being more cost efficient than your rival. Until 1986, this struggle was severely hampered in Britain by the disruptive pressures that were skillfully used by printing trade unions, who could kill or maim a night's circulation with a single carefully timed meeting, let alone a walkout.

Newspaper workers enjoy powerful leverage: if they stop work for an hour at a sensitive moment in the publication cycle, sales the next day are irreparably damaged. There is no compensation or catch-up. British printing unions traced their ancestry back to late medieval guilds and their branches were quaintly known as 'chapels'.[23] There were separate unions for separate functions and each management had to deal with a group of competing union representatives.[24] The unions were notoriously reluctant to follow the orders of the national trade union movement. These unions, starting with the first restrictive practice in 1587, had arranged secure employment at inflated wages for their members. In effect, the owners did not control their own printing; stoppages were frequent.

By the late 1970s, national newspapers were overpaying their production staff, the press halls were overmanned and the machinery was out of date. In the three months before *The Times* and the *Sunday Times* ceased publication for nearly a year in 1978, *The Times* had not completed a full print run on 21 occasions, the *Sunday Times* on 9 occasions. Publishers wanted to install new photocomposition systems that would allow newspapers to be produced with smaller workforces.

Most publishers could see no way to reach this promised land and preferred to pay the ransoms demanded. By the time that Margaret Thatcher had been elected at the head of a relatively radical Conservative Government in 1979, accumulated public resentment of trade unions ran high and laws on strikes and industrial disruption were stiffened. In early 1986, Rupert Murdoch moved his four newspapers to a single print works in a part of east London that had once been docks.[25] The entire printing staff was declared to have dismissed itself because of its unwillingness to negotiate new working practices, and members of the Electrical, Electronic, Telecommunications and Plumbing Union produced the papers.

Some of the ground for this coup had been laid by Eddie Shah, a north-west England publisher with a new newspaper produced by non-union labour. A sample 'dummy' edition of his planned paper, *Today*, carried the astutely prophetic headline: 'So Will It Be Goodbye to Fleet Street?' Murdoch's move had been carefully planned for months beforehand.[26] The plant of the new four-newspaper company, News International, was picketed and, for a year, attempts were made to blockade it. But the papers were published and their circulations and staffs grew. The power of the print unions had been broken and the cost of producing newspapers fell. The profits of *The Sun* were transformed for a few years before beginning to slide under new pressures.

I really loathe people with power

The news media of the 1950s was, by present standards, almost comically deferential and cautious. BBC Television, when it began broadcasting in Britain in the 1930s, was forbidden to discuss government announcements on the day they were made. The corporation's news coverage was gradually sharpened by internal competition and especially by the creation of Independent Television News in 1955.

Journalists chafed at ideas that they should police their work according to ideas of separating fact from comment, and were suspicious of deferential collusion between correspondents (particularly political specialists) and politicians with power. The inspection and monitoring of power in all its forms became the broad aim common to journalists in most newsrooms, however much their techniques or targets might differ. In post-war societies, newly powerful institutions proliferated. Power could be inspected and investigated not only in parliaments but in private companies and in public bodies (such as the National Health Service in Britain) now in charge of sizeable taxpayer-funded budgets.

Throughout the 1960s and 1970s, the majority of broadcast or printed journalism remained respectably routine. But a layer of more ambitious, expensive and occasionally spectacular reporting was added and it was driven by the conviction that relatively rich, open societies had a good deal to hide and that by patient inquiry it could be discovered and disclosed. This investigative journalism drew on the tradition of the American 'muckraking' reporters of the early 20th century who had exposed corporate malpractice. On average, the powerful acted better if they knew they were being watched. This motive was perfectly captured by the leading investigative reporter Nick Davies:[27] 'I do have an agenda when it comes to selecting stories,' Davies said, 'I quite specifically became a reporter to cause trouble to powerful people who deserved it. In quite a deep way, I really loathe people with power, and journalism gives you a licence to criticize them.'

In the 1970s Davies had been inspired, like many of his contemporaries, by the most powerfully symbolic event of its era, the Watergate story. The investigation by the *Washington Post* into the illegal acts committed by President Richard Nixon and his lieutenants was iconic in dramatizing the press's ability to hold power to account. A single newspaper had taken on the holder of the most powerful political office in the world and won by forcing the president's resignation. Or so it appeared.

But Watergate posed two uncomfortable questions, one much debated, the other less so. Did the journalists of the *Washington Post* bring down Nixon? In one sense, they clearly did: if they had not tripped over a clue and investigated it, the wrongdoing might have gone unrevealed. But in another sense the heroic, short version of what happened obscures a more complex cause and effect. The information published by the *Washington Post* led to Senate hearings. Those hearings, televised from 'gavel to gavel', dislodged new evidence and brought forth important new witnesses who sank any chance that Nixon might survive on the benefit of the doubt. The hearings dramatized and extended the knowledge of what the White House had been up to on a scale that even the *Washington Post* could never achieve. Famous and well-regarded as the newspaper may have been, it was – when compared to the television networks – a daily parish magazine for a political city. To acquire political clout and momentum, the scandal needed the accountability mechanism of the formal political system and the reach of television. But to be known about at all, it first needed the catalyst of the newspaper's disclosure.

This is not to diminish the pivotal role played by the original reportage, but to highlight the timeless dilemma involved: journalism supplies information on which others act. Journalists want to see and to be able to measure the effect of what they have done; the evidence is often elusive or at least not decisive. In the wake of Watergate, this had a long-lasting effect on reporters everywhere. The decline of print had begun before the Watergate drama in the early 1970s. Financial pressures were exacerbated by increasing competition from the proliferation of news outlets and platforms as well as by management ineptitude and shortsightedness. This restricted the resources available for long, difficult reportage with uncertain results. Reporters and editors tended to react by casting much journalism that did not deserve the term into the heroic mould of 'investigation'. In 2002 the *Daily Mirror* asked: 'Which is the greatest exclusive, Watergate or Burrellgate?',[28] while publishing the claims about the British royal family made by Paul Burrell, who had worked as butler to the late Diana, Princess of Wales. Mr Burrell had been handsomely paid for supplying this 'exclusive'.

The second awkward issue raised by Watergate, but much less debated, was the supervision of ends and means in reporting, an issue that would haunt newsrooms for years after Watergate and which still does. As often, the difficult question was asked by an outsider. Commenting on the book written by Bob Woodward and Carl Bernstein, the reporters who broke Watergate, the philosopher Sissela Bok drew attention to a passage in which the reporters described how they had lied to their most important source, known as 'Deep Throat',[29] to trick him into confirming something. Bok did not object to the deception as such. But she was bothered by how casually this had been done. 'No one seems to have stopped to think that there was a problem in using deceptive means,' she wrote.[30] This would be a problem in years to come, Bok added: it would shape the view of the public and of those about to become journalists. In retrospect, this was a perceptive warning. At the time, no one took any notice.

Deregulation

Ideas of what journalism ought to be were divided and moved in distinct directions. There were movements that entwined journalism with political activism, for 'social responsibility journalism' (not quite the same thing), regulated broadcast journalists expanded their freedom of manoeuvre within formal requirements for impartiality, recurrent attempts were made to give news – especially broadcast news – greater depth (fighting what had been called 'the bias against understanding') and there was a brief fashion for upending the authority of editors and publishers with 'newsroom democracy'. This last slogan usually meant left-wing editorial policies or slants. That ideal was fatally undermined by the actual outcomes on the few occasions when newsroom democracy was attempted as an experiment.[31] As the broadcast networks consolidated their reach and hold in developed societies, forces in each society pushed and pulled to produce a cultural and legal compromise between editorial independence and regulation. Most countries were content to evolve a combination of both highly regulated broadcast and more lightly controlled print. Most European states gave news subsidies, varying the amounts and the platforms to which subsidy was given according to precedent and political preference.[32]

For at least two decades after the start of television broadcasting in most developed states in the 1950s or 1960s, the news media appeared to be a stable oligarchy that did not face disruptive challenges because control of the platforms was protected by high entry costs (in the case of print) and regulation of licences (in broadcasting). This pattern was consistent across many countries. This stability was upset by the arrival in the 1980s of new television technologies that offered governments so inclined fresh opportunities to deregulate and disperse control of new channels and platforms to new entrants to the field. Depending on the country and colour of the government – the 1980s saw the political tide in Europe and America running in favour of free-market parties – those new entrants usually needed capital and good political connections to succeed.

Technology opened the door to change. Satellites, originally put into space during the cold war in case of an arms race miles above the earth and for spying on enemies, evolved to the point where they could, at a price, carry television signals over large distances. Consumer choice was extended by the discovery that underground cables could carry hundreds of channels to a screen at low cost. These technologies transformed the economics of television and gave states new ways to influence populations outside their own borders. Until the arrival of web 2.0 and its ability to transmit audio-visual files, nation states retained supervisory control of broadcasters even as they deregulated and the channels proliferated. The power of cross-border television was never better illustrated than in the Arab insurgencies of 2011. The fall of the governing regimes in Tunisia and Egypt has often been attributed to social media such as Facebook and Twitter. These net-working platforms were important to the protest organizers, but a case can be made that transnational broadcasters such as Al-Jazeera had at least as great an impact on events by being able to capture and relay the events to significant audiences in defiance of the wishes of the national government.[33]

In Britain, the delivery of broadcast news and entertainment became more plural and audiences fragmented, but the strength of the BBC remained very largely unimpaired. The defection of mass audiences for major news programmes can be measured by the falling numbers for the rival mid-evening television news bulletins on BBC1 and ITV (see Figure 3.2). But the fragmentation of the television audience across many channels was not the same as the long fall in print circulations. Irrespective of rows, court cases, stand-offs with governments and the recurrent tense negotiations over the setting of the BBC's licence fee income, *BBC News* kept its leading position measured by audience 'reach' and trust figures better than any other news provider. New platforms and competitors did not displace incumbents; they crowded the markets alongside each other.

This mixture of a carefully preserved BBC, the creation of satellite broad-casting dominated by BSkyB and the degrading of ITV's capacity for news and current affairs was the result of a political compromise in the Con-servative cabinet of Prime Minister Margaret Thatcher. Thatcher had helped Rupert Murdoch to a leading position in satellite broadcasting and was viscerally hostile to the BBC's opinion-shaping power. But she was frustrated

FIGURE 3.2   BBC and ITV News viewers 1998–2012

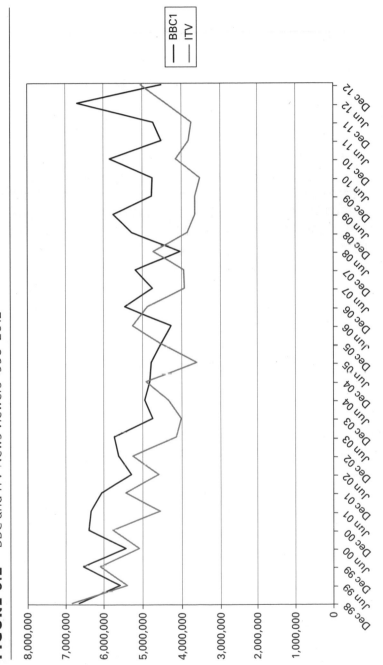

SOURCE: BARB

by her powerful, if less vocal, colleague William Whitelaw who was committed to protecting a broadcasting structure that preserved quality. 'I am always disturbed by talk of achieving higher standards in programmes at the same time as proposals are introduced leading to deregulation and financial competition because I do not believe that they are basically compatible,' Whitelaw wrote later, illustrating that deregulation of television had hit its limits.[34]

The true victims of the British deregulatory changes of the 1980s were the current-affairs programmes on the country's second network, ITV. The importance of quality and public service criteria in the allocation of franchises was watered down in the new Broadcasting Act in 1990. The current affairs programmes affected included *World in Action*, long famous for investigative documentaries. In 1985, *World in Action* had broadcast a film that undermined the evidence behind the conviction of six men who were in prison for detonating bombs in two Birmingham pubs in 1974, which had killed 21 people. Given the public revulsion at the time of the bombings (182 people had been injured, some of them dreadfully) and the fact that the convictions were over a decade old when the *World in Action* film was aired, it would be difficult to imagine a less popular theme for a mass-audience programme. But after further programmes and a long public campaign by the journalist (and later MP) Chris Mullin, the convictions were set aside. Permanent changes to police and criminal justice procedures resulted.[35]

World in Action's editor at the time, Ray Fitzwalter, has said that few if any of the programmes made on his watch could be broadcast on ITV now. *World in Action* came to an end in 1998. Andrew Neil, former editor of the *Sunday Times* and an enthusiastic fan of competition in broadcasting, wrote that ITV's pretensions to being a public service broadcaster were at an end since its current-affairs programmes were following a 'tabloid agenda with an emphasis on consumer concerns and stunts'.[36]

Deregulation of television in the United States at the same period brought many new competitors into the news business – and changed it at the same time. Cable news providers concentrated on 'talking head' reactions and arguments about news and did not use success, when they achieved it, to increase the amount of original reporting. The slide in the fortunes of many American news organizations during the 1980s, when the economy and advertising were healthy, raised the grim possibility that people were starting to disconnect from news altogether. Network television news audiences fell from 52.1 million viewers in 1980 to 25 million in 2008. The US population grew by 80 million in that period, so the fall in the number of TV news watchers per 1,000 fell from 229 to 82, or 64 per cent. Circulation of the largest three news magazines (*Newsweek, Time* and *US News & World Report*) fell 38 per cent on the same basis in the same period.

Boom and decline

The most significant long-term force of change in the news media of the late 20th century was the steadily weakening appeal of established news outlets, both broadcast and print. Mass readerships and audiences are coalitions and these coalitions fragmented as new choices for news and information became available, whether they were magazines, multiplying radio stations or new television platforms. Overall profitability did not fall markedly until the 1990s, but the multiplication of channels and fragmentation of audiences had financial effects nevertheless. The steady erosion of regular newspaper reading habits meant that advertising income in the 1980s – despite generally good economic conditions in the developed world – was starting to be volatile, vulnerable and less reliable. Company managements began to squeeze editorial budgets in order to maintain profit levels at lower incomes. As many managers saw it, there was plenty of fat to squeeze. The truth of that assumption varied. Few managers had any idea of when to stop squeezing once they had started.

Profitability was also sustained by the dwindling number of competitors. Papers died and were swallowed. Paris had 31 daily papers in 1945, down to 9 by 1975 and up to 11 by 2000. At that date, the number of newspaper copies sold in France per 1000 inhabitants was 157, one of the lowest rates in Europe (the equivalent figure for Britain was then 314). Germany had 255 newspapers in 1954 and close to one-half that (121) by 1975. The fall in Denmark was even steeper: from 150 newspapers in 1945 to 45 in 1975.[37] Such fluctuations are more common in media history than often supposed. But no such number of newspapers has yet disappeared in the internet age.

Well before the internet and digital communications brought news to people in a handheld device at the time of their choosing, attitudes to the consumption of news were being changed not only by the growth of new outlets but also by the shortage of time. From the mid-19th century until the 1970s, two long trends held good for much of Europe: total hours worked fell gradually and the affluent worked less than the poor. In the 1980s, this trend changed in Britain: working hours began to increase and social scientists began to talk about 'time famine'.[38] Various factors combined to the same effect. Working mothers entered the workforce in larger numbers and

FIGURE 3.3 Share of advertising taken by various US media 1949–2009

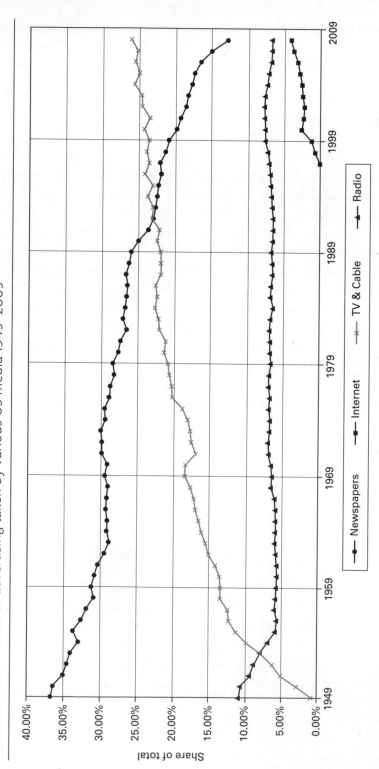

SOURCE: Google and Martin Langeveld at Nieman Journalism Lab; data from NAA, TVB, IAB, McCann

found themselves especially short of time; during the 1990s, the number of working mothers putting in unpaid overtime rose from 18 per cent to 47 per cent. Capital-intensive businesses employing manual labour on fixed wages began to give way to service industries relying on human capital and talent working long hours.

These shifts affected print more than television. By the 1990s, national newspapers were milking an advertising boom by ramping up the numbers of pages – to levels that some readers, at least, found daunting. The temporary surge in newspaper profitability in the 1990s was mostly the result of a two-thirds fall in the price of paper. I remember watching a focus group of young women in Yorkshire in the late 1990s on behalf of *The Times*. One woman in her mid-30s said that she liked the newspaper, but read it irregularly. The researcher asked what made her decide to buy the paper when she did. She bought it, she said, on days when she knew that she wasn't going out in the evening. Then she would spread the paper out on the floor when she got home from work and 'have a really good read'. For some people, the size of the paper and the shortage of time had combined to make newspaper reading a part-time, occasional activity.

Economic pressures had been bearing down on newspapers for a long time. Figure 3.3 shows the share of advertising taken by various media in the United States from 1949–2009. Apart from a few brief rallies, the newspaper share had been in decline from the start of the period. Figure 3.4

FIGURE 3.4   Newspaper ad revenue and GDP (constant dollars)

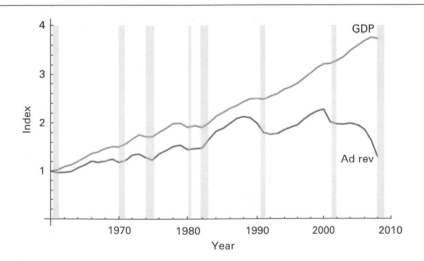

SOURCE: Hal Varian, Google and Newspaper Association of America

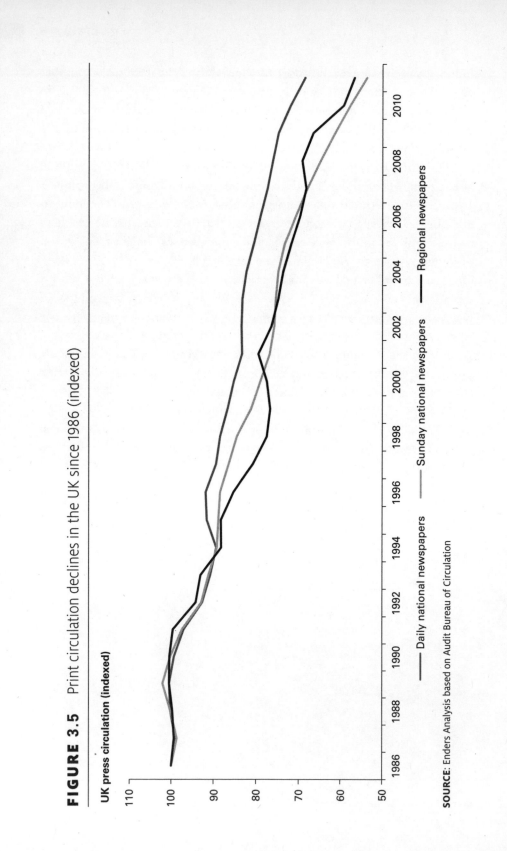

FIGURE 3.5 Print circulation declines in the UK since 1986 (indexed)

UK press circulation (indexed)

— Daily national newspapers ——— Sunday national newspapers ——— Regional newspapers

SOURCE: Enders Analysis based on Audit Bureau of Circulation

compares American GDP with newspaper advertising revenue (adjusted for inflation). The graph shows that both lines drop or run flat during recessions. But newspaper advertising did not match GDP growth from 1960 onwards, began to stagnate in the late 1980s and slipped off a cliff around 2000. Competitors entered the American newspaper market at regular intervals, starting with radio in the 1920s, continuing with television in the 1950s, cable and satellite broadcasting in the 1980s through to the internet in 1990s. Readership declined from the 1960s, circulation from the 1980s; profits did not fall until the 1990s.

The aggregate circulation of British national newspapers had been falling since 1955, and from the mid-1980s – 10 years before the dial-up internet was launched – the trend was followed by regional newspapers and consumer magazines[39] (see Figure 3.5 and 6.1). In a number of OECD (Organization for Economic Cooperation and Development) countries, total circulations held stable until the 1990s, or even the turn of the century, but profitability did not. In some cases, the arrival of free newspapers kept overall circulation rates from falling; in others, government subsidy kept the figures artificially healthy. France, with one of the highest direct subsidies to newspapers in Europe, was one example of a stable aggregate circulation masking a slide in profitability. By the start of the 21st century, newspaper circulations were falling in Europe and America; in countries such as Britain and America, where the decline had begun earlier, the rate of decline accelerated.

A great deal of commentary written from inside the printed press in the last quarter of the 20th century rejoiced that the prediction that neither radio nor television would kill newspapers had been proved wrong. This reassuring surprise obscured developments that were the result of print being forced to compete for attention with broadcasting and that fell short of wholesale collapse. Three key changes flowed from the long trends of falling readership and profits.

Owners, news and celebrity

The first change was consolidation of ownership and a new kind of owner. From the moment that publishers emerged from the restrictions and rationing of the Second World War, cross-subsidy of newspaper operations became steadily more necessary and more common. For 25 years after 1960 in Britain, a combination of capital and labour costs made starting a new newspaper – a common event in the second half of the 19th century – a rare occurrence, because it was prohibitively expensive. Costs were reduced but profitability was weaker than had been assumed. When the specialized newspaper trade unions were defeated by News International in 1986–87, eight papers were founded in the next few years. Two still survive – *The Independent* and *Sunday Sport*; *The Independent on Sunday* was absorbed by its daily counterpart. Five were closed.

The need for cross-subsidy meant that large and diverse companies were more likely to become owners of newspapers – or that owners of newspapers saw that they had to diversify their companies in order to acquire the strength to cope with losses in print. The latter tendency is the story of Rupert Murdoch's News Corporation, which began as an Australian newspaper company, became a multinational newspaper group and then grew to acquire television, magazine, book and online properties. Far-sighted owners such as Murdoch could sense that skilfully managed newspaper operations could be profitable even in the context of long decline, particularly by holding large market shares built in earlier eras. If newspapers were dinosaurs, Murdoch was determined to prove that they have long tails. He could cross-subsidize, buy and sell print properties and improve economic efficiency. But he could not alter the long trends, particularly when they were accelerated by digital.

Britain's national newspaper market offered a large prize to any publisher who could secure a share of the lucrative advertising market, worth a total of £5 billion per year by 2000. But the costs and and risks were formidable. Businessmen and women considered purposeful and successful in other sectors would occasionally end up in charge of newspaper groups and discover that newspaper companies involved complex choreography involving editors, journalists and printers, all of whom were semi-independent of the company's management and who often thought that they were entitled to be completely independent of it.[40] Creative success and passion could not be ordered or bought from a supplier; they had to be found, cultivated and paid. Many captains of other industries who were suddenly brought into news publishing found these tasks baffling and infuriating. Newspaper closures damaged company's reputations, as the Cadbury family discovered when closing the much-loved but loss-making *News Chronicle* in 1960. Governments were likewise nervous of being seen to preside over newspaper closures.

The second change brought about by the long, barely noticed declines was nothing less than a slow rewriting of the definition of news. In most countries with broadcast news, by 1970 a majority of people took their first news from radio or television. Very slowly this shift in habits altered the way in which newspaper readers saw and used their papers. Newspapers had to look in other directions to give value. The definition of a newspaper as a summary of what makes today different from yesterday gave way to a template that made a newspaper something closer to a daily magazine.

Quality papers increased the proportion of editorial given to opinion. In Britain, this first showed as an expansion of 'op-ed' pages in the 1980s and later as the regular use of opinion or analysis in pages of news. Investigative journalism, while always sensitive to budget-cutting because of the very high costs involved, at least guaranteed that the resulting story was original and could not be duplicated by a rival. Serious journalism shifted its weight away from 'hard' news and towards fuller context, analysis and background, delivered if possible with writing of quality that marked it as distinctive. The CVs of daily newspaper editors increasingly came to feature years spent in features departments (small and often derided by news reporters in earlier eras) or on Sunday titles.

Popular newspapers found their own ways to fill the gaps left by television. They too acquired more columnists. Sports coverage increased as a proportion of all newspapers as the broadcasting of sport expanded with the arrival of satellite channels in the 1980s and rapid growth in the audience for live sport.

For popular titles, by far the most promising experiment lay in the private lives of celebrities. This was material that regulated broadcasters could not touch and where newspapers could create a trading market in publishable revelations. Revelations were often confected with the aid of the growing public relations industry, which attached itself to the entertainment television boom of the 1980s and 1990s. Disclosures were bought from the disaffected, from agents specializing in disaffected people with revelations to sell, from private detectives and from anyone who knew how the system worked and how to make sure that you got paid for a tip, a picture or even just an undisclosed address or phone number.

This became a small, networked industry with its own key players, rules and rituals. Sunday popular papers, dominated by the market leader the *News of the World*, needed even more striking revelations than dailies, and the stories had to be kept secret until the end of the week. So relentless was the stream of negative stories that a quite separate branch of celebrity information-trading grew up. Magazines based on the original formula refined by *Hello* magazine struck exclusive deals with celebrities large and small for uncritical and sycophantic coverage of their houses or weddings. The subjects had only to deal with one publication and enjoyed a degree of control over the coverage. That coverage was usually so extensive that the value of further, perhaps less flattering, stories about the individual or couple lost their appeal.

Over years, newspapers acquire layers of different functions and material. Old, less fashionable items rarely disappear completely: they shrink to make room for new elements. So by around the year 2000 British popular papers contained political, international and economic news and comments but in carefully rationed and slightly different amounts. The *Daily Star* contained little or none; *The Sun* contained some; the *Daily Mail* considerably more. But this content was not what acquired new readers or held the loyalty of more than a minority. All these newspapers competed to produce celebrity revelations in their particular style. The *Daily Mail*'s printed version contained a slice of angry political stories in the mix, but when the paper began an extraordinarily successful online site, celebrity coverage predominated to a far greater degree. In less than a decade, the combination of slick, skilful editing and careful handling of the soft pornography involved in much showbusiness and celebrity reporting took *MailOnline* from nowhere to being the most visited newspaper site in the world.

Notes

1 Cecil King, Granada Lecture 1966, cited in Smith, A (ed) (1974) *The British Press Since the War*, David & Charles, London.

2 Churchill, W (1930) *A Roving Commission: My Early Life*, quoted in Koss, S (1984) *The Rise and Fall of the Political Press in Britain*, vol 2, Hamish Hamilton, London.

3 Later Lord Northcliffe.

4 Quoted in Koss, *The Rise and Fall of the Political Press in Britain*.

5 Chapman, J (2005) *Comparative Media History*, Polity, Cambridge.

6 Wells, H G (1932) Liberalism and the Revolutionary Spirit – Address to the Liberal Party Summer School, Oxford. Reprinted in Wells, H G (1932) *After Democracy*, Watts & Co, London; quoted in Hampton, M (2004) *Visions of the Press in Britain 1850–1950*, University of Illinois, Illinois.

7 From Reith, J C (1924) *Broadcast Over Britain*, quoted in Briggs, A and Burke, P (2009) *A Social History of the Media: From Gutenberg to the Internet*, Polity, London.

8 In America, this involved blithe disregard of the First Amendment. In Britain, the measures included the Official Secrets Act of 1911, the subject of particularly heated criticism from the 1970s until its replacement in 1989.

9   Chapman, *Comparative Media History*.

10 Barnett, S (2011) *The Rise and Fall of Television Journalism: Just Wires and Lights in a Box?*, Bloomsbury, London.

11 Quoted in Curran, J and Seaton, J (2010) *Power Without Responsibility: Press, Broadcasting and the Internet in Britain*, Routledge, London.

12 Chapman, *Comparative Media History*, p 184, quoting University of Sussex, Mass-Observation Archive, file report 375.

13 Curran and Seaton, *Power Without Responsibility*.

14 Quoted in Greenslade, R (2003) *Press Gang: How Newspapers Make Profits from Propaganda*, MacMillan, London.

15 Adrian Bingham, 'Monitoring the popular press: an historical perspective', May 2005. **http://www.historyandpolicy.org/papers/policy-paper-27.html**. (accessed 20.05.12)

16 Smith, *The British Press Since the War*.

17 Halberstam, D (1979) *The Powers That Be*, Knopf, New York.

18 The story was introduced to a new generation by the movie *Good Night and Good Luck* (2005) directed by George Clooney.

19 Campbell, W J (2010) *Getting It Wrong: The Ten Greatest Misreported Stories in American Journalism*, University of California Press, California.

20 The launch advertising for *The Independent* in 1986 read simply: 'It is. Are you?'

21 Some estimates (see Figure 3.1) put the peak at 1950. The Audit Bureau of Circulation (ABC) archive figures record the highest combined sale of national daily and Sunday papers in 1955. But the ABC did not at the time include every paper; it did not then, for example, audit the circulation of the *Daily Telegraph*.

22 Picard, R G (2010) *Value Creation and the Future of News Organisations*, Media XXI, Lisbon.

23 The origins of this name remain obscure: it may be connected to Caxton's start at Westminster Abbey.

24 When *The Times* and the *Sunday Times* management suspended publication in an attempt to reform their working practices in 1978, the workforce of more than 4,000 was represented by eight unions divided into 65 chapels.

25 *The Times*, the *Sunday Times*, *The Sun* and *News of the World*.

26 This included a not entirely successful deception involving dummy preparations for a new London evening newspaper. The unions learnt the truth of what was happening but refused to believe that any publisher would attempt to outplay them so boldly.

27 In 2009 and subsequently, Davies was the reporter who led *The Guardian*'s exposure of the phone-hacking scandal at the *News of the World*.

28   14 November 2002.

29   Revealed many years later to have been Mark Felt, associate director of the FBI.

30   Bok, S (1999) *Lying: Moral Choice in Public and Private Life*, Vintage, New York.

31   An emblematic example was the short and unhappy life of *News on Sunday*, which was designed to be run as a workers' cooperative when launched in 1987. It died the same year amid losses and acrimony. See Greenslade, *Press Gang: How Newspapers Make Profits from Propaganda*.

32   Levy, D and Nielsen, R K (2010) *The Changing Business of Journalism and its Implications for Democracy*, Reuters Institute, Oxford.

33   See also Chapter 5.

34   Barnett, *The Rise and Fall of Television Journalism*.

35   Barnett, *The Rise and Fall of Television Journalism*.

36   *Daily Telegraph*, 1 December 1998 (quoted in Barnett, *The Rise and Fall of Television Journalism*).

37   Smith, A (1980) *Goodbye Gutenberg*, Oxford University Press, Oxford.

38   Reeves, R (2001) *The Observer*, 27 May.

39   Defined as magazines on sale to the general public.

40   For an entertaining example, see Greenslade, *Press Gang: How Newspapers Make Profits from Propaganda*, pp 317–25 for an account of Victor Matthews taking the helm of Express Newspapers.

The engine of opportunity

04

> We lived on farms, then we lived in cities, and now we're
> going to live on the internet!
>
> **SEAN PARKER (PLAYED BY JUSTIN TIMBERLAKE),**
> **IN THE FILM *THE SOCIAL NETWORK*, 2010**

In the space of a little more than a century, four electricity-powered inno-vations set off successive waves of change in the way that information moves. In all but a few societies, the telegraph, the telephone, radio and television had shortened the interval before news became known, made events that people did not witness themselves both audible and visible and, in combination, helped to strengthen the agenda-setting power of the news media. The cumulative effect of these four inventions reshaped the public sphere. Even though people travelled steadily faster and in greater numbers in the 20th century, they did not have to travel to see and hear things they were curious about. 'While communication was once an inferior substitute for transportation,' Daniel Boorstin wrote in 1978, 'it is now often the pre-ferred alternative.'[1]

In the period described in the last chapter, scientists began dreaming of yet better and faster ways of transmitting information. The telegraph and telephone were bilateral; radio and television broadcast to mass audi-ences and in one direction only. Scientists were thinking of a future in which information travelled interactively on a more interesting scale. In the 1940s they did not foresee the future, but a few grasped the problem. 'The fundamental problem of communication is that of reproducing at one point either exactly or approximately a message selected at another point,' wrote Claude Shannon, a researcher at Bell Telephone Laboratories in New York, imagining in 1948 a version of what we would now call 'downloading'.[2]

A sequence of fresh innovations – the transistor, digitization or the breaking of information into 'bits', increasingly powerful microchips, personal computers, mobile telephony – enabled a series of advances in media between the 1960s and 1990. Journalists reaped the benefits of lightweight (and therefore mobile) television equipment, a vast increase in the number of television channels, remote printing, satellite and cable broadcasting and computerized typesetting. There were blind alleys and unfulfilled predictions. But no invention unleashed as much disruptive change as the internet, the child of a marriage between computers and telephone networks.

The origins of the discovery that huge quantities of information could be stored, searched, distributed and copied almost instantaneously and at very low cost lay back in the 1960s when American military researchers reached a point of terminal irritation with computers that could not talk to each other. It was, one officer said at the time, like having a different television set for each channel that you wanted to watch. Solving that problem created private closed networks of computers that were later linked into a more extensive worldwide web. The web transmitted information by breaking it into 'packets' and was designed to be resilient and open by being designed without central control.[3] As the uses of the new network became gradually more obvious in the early 1990s, many people – myself and many journalists included – treated the internet as a new publishing system. It was faster and cheaper, but did people really want to read on computer screens what they could get on paper? We had, initially at least, very little clue that successive cycles of disruption were about to hit the news media – and to hit a great many other things.

It may one day in the future seem odd that societies had a large group of well-paid professionals whose job it was to select and provide the words and images that people looked at in order to know the world beyond what they could see and hear with their own eyes and ears. It would certainly have seemed very odd to anyone alive anywhere before 1800 and quite strange to many before 1900. In the 20th century, journalism extended its provision of information and understanding thanks to several decades of cross-subsidy from advertising (and from taxation in the case of some broadcasting). Now the mechanism for carrying journalism is changing again. That has had, and will have, effects on how journalism is done and organized. But the most immediate effect of the latest disruptive technology is on the business model that has sustained journalism recently. Over the long term, the price of most goods tends to fall. The cost of good journalism is an exception to this rule.

Chain reaction

News organizations, for many reasons, failed to grasp the threat and the opportunity of the internet. Among them was the deceptive stability of the four decades before 1990. As I argued in the last chapter, much of this stability was illusory and masked decline in the public engagement with mainstream journalism produced in print and on terrestrial television. Leaders of the news media were accustomed to readers, audiences, legal frameworks and business models that were challenging. But none of those had threatened to turn the world upside down.

Transformative change comes in the form of a chain reaction and successive cycles of pressure and chaos. Two decades from the moment when the internet became widely used, changes in opportunities and possibilities are still being created, as research and experimentation refine new techniques and open new avenues. The internet has seen or holds the possibilities for change in political campaigning, constitutional systems, cash, books, education at all levels, the capacities and configuration of the human brain, surveillance, crime, broadcasting, travel, auctions and market making, news and journalism – to name only a selection. The social adoption of new technologies often does not follow either the prescriptions or the timetables drawn up by inventors or first-adopters. In 1999, on the eve of the millennium, Britain was hardly an internet society: 13 per cent of households then had internet access. By 2008 that number had risen to 65 per cent – as rapid and significant a change as the coming of radio or television. By 2012, 80 per cent of British households had internet access; 33 million people accessed the internet every day, a total that had doubled in six years.[4] As we will also see, technologically driven optimism often conceals drawbacks not obvious in the first flush of enthusiasm for new breakthroughs.

Before looking in detail at why the global linkage of computers (smartphones are included in that category) rewrites yet again the rules of journalism, it is worth breaking down the broader changes in knowledge and its circulation. Now that the internet is a utility in wide global use, it is easy to take its disruptive possibilities for granted or wrongly to assume that change has finished. These broad changes are itemized below.

Scale

The quantity of information has grown by a very large order of magnitude. In 2008, Google was trawling 1 trillion web pages in its searches; five years later, the total is 30 trillion. When the publishers of the *Oxford English*

Dictionary began digitizing in 1987, they reckoned the dictionary's size then to be one gigabyte (1,000 gigabytes is a terabyte). The US Library of Congress represents 10 terabytes and in its attempt to archive websites, the library had collected 160 terabytes of material by early 2010. Eric Schmidt of Google says that his company's researchers reckon that between the birth of the world and 2003, 5 exabytes of information were created (an exabyte is 1 billion gigabytes and written with 18 zeroes). The human race is now, according to Google, creating 5 exabytes every two days. One internet expert reckons that 37 per cent of internet content is x-rated pornography, only exceeded as proportion of the whole by spam.[5] When news publications first came into existence the information they contained, both good and bad, was in short supply. What was scarce is now in glut; good and bad are still mixed. A new challenge for journalists – assuming that the idea of journalism survives, as it should – is coping with abundance.

Nodes and networks

The transmission of information has become decentralized and distributed. The existence of the internet does not abolish the possibility that small numbers of people can control what other people learn about the world. But the ability for many millions of people to send messages and to distributes links, images and files 'peer-to-peer' is an important change to the routing of information and the new power for individuals to form their own nodes and networks. A smaller proportion of the world's information about itself passes through major media outlets. Those outlets may remain, in relative terms, large and influential; new media giants may displace older ones. But the dominance of an oligarchy of mainstream media institutions had been undermined by multiple innovations before the internet (such as the proliferation of television and radio channels) and peer-to-peer communication alters the balance of power yet further. The power to publish is now widely dispersed; this has already led to adjustments in supply and demand for information and news, and more will occur. Society does not automatically gain. Jack Balkin of the Yale Law School says: 'People routinely praise the internet for its decentralizing tendencies. Decentralization and diffusion of power, however, is not the same thing as democracy... The fact that no one is in charge does not mean that everyone is free.'[6]

Impermanence

Interactivity has made information more open to challenge and change. Net utopians celebrate this as allowing the crowd-sourcing of information and can point to numerous examples of information enriched, better-focused and of decisive impact when it is from plural sources.[7] But information is also changeable and impermanent: the authority that went with the fixed nature of print has gone.

Choice

Interactivity also covers the shift from 'push' media to 'pull': the consumer acquires more power to choose what to consume. The user can decide what is her or his news.

Splintering the conversation

The ability to pick and choose what information to consume, when and how, must over time weaken the socially unifying effects of mainstream media, particularly of television. People in the second half of the 20th century made appointments with news media: a nightly habit of watching the main television news being the commonest. When listening, watching or reading, they could know that millions or thousands of others were getting the same version. Newspapers were read in the morning and television news seen in the evening, bracketing the working day. Digitization and the internet eroded these patterns by bringing news to be consumed on a phone or PC at the time of the consumer's choice. Developments such as the proliferation of broadcast channels, TV recording and playback devices, the growing perception that people had less time in the day (reinforced by many more mothers at work),[8] the internet's limitless ability to store material that can be revisited – all these helped to strengthen the news audience's ability to choose, but also to splinter the 'national conversation'.

Search

Thanks to the power of the giant search engines, information is not only found more easily but classified differently. Our relationship to what we know and what we might want to know alters. We need to retain less because information can so easily be found. We consume it in smaller fragments. Gradually searchable databases will make larger quantities of data – held, say, by governments and public bodies – publicly available. Governments are unlikely to surrender such data willingly. The power to make data accessible and useful lies in the hands of both information architects and journalists: breakthroughs in public understanding will be made at the junction where these two skills meet. But everything suggests that active citizens will gradually be able to use and analyse more reliable public data, which will make government more legible. Whether transparency increases or helps accountability is another question.

Everyone edits

Consumers can converge both platforms and content. The frontiers between audio-visual and text have dissolved: the internet platform can carry them all. That convergence allows immediate comparison and allows anyone with the time and a little skill to re-edit or mash-up content.

Narrowcasting

Broadcasting can be replaced by narrowcasting. The internet's ability to identify who is consuming what, for how long, and from where, allows content of all kinds to be targeted and tailored to specific segments chosen by mutual interests, demographic characteristic or any other criteria.

Utopia or dystopia?

The list above is not a catalogue of every change driven by the rapid spread of the internet: it is confined to those shifts that have implications for information for news and journalism. Those consequences are analysed in greater detail below.

But first, a context for technology. Change in journalism has often been triggered by new opportunities opened by science. New technology can influence the way that journalism is done: storytelling takes different forms in print, broadcast and online and the platform helps to shape the style. The widely spread style of a newspaper 'news story', which opens with the newest and most significant item of information and goes into lesser facts or background in a modular, top-down sequence, was derived from the typesetting and page-assembly technology developed for 19th-century newspapers. Type was grouped into blocks of a single paragraph or sentence and blocks. Cuts needed to be made at short notice in order to fit the jigsaw of a page together. The risk of mistakes was lowered by ensuring that stories could be cut from the bottom upward and paragraph by paragraph. That style of writing began to fade in importance from the moment that measurement of writing length could be done on a screen. But the imprint of that discipline lasted well beyond the technology that had formed it. Many stories are still written to that template: readers are familiar with it and, besides, it is an effective way of organizing facts.

Developments in technology open possibilities; internet software is an engine of opportunity. People decide whether the opportunities are taken and whether for good or ill. Technological advance and openings occur in and interact with a social, economic, political and legal context. Technology is not wholly neutral, because each new development will favour certain ways of doing journalism. But human minds assemble and shape information and news. In short, the internet opens new issues; it doesn't settle them. People make those decisions.

The history of news and its technology is not a story of the complete replacement of old machines by new ones. When I first became a full-time newspaper journalist in the early 1970s, I worked in a newsroom right next to a composing room packed with clattering linotype machines, the essential technology of which had not changed for half a century. During that half century, both radio and television had entered the news business. Instead of replacement of one technology by another, what more frequently happens is that the relative power and importance of one platform or another may change but that new technologies are layered on top of the old. The internet greatly exacerbates the business problems of daily, general-interest newspapers. That does not mean that such papers will disappear any time soon across the world 'because of the internet'. The impact of the internet on news is felt at different speeds in different places. Still less will print in general collapse or vanish.

No sooner had the internet's potential been grasped than its pioneers began predicting the rapid death of newspapers. The vulnerability of their infrastructure had been noticed long before that. The classified ads (and stock market quotations) are the bedrock of the press, Marshall McLuhan wrote in 1964, and 'should an alternative source of easy access to such diverse daily information be found, the press will fold.'[9] A book called *The Vanishing Newspaper* predicted that the last newspaper would print its last copy in the United States in the first quarter of 2043.[10]

The new platform for classified advertising that McLuhan imagined was found in the 1990s, leaving newsprint vulnerable. Journalists and their audiences are interacting with each other according to new rules that neither side entirely understands. But this is a long process of discovery made by trial and error. That process is taking place both inside and outside the existing news media system in each culture. Established mainstream media organizations are adapting to new realities and bringing to them assumptions, histories and values from the pre-digital era. Some will adapt and prosper; some will fail. Internet traffic is dominated by recently founded search and social-networking businesses such as Google and Facebook, but the consumption of news still leans towards well-known institutions such as the BBC, the *New York Times* or sites that aggregate their output (see Figure 4.1). New and old are mixed in unpredictable ways against a rapidly changing business and technical backdrop. In short, the effects of technology are ambiguous. In the words of David Noble, 'technology leads a double life, one which conforms to the intentions of designers and interests of power and another which contradicts them – proceeding behind their backs of their architects to yield unintended consequences and unintended possibilities'.[11]

FIGURE 4.1   Top news websites (2013)

1) Yahoo! News
2) CNN Interactive
3) MSNBC
4) Google News
5) New York Times
6) Huffington Post
7) Fox News
8) Washington Post
9) Los Angeles Times
10) MailOnline
11) Reuters
12) ABC News
13) USA Today
14) BBC News
15) Drudge Report

SOURCE: http://www.ebizmba.com/articles/news-websites (accessed 5.5.13)

Feverish early hyperbole about new advances in communication has a long history. Technologists often exaggerate the early impact of innovations (and expect them to come into wide use sooner than turns out to be the case) but equally often underestimate or misunderstand the long-run impact. This pattern has held true for the initial bursts of enthusiasm for railways, air travel, radio, television and the internet. Karl Marx believed that railways would do away with the Indian caste system. The laying of the first transatlantic telegraph cable between Britain and America in 1861 was an event of lasting importance, but Edward Thornton, the British ambassador to

Washington, inflated even that in 1868 when he said that the telegraph was 'removing causes of misunderstanding, and promoting peace and harmony throughout the world'.

In 1915, *Flying* magazine announced that the First World War would be the last great war in history because air travel would usher in a 'new period in human relations'. Guglielmo Marconi thought that his invention, radio, would render war 'ridiculous'. The first television critic of the *New York Times* asserted that the new device would generate a new harmony between the nations of the world.[12]

Potential drawbacks of new technologies are not always as immediately obvious as the gains. Evgeny Morozov,[13] whose examples of utopian optimism are quoted above, compiles a list of groups who have found the internet useful. It includes polygamists, nationalists (from the Circassian to Chinese varieties), Mexican crime gangs and traders in both near-extinct species and human organs. Text messages or e-mail are well suited to organizing a cleaning rota; they are equally useful for coordinating ethnic cleansing. The ease of distributing information via e-mail and the web may allow dissidents and activists to mobilize in authoritarian and totalitarian states. But digital-based systems also afford those authorities unprecedented ways to trace communications and organize surveillance. The internet can give us unprecedented knowledge to hold governments and corporations to account, Julian Assange said in 2011, but it is also 'the greatest spying machine the world has ever seen'.[14]

What the internet does to the business of news

Many studies of company history find that disruptive changes of technology, taste or demography are rarely recognized as threats by those whose job it is to assess dangers and to react to them. The internet is no different. Many news companies reacted very slowly or wrongly to the internet and its implications for their business. In truth, the producers of news were no longer in control of the space in which they communicated. It just took them years to see the scale of their problem.

The root cause of the failure to see clearly what might happen was complacency. Executives were so preoccupied with squeezing falling profits from a business model already ground down by earlier developments, they did not spare the time and energy for what they considered to be idle speculation.

Journalists, who often lectured politicians and business people on the need for adaptability and openness to change, mostly did no better: they were in favour of change in theory, provided that in practice it affected someone else.

It is not possible to compile a full list of every change visited on the media business by the world wide web, simply because those changes will continue to reverberate in successive cycles of change for years to come. These will not be changes confined to what we loosely call 'media'. Here is one view of the breadth of the alterations that we may yet see, in this case from an economist working for the Bank of England:

> Information is streamed in ever-greater volumes and at ever-rising velocities. Timelines for decision-making appear to have been compressed. Pressures to deliver immediate results seem to have intensified. Tenure patterns for some of our most important life choices (marriage, jobs, money) are in secular decline.
>
> These forces may be altering not just the way we act, but also the way we think. Neurologically, our brains are adapting to increasing volumes and velocities of information by shortening attention spans. Technological innovation, such as the World Wide Web, may have caused a permanent neurological rewiring, as did previous technological revolutions such as the printing press and typewriter.[15]

The debate over whether the web is rewiring the circuits of our brains, or to what extent, lies beyond the scope of this book and remains disputed. It is not even possible to identify exactly which business models have the best chance of success in the future (although there are some clues in Chapters 9 and 10). But to work out what will occur next, it is well worth looking at what happened when new ways of moving information began to undermine – and then rip apart – the industrialized business model for news publishing.

Monopolies busted (1)

The most basic effect of peer-to-peer distribution of information on media businesses is to destroy monopolies. In general, the value of news had been lifted by its relative scarcity until communications channels began proliferating in the 1980s, just ahead of the internet's arrival. Monopolies are created either by dominance of a market, which may be technically open but which has very high barriers to entry, or by state regulation (such as the granting of broadcasting licences). The most striking case was the conversion of most American cities to single-newspaper markets in the period

1950–75. This had a marked effect on local city journalism, because the surviving newspaper in each district was usually the one with the widest reach across which to spread its costs of printing and dispatching copies of the paper.[16] (Not all markets were affected in this way: countries such as Britain and Japan had national print markets.) Advertising on the internet threatened city newspapers' dominance in getting classified advertisements to large numbers of people quickly and cheaply. The impact was faster on newspapers because the internet reproduced static advertisements immediately. The effect on television monopolies, where they existed, was slower until broadband began to carry video advertisements down new routes.

Monopolies busted (2)

A richer supply of information alters what people require or desire from their news media. Print media based their appeal on a mixture: some news you need, some you just like to read. The internet provides specialized, deep and accessible sources of information. This tends to be information people require for their work: graphs of gas prices on demand, instruction manuals, detailed discussion forums. Newspapers cannot provide information of the same quality in specialized depth. The reader may continue to enjoy the newspaper for information they desire. The reader's loyalty weakens as the awareness grows that the newspaper is no longer the best or only provider of what they need.

Classified and Craigslist

For newspapers, the impact of the internet was greatest where the dependence on classified advertising was heaviest.[17] Doing classified bigger and better than newpapers could ever manage was perhaps the first 'killer app' that made money. Newspaper dependence on either display[18] or classified advertising varies widely across the world, from well over 80 per cent of income in the United States to below 40 per cent in Japan.[19] Evening and local newspapers, which depend particularly heavily on classified, were under most threat. The internet has almost no restriction on space, so it was quickly possible to assemble larger quantities of ads in one place, which could be instantly and painlessly searched. People looking for cars, jobs and houses could register with a site and be automatically e-mailed advertisements that fitted their requirements. The cost was tiny because a small number of ad-carriers had suddenly been replaced by a crowd of competitors. Specialist sites soon emerged. In 1995, Craig Newmark started an e-mail list of events in San Francisco. The e-mail became a site, craigslist. com, which charged for job or property listings but allowed personal ads for free. By 2004, Craigslist was estimated to be taking at least $50 million in annual advertising revenues from newspapers in the San Francisco area and was the 'go to' destination for small ads in many American cities – it now operates in 70 countries. As the Craigslist formula was varied or imitated across the digitally connected world, a large segment of dependable newspaper income evaporated. Classified advertising in US newspapers fell by one-half from $18 billion in 2005 to $9 billion in 2008. Even in Germany, with a strong advertising market that was only slowly hit by digital, the print share of total advertising revenue fell from 48.1 per cent in 1998 to 37 per cent in 2008. In the same period, the internet share of advertising climbed from 0.2 per cent to 15 per cent.[20] Globally, online advertising is due to outstrip newspaper print advertising in 2013.

Style

The neutrality and impartiality that American newspapers had learnt to practice to capture the widest metropolitan urban readerships made print journalism look stiff and solemn in the new conditions. The earlier deregulation and subsequent proliferation of talk radio had shown that opinion pulled in new audiences. Fox News demonstrated the same for television. This impact was much weaker in countries such as Britain and France with a longer tradition of journalism founded on opinion and whose newspapers had always differentiated themselves by their political stance.

Decline accelerated

In the early years of internet disruption, the claim could be heard that the internet was not disruptive at all. Perhaps American newspapers were being hit, but they were uniquely vulnerable, the argument ran, because of their unusual market conditions. Internet editions were widening readerships and not 'cannibalizing' print readerships. In the 1990s there was some small truth in this, but the internet's full effect was merely delayed. Figure 3.5 (see p. 76), showing British newspaper circulation, makes clear that the decline began well before the recession of 2007, which simply made things worse.[21] The internet's effect on print circulations is to gradually weaken loyalty, habitual purchase and engagement. The effect is also ambiguous. Young readers buy fewer newspapers but loyal print readers are also among the most eager consumers of online information.

Advertising economics

Newspaper executives with new websites to go alongside their print operations assumed that even if they had lost some classified advertising, they could still charge for display ads on the sites and reproduce something resembling the business model for print. But they were frustrated by the law of supply and demand. The supply of print advertising space in a given market is limited: only a number of businesses will have the capital and content to survive and there is a limit to the number of pages that printing machinery can handle, or that readers can tolerate. If the space is rationed, its price can be pushed up as long as advertisers compete to appear on the page. With the advertising 'inventory' on the web of infinite size, that supply and demand equation ceased to work. Advertising managers hoped and assumed that as print ad revenue fell, internet revenue would rise to replace it: the lines would cross as an 'X' on the graph. It did not work that way (see Figure 4.2). Twenty years after the internet disruption began, a few advertising-supported models are succeeding. But they tend to be start-ups with low costs.[22] Legacy newspapers, particularly of general interest, have not been able to replace lost print ads in order to cover their costs.

FIGURE 4.2   *Washington Post* print and online revenues

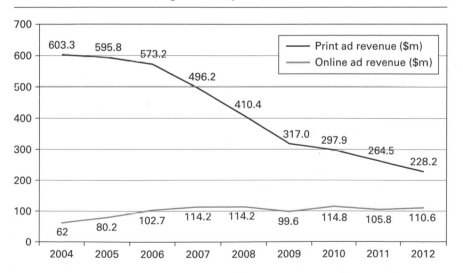

SOURCE: http://www.washpostco.com/phoenix.zhtml?c=62487&p=irol-reportsAnnualArch

'Native advertising'

The difficulties of winning conventional advertising for online news sites has generated pressure to blur the distinction between editorial and advertising. This pressure has always been present in print, usually in the form of 'advertorial', editorial coverage that is supposed to be written independently of advertisers but that would not be in the newspaper at all if advertising was not there to support it. US sites Buzzfeed, Gawker Media, *Forbes*, *Washington Post* and Atlantic Media have all experimented with 'native advertising', which goes further than covering a subject chosen by the advertisers. Some allow advertisers to create online content; some sites help to create content for advertisers. Critics allege that the labelling for this material is unclear.[23] Atlantic Media hit a squall of protest when it sold space to the Church of Scientology and deleted negative comments below the post. Atlantic took down the material after less than 12 hours and apologized.[24]

TV advertising

Although the internet mounted a slower challenge to television advertising, much the same logic was at work. The scarcity of national or network channels in the early television age had pushed prices to highly lucrative levels. Cable and satellite channels multiplied outlets and drove down prices; falling audiences did the same. But while TV news audiences had fallen since the multiplication of channels in the 1980s, the fall was not as steep as the defection of readers from print.

Digital optimism

John Paton, who runs the second largest local newspaper and website chain in the United States, takes a more robust view of the potential strength of advertising income and is testing his view on a large scale. He maintains that the problem with raising local online advertising revenue is that it has not been tried with enough vigour and skill. He reverses the normal publisher's complaint that journalists with their fixed mindsets and high costs are the issue. The people who need to think differently, Paton says, are on the business side.

Journalism overproduction

The colossal increase in the quantity of available information raises a possibility – and a strategic dilemma for publishers – never previously encountered in journalism: overproduction. What was scarce is now in glut. Far more reporting is copied from other media than journalists generally admit and this was the case long before the internet made it easy. The internet revealed to a global audience how much journalism is a variant or a direct copy of a template produced by the first story into the field. This has huge consequences for newsrooms and the deployment of journalists;[25] it touches the business as well. If 50 reporters turn up to hear a major political announcement live, will democracy suffer if 20 of them are not present? Considering that nowadays the politician making the announcement will immediately release audio, video and text of her or his own, and that rolling news channels will carry the event live, 20 reporters more or less cannot make much difference to the information being available. So managements must ask themselves how the resources for doing journalism can be concentrated where the value can be highest. The inhabitants of mainstream media newsrooms are, in my experience, extraordinarily reluctant to focus on this.

Wastage falls

The internet tends to split what previous technologies have lumped together. Much advertising in the mass media era was wasted. Advertisers bought large bundles of viewers or readers, which included many people they weren't interested in. There was no other choice. Internet search engines such as Google quickly saw that they could write software to 'push' ads towards the interest that the searcher revealed. You put 'lawnmower' into the slot on the Google front page: alongside and above your search results will be ads for garden centres. And Google was rapidly gathering much more detailed information from its users. Advertisers using Google could measure with greater precision and efficiency how well a particular ad was working. Google's founders, Sergey Brin and Larry Page, held a meeting early in the company's life with Mel Karmazin, then the president of Viacom, and an advertising salesman of legendary success and experience. Advertising prices could be driven up, Karmazin explained to the Californian pair, because 'advertisers don't know what works and what doesn't. That's a great model.' Brin and Page were shocked by what they considered a business based on deception and were sure that Google could do better. 'You're fucking with the magic!' Karmazin warned, entirely in vain.[26] The old system was upended by a company whose name was either a joke or a spelling mistake.[27]

Technology trap

An often neglected consequence of internet publishing on mainstream news businesses was a wholly new stress on technology. Mature print or television businesses knew their technologies and adapted them as more cost-efficient innovations came along. But no rethinking was needed. The need to master and experiment with the possibilities of the internet required almost every assumption of company organization and cost to be examined from first principles. New kinds of expertise needed to be hired, technology needs had to figure higher in priorities, new capacities had to be paid for, investments had to be made in machines with uncertain life cycles. Technology needed to be moved from the margins to the centre. In the 1990s, few established news organizations grasped this and acted quickly. Take the contrast between two different parts of News Corporation in Britain in that decade. News Corp held a commanding stake in the satellite channel Sky, and owned News International, which published four national newspapers.[28] Sky made technology a very high priority and led the field with several developments in set-top boxes. News International at first tended to treat the internet as a different means of distribution, not something that would force every aspect of the newspapers to be rethought.

Bundles

The internet shone a new light on how news businesses thought – if they thought at all – about cross-subsidy. News reporting is subsidized at many different levels. Newspapers that get the majority of their income from advertisements are paying for the correspondent in Cairo or Tokyo with the advertisements for Alfa Romeo or Yakult. The business survives if the bundle of income exceeds the bundle of costs. The newspaper may run at a loss if another division of the company makes a profit larger than the loss. If circulation or subscription revenue is the majority, the reader or viewer is still paying for a bundle and not valuing each item separately. At first, net gurus speculated that the bundles that make up newspapers, news and current affairs on radio or television would be broken up into a range of individual items from which audiences could choose. But the internet's natural centrifugal tendency was checked by the effort involved and the need for a consumer of news to be sure that it comes from a trusted source. So bundles of news have survived but individual stories, videos and links are shared as individual fragments, if the publisher allows it. The overall effect was to expose journalism to direct valuation. Journalists were reminded that their work was made possible by a balanced business that generated enough cross-subsidy to keep them on the road. Asking readers and viewers to pay for news journalism directly and at the cost it takes to produce did not work. And it never has.

Monopoly complacency

One of the most powerful shocks administered to newsrooms by the internet was the reminder that many editors and journalists took their readers for granted. The declines of the decades before 1990 had been just gradual enough to conceal to many editorial employees the growing weakness of the platform on which they operated. British national papers, operating in what had always been a fiercely competitive market, had for years been endlessly anxious about their readers, active with opinion research surveys and were hardly complacent about print readers, even if indifferent to the internet. But in monopoly markets, readers had nowhere else to go. And in many of those local monopoly markets, newspapers had often hollowed out their content by employing fewer reporters, training them less or not at all and by reducing original content. Over time, all these weaknesses were to be attacked by insurgent internet news businesses.

Measuring value

Interactive, peer-to-peer communications shift the balance of advantage from producer to consumer. Feedback, comparison, obtaining market intelligence, measurement – all are easier for consumers and customers and increase their relative power. In media in general and in journalism in particular, this puts a premium on high-calibre knowledge of what exactly will represent value to the user. Executives, innovators and planners must become better anthropologists: how, why and when will someone need what I can deliver? Earlier generations of media business would think of a 'product' and deliver it to a captive audience with a fair, but not certain, chance that it might work. With audience attention now endlessly fickle and able to flow back and forth like liquid, that technique will work less often. Much more intimate knowledge of potential need and value is essential. Supply and demand will work differently in an altered context.

Targeting

Much effort has gone into gathering data about website customers, most of it covert and some of it controversial.[29] The idea was to make advertisement targeting more and more precise, assisted by greater volumes of data about individual users and their habits and tastes, as revealed by their patterns of web use. But, so far, the returns on this have not matched up to the hype. Reuters blogger Felix Salmon thinks that this shortfall on expectations is due to one of two possible causes: either consumers' resentment at both being 'spied on' and pestered on the web by repetitive ads triggered by a keyword they have typed, or in that targeted advertising is becoming like direct mail shots. Hard-copy direct-mail ads have, even if sent in their millions to the right demographic group interested, always had low response rates.[30]

Personal brands

The generation of editorial content, distribution and marketing are now mixed together in a new way. Search allows a user to go to the item or journalist they choose directly and not through the organization they belong to. Newsrooms thus become something closer to platforms for individuals who can market their work on networks that they can create, maintain and develop. Lewis Dvorkin, chief digital officer of *Forbes* magazine, insists that his journalists and blogging contributors push their own work and generate traffic as part of their deal with the magazine site.

New players

The internet, by virtue of its ease and low cost, made it possible for many other players to enter the business of creating content. Private-sector companies began by sending uplifting video messages to their staff scattered across the world, but quickly moved on to what would once have been called television programming. Charities and non-government organizations (NGOs) began telling their own stories unmediated by news organizations, replacing what might have been expert commentary on events in an earlier era. Think tanks or activist organizations could compete for a reputation for being a reliable source, supplying both the media and the public.[31] Brand advertising came to embrace material indistinguishable from news, sport or current affairs. Red Bull, the energy-drink firm started in Austria in 1987, has sponsored adrenaline-junkie extreme sports from the start and is now the world's main producer of such coverage, having been archiving the video from the start. They ran a seven-year project on free-falling, which culminated in three world records for free-falls from more than 128,000 feet. The coverage has generated magazines, a syndication deal with NBC and X-Box games. In December 2012, their YouTube channel had 1 million subscribers and had logged 5 billion views in the previous six years.[32]

Trust and attention

Trust and attention are important currencies for anyone producing news, and the internet has important effects on the business aspects of both. An information-rich world means that journalists cannot function without producing value. Most journalists want to be trusted and most want attention; the aims can be in tension or conflict with each other. Both trust and attention are being measured in different ways in social networks that enable sharing. The mere act of sharing something does not mean that whoever you share it with is necessarily being told to trust it; you may just be calling it to their attention. If you share a blogpost about a man marrying a goat, or a picture of a skateboarding cat, you may just be saying: look at this! But the measurement of trust and attention – or engagement – on networks, and on the web in general, is in its infancy and will grow much more sophisticated much more quickly. The cumulative effect of assembling your view of what's happening from shared links will be to shrink the attention paid to the major channels that produce the material in the first place. News is likely to feel 'channel-less'.[33]

Delayed acceleration

Publishers trying to cope with internet disruption faced a dilemma much more complex than many cyber-utopians thought. When a business model begins to disintegrate, it can do so quite slowly and at uneven speed. This might be called the technology cycle of deception and acceleration. Technologists often confuse their ability to see a potential change with the, quite different, rate at which the innovation will be adopted by large numbers of people. Thus, many dramatic predictions about the future are often followed by a long period in which little seems to happen; there is then often a later moment at which the apparently sluggish change speeds up. Managements are therefore trying to run two different models at the same time. Professor Clayton Christensen of Harvard, a scholar of business disruption, puts it like this:

The new business with the new technology emerges and becomes quite substantial even as the old technology and old business model is still very strong. So you have to preside over two business models simultaneously and not hold the new to the standards of the old.[34]

That last injunction is the piece of advice most often ignored in journalism. Mainstream journalists look at start-ups and sneer at their modest size and inability to do much 'original reporting'. Sometimes they may do so with reason, but they also fail to see a future in which competitive start-ups will grow and discipline themselves as they go, gradually becoming tougher competition for established players.

Tablets

Change can occur very fast when it acquires real momentum and people feel comfortable with new devices and software. The arrival of the iPad and its rival tablets was a game-changing moment, not because of the technical attributes of the device, but because of the overall message sent by both the hardware and the software. The applications were easy and unfrightening to use, the screen's optical quality came close to being as attractive as paper (even better for people with poor eyesight). Switchover to digital reading was accelerating, also helped by the growth of e-readers such as Amazon's Kindle. When readers of *The Economist* were asked in 2012 how they were accessing the magazine's output, four were reading in print to every one reader online. But asked how they would be reading in 2014, 70 per cent said online and only 30 per cent expected to be using print.

New markets, new gaps

Fast-evolving innovations require agility and deeper knowledge in the organizations affected by them. Manoeuvrability is not worth much if the organization cannot know or understand what is going on around it. This may sound obvious, but it is surprising how little the media companies in Europe thought they needed to know about the internet, search and software during the 1990s. People who wanted to go out to California to find out about it were frequently thought eccentric. Yet online readerships were not confined inside frontiers. Online does not abolish barriers of language or national culture: advertising remains largely national and international advertising earns less. But the web jumps some of geography's limits. Online user communities do not have to meet in the same place. Spain's *El Mundo* trails a long way behind *El País* in print circulation, but led for years online because of Spanish-speaking Latin America. Forty-two per cent of *El Mundo*'s readers are overseas; though it sells no print copies outside Spain, it is among the top two or three news sites in every Spanish-speaking country in Latin America.[35] Online usage took off very slowly in Russia, but Russians enthusiastically adopted social networks – mostly using smart-phones. In effect, Russia skipped the e-mail stage. In whole regions such as southern Africa and South Asia, the internet has never really happened on personal computers on any scale. Purchasing power and poor networks stopped PCs spreading very far. So in those large areas, the internet is held in the hand and used on smartphones or tablets.

Journalist obstacles

News organizations coping with disruption face the normal constraints that can delay or prevent change: cautious shareholders, unions and customers who, in the case of news media, are mostly conservative. But they often face an additional inhibition from journalists themselves. There are many excep-tions, but in the main journalists are convinced or easily persuaded that what they do is so good and important that someone should pay them to do it. They rightly often place their faith in institutions large enough to protect them from legal or other attack, which builds and maintains traditions with high standards. But they less frequently see that independence, which they also value, requires financial self-sufficiency (or at least cross-subsidy). As the business models of mainstream media have sunk deeper into trouble in more and more parts of the world, the odd journalist has been heard to say that journalism is threatened but that it is important that people *should* pay for it. This feeling is not a business model.

Overborrowing

One shock administered by the internet revolution was a function of unusual historical circumstances. In the 1980s and particularly in the 1990s, developed economies were doing so well that many publishing companies had borrowed very heavily. The advertising boom in some countries such as Britain and the United States in that decade was short and misleading: advertising slumped in the new century. When that slump came, the most highly leveraged companies found themselves in the deepest trouble. The long-standing problems of newspapers such as the *Chicago Tribune* and the *Los Angeles Times* have multiple causes, but high borrowing in a time of falling revenue is a significant one.

Any one of these changes would have been a major disruption to a news company. Taken together, they were destabilizing, albeit slowly. The positions built over the previous five or six decades were not likely to crumble immediately. But as the figures under the old business models got worse, the realization dawned that there is no law that guarantees that a departing business model will be replaced by another one. As business managers were grappling with a complete change of their ecosystem, journalists were trying to adjust to changes equally large in their world.

Notes

1 Boorstin, Daniel J (1978) *The Republic of Technology*, Harper & Row, New York.

2 Quoted in Gleick, J (2011) *The Information*, 4th Estate, London.

3 Naughton, J (2012) *From Gutenberg to Zuckerberg: What You Really Need To Know About the Internet*, Quercus, London.

4 Family Expenditure Survey 2012, Office for National Statistics, London.

5 Howard Rheingold, author of *Net Smart*, quoted in the *Sunday Times*, 10 February 2013.

6 Balkin, Jack M (2010) *Information Power: The Information Society from an Anti-Humanist Perspective*, Social Science Research Network eLibrary. Quoted in Morozov, E (2011) *The Net Delusion: How Not To Liberate the World*, Allen Lane, London.

7 Shirky, C (2008) *Here Comes Everybody*, Allen Lane, London.

8 See Chapter 3.

9 McLuhan, M (1964) *Understanding Media: The Extensions of Man*, McGraw-Hill, New York.

10 Meyer, Philip (2004) *The Vanishing Newspaper*, University of Missouri Press, Missouri.

11 Noble, David (1986) *The Forces of Production*, Oxford University Press, Oxford.

12 Morozov, *The Net Delusion: How Not To Liberate the World*.

13 Morozov, *The Net Delusion: How Not To Liberate the World*.

14 http://www.guardian.co.uk/media/2011/mar/15/web-spying-machine-julian-assange (accessed 2.12.12).

15 Andrew G Haldane, quoted at http://gigaom.com/2011/05/10/the-distribution-democracy-and-the-future-of-media/ (accessed 24.1.13).

16 Knee, J, Greenwald, B and Seave, A (2009) *The Curse of the Mogul*, Portfolio, New York.

17 Small ads, most usually for houses, flats, cars and jobs, usually costed by numbers of words or lines and normally text only.

18 Larger advertisements using pictures and text, usually for retail or brands.

19 Levy, D and Nielsen, R K (eds) (2010) *The Changing Business of Journalism and its Implications for Democracy*, RISJ Oxford.

20 Esser and Bruggeman, 'The strategic crisis of German newspapers' in Levy and Nielsen, *The Changing Business of Journalism and its Implications for Democracy*.

21 Slide 8 in **http://www.scribd.com/doc/85024991/Enders-Analysis-slide-presentation-to-News-on-the-Move#download**.

22 See Chapter 9.

23 **http://dish.andrewsullivan.com/2013/02/21/guess-which-buzzfeed-piece-is-an-ad/** (accessed 8.3.13).

24 **http://www.forbes.com/sites/jeffbercovici/2013/01/15/the-atlantic-on-that-scientology-advertorial-we-screwed-up/** (accessed 8.3.13).

25 Discussed further in Chapter 6.

26 Auletta, K (2010) *Googled: The End of the World as We Know It*, Virgin.

27 **http://googlesystem.blogspot.co.uk/2006/07/5-different-stories-about-googles-name.html** (accessed 25.1.13).

28 *The Times*, the *Sunday Times*, *The Sun* and *News of the World*.

29 **http://online.wsj.com/article/SB10001424052748703940904575395073512989404.html** (accessed 26.1.13).

30 **http://blogs.reuters.com/felix-salmon/2011/04/28/the-uncanny-valley-of-advertising/** (accessed 26.1.13) and interview with the author.

31 A good example might be the much-consulted International Crisis Group, based in Brussels: **www.crisisgroup.org**.

32 **http://www.forbes.com/sites/aliciajessop/2012/12/07/the-secret-behind-red-bulls-action-sports-success/** (accessed 25.1.13).

33 **http://gigaom.com/2011/05/10/the-distribution-democracy-and-the-future-of-media/** (accessed 24.1.13).

34 **http://www.themediabriefing.com/article/2012-09-09/clayton-christensen-on-the-threat-of-innovation-and-transition-to-new-technology** (accessed 3.2.13)

35 **http://www.economist.com/node/21550262** (accessed 26.1.13).

05 Rethinking journalism again

> *No institution wants to dissolve itself. Getting that old mindset to accept that everything that it has done as a business and editorial model is now over, pffft, gone, is very, very hard.*
>
> ANDREW SULLIVAN, *THE DISH*, 2012

News media were once easy to recognize. They were simple to identify by virtue of the capital-intensive machinery involved, whether that was broadcast equipment or rotary printing presses. Journalists were people who worked for these quasi-industrial organizations. Digital communications have also demolished, or at least blurred, many frontiers and barriers that defined many familiar and well-known activities. The internet collapses both time and space for those who have access to it. Information is available faster, in quantity and at low or no cost; geography is no hindrance. The technology and distinctions that underpinned the exclusiveness of journalism and journalists have gone, and some of the social and professional prestige has evaporated with it. The business model of some parts of the established news media is being eroded, principally with daily, general-interest newspapers at highest risk. The term 'newspaper' is now awkwardly stretched to cover print, tablet editions, mobile-compatible output and millions of pages in the online archive.

The consequences are not all good or all bad. The history of what has happened to journalism so far cannot be written as a *Wired* version of Whig history,[1] a story of never-ending progress. Journalism has always existed in messy and often controversial circumstances, regardless of rows and disruptions caused by what is said or written by journalists. This is for two reasons. First, open societies assume that journalism functions better if it is independent of the state, even if there are many variations of that belief in practice. Being reliant on the market is inherently unstable and carries its own risks. Second, the intersection between a social, democratic purpose and the market is a place that guarantees only one regular thing: change. Journalism is exposed to changes in means of communication, political and social beliefs, law and the distribution of power. Periods of stability are the exception and not the rule. Journalism today can be better described as a living experiment than a ruinous decline. But that rests on a hope that what is of value in journalism can be adapted to new conditions. We can be certain that the future will not resemble the past. But there is no law that says it will be better. We must try to make it so.

Among the predictions that are often made with confidence is that 'the age of mass media is over'. Given both the fragmentation and proliferation of media platforms and the weakening of the hold on big audiences of mainstream media, it is tempting to simplify the future in these terms. But we are living in a moment of transition and that 'demassification' of the media may turn out to be temporary. Some established media outlets are succeeding in using their advantages and skills to amass huge audiences online.

Perhaps the most remarkable worldwide example of this is the late-starting, global success of the *Daily Mail*'s website *MailOnline*. The London-based paper held off from more than a few tentative experiments on the web in the early years, but secured a colossal, if transient, readership when *MailOnline* refined its formula of expanding celebrity gossip coverage to dominate the online offering. The *Mail*'s long-practised skills in presenting entertainment stories in a style that is readable but not offensive (and doing so at tightly controlled editorial cost) drew the world's largest number of monthly unique visitors at 50.1 million in 2012.[2] When that figure passed the *New York Times*, a spokesman for the *New York Times* sniffed that 'it's a roll-up of their properties. We remain the number one *individual* newspaper site in the world. The *Mail* is not in our competitive set.' Neither the *Daily Mail* nor the *New York Times* have shown that they can turn these numbers into sustainable profit.[3] Neither newspaper has yet shown that they can either charge subscribers enough to make up falls in advertising income or deliver consumers to advertisers more effectively than Google.

The increase in choice provided by the internet does not mean that people will use all the choices, or that choice will be distributed evenly. Common sense tells us that people like to do what other people do, that they like to be able to discuss common experiences. Research confirms that this holds good even in the web's cornucopia. Researchers looking at the numbers of people reading newly minted blogs by the millions rapidly discovered that a few were read by very large numbers. Clay Shirky summarized this brutal truth: 'In systems where many people are free to choose between many options, a small subset of the whole will get a disproportionate amount of traffic (or attention, or income), even if no members of the system actively work towards such an outcome.'[4]

The basic effect of the internet on news publishing is the huge increase in participation. Barriers to entry in communication, in becoming a 'publisher', in distributing information globally, barriers to access to innovation and to audiences that can be addressed without permissions or switches – all these inhibitions have been lowered or have disappeared. That is what lies at the root of the explosion of information, the scale of which alters many aspects of journalism. The next sections of this chapter look at the fallout from the detonation.

Complexity

It tempts ridicule to point out that one effect of digital communication has been a sizeable increase in complexity. But the effect on established news organizations is poorly understood. All changes in communications have brought new complexity, but the quantity of information put into circulation by the world wide web represented a new scale of challenge. IBM estimates that 2.5 quintillion (17 zeroes) new bytes (sequences of eight binary digits that each encode a single character of text in a computer) are being created every day.[5] One-third of the world's 6 billion population is connected to the internet. One inhabitant in every seven on the planet is on Facebook. Hundreds of millions of blogs are live. An hour of video footage is uploaded to YouTube every second; globally, YouTube is viewed 4 billion times each day.[6] During the airing of the Japanese anime film *Castle in the Sky* in December 2011, Twitter counted just over 25,000 tweets being sent per second.[7] In any 20 minutes, Facebook typically sees 1 million shared links, 2.7 million photos uploaded and 10.2 million comments.[8] This is the scale of the information ecosystem in which news publishers operate.

I took part in early efforts of one big news company to cope with this huge increase in complexity.[9] Looking back, our failure to understand what was happening to the world in which we were operating is humiliating to recall. I doubt if the experience of other such organizations in Europe and America was very different. A long period of relative stability had made newspapers conservative in structure, processes and recruitment. We were hesitant about experiment, we assumed that mass was compulsory and niche a disaster, we assumed that advertising income would arrive naturally on the internet. Above all, we did not see the pivotal importance of investment in technology and that we needed to recruit – and not just to call in as consultants – a wide range of new skills. Many people in charge did not even see the issue of complexity, let alone have the capacity to solve the problems.

The technology writer John Naughton argues that media companies require an internal cultural revolution to equip themselves to live with instability and complexity. He quotes the management scientist Jonathan Rosenhead warning against the negative consequences of 'common internal culture'.[10] News organizations develop very strong internal cultures mostly because they have unusually pressured daily rhythms. This has produced a paradox in many media companies wrestling with the digital disruption. Journalists and publishers can talk freely about the future, change and what needs to be done, yet as soon as they return to their busy desks in the newsroom, the ideas evaporate in the face of daily or hourly deadlines.

In this atmosphere it is hard, and often impossible, for experiments to be mounted in sufficient quantity to meet the challenges of disruption. Large media companies are accustomed to mature, stable markets in which to brainstorm a new magazine or programme: a winning idea is chosen and money is set aside to work up and market-test the chosen option; yet more funds are earmarked for launch and promotion if the focus groups like what they see. This method worked well for years. But it is slow, cumbersome and costly in disrupted conditions. Such companies struggle to understand that it might have been better to split the budget among 10 experiments in order to cover more ground and to create competition for quality of experiment. Media executives rarely realize how many obstacles they place in the way of generating enough trial and error to learn how to cope with new threats. 'Dandelion-seed strategy' (scatter lots of ideas, expect many to fail) was not an expression in use in media boardrooms when it mattered.

Frontiers fade and vanish

Repeated, continuous change and uncertainty have seen walls, barriers and distinctions disappear. For half a century, print and broadcast journalists worked in separate newsrooms and cultures. Is online a medium of words, as it briefly began, or a broadcast medium, as increased bandwidth has made it? Both and neither. Journalists are now trained to be 'multi-platform', moving seamlessly from one technique to another and using the most appropriate combination to the story and the audience.

One division, not to say rivalry, which may yet disappear is the one between print and digital. In the 1990s, the first flush of enthusiasm for reading on the internet died with the dawning realization, soon confirmed by research, that screens were tiring and no fun to read, particularly if the text was more than 200 words long. A few wishful thinkers constructed a theory that newspapers could thus survive the threat that the internet represented to their livelihood: no one would read news on screens. Two developments knocked this hope sideways. Screens do not have the light-reflecting qualities of paper (and this has certainly helped magazines retain their distinctive appeal) but they improve all the time. The appearance of the iPad alone converted many sceptical older readers who found the highly evolved and engineered screen more attractive to read than newsprint. Easily portable tablets allowed online news to get to readers when they are on the move, thus capturing the part of the day that PCs had not been able to reach.

In the end, screens will be likely to mimic the optical qualities of print. And the robust, portable qualities of paper as well: the engineers at Fujitsu and at Samsung have been working on bendable or foldable screen for some years. Only a decade ago, website designers advised that text should always use sans-serif typefaces, as they were easier to read on the screen quality of the time. Even relatively small mobile screens are now sufficiently bright and readable to take serif typefaces (such as the one you are now reading).

Ink marks on squashed trees

For 20 years people have been asking if 'print' will disappear. It will much more likely shrink and do so unevenly. Where and how that shrinkage occurs will depend on the economics of three different uses for print: news-papers, magazines and books. Think of the information you consume on a range from the fastest to the slowest: at one end of the scale, books, with long gestation and publication cycles for leisurely reading in no hurry. Traverse across the scale and the pace picks up with magazines (quarterly, monthly, weekly) and accelerates further with newspapers. At the fastest end of the scale are 24-hour news channels and constantly updating websites. We do not yet know for certain how digital will impact on the supply and demand in each of these areas. We already know that the distribution and retail costs for bookselling are reshaping the book trade: but reconstructing, not abolishing it. Physical books tend towards a length and size that feels like value for money, but which can be held in the hand. E-books have no such constraint and can be as long or short as the author can make appealing.

Newspapers have struggled to define where they belong on the scale that varies speed and depth. One safe prediction is that daily newspapers will continue to be under severe pressure, even if a digital business model does not come into view for some time.[11] There are many variations on this theme:

> If you were starting from scratch, you could never possibly justify this business model. Grow trees – then grind them up, and truck big rolls of paper...?
> Then run them through enormously expensive machinery, hand-deliver them overnight to thousands of doorsteps, and leave more on newsstands, where the surplus is out of date immediately and must be thrown away? Who would say that made sense?[12]

This does not mean that no new print journalism will start. There are occasional examples of successful websites that start print editions,[13] but they are rare and often function as marketing arms for the website rather than as businesses in their own right. Newspapers face a triple crisis of lost classified advertising revenue, falling income from larger 'display' advertisements and falling circulation. They do so with sizeable cost structures that are hard to reduce. Over time, environmental pressures may add to these difficulties. The hefty Sunday edition of the *New York Times*, one of the largest of its kind in the world, is estimated to consume 27,000 trees per week.[14]

Comparison and choice

Consumers of news have been conditioned by digital information to be able to get to what they want at speed without having to sit through a menu decided by someone else. They also expect to be able to check or consult the news whenever it suits them. News is a river of endlessly renewed material that never stops flowing; it is no longer an occasional event. You dip into it at the time and place of your choosing. These active and choosy users tend to be younger users. Even older members of the audience look at television news with impatience. Conditioned by being able to find the key bit of news I'm looking for at will and at speed, I now find the conventional pattern of mainstream television reporting to be slow, mannered and ritualistic. I suspect that I'm not alone.

The internet let the light in on a confidence trick. Many newspaper journalists did not realize, and some still don't, that they have been rumbled. Readers gained a power of comparison that they did not previously have.

The full effects of this have still probably not been explored. For the effect on journalism has been and will be profound. Journalists naturally converge on the event that they consider to be the biggest news. But in the future, readers will find less and less attraction in news media that produce the same story. Media that look as if they do little but duplicate each other cannot possibly secure the kind of loyalty and engagement that they are going to need. Journalists who end up writing much the same story as their competitors did not have to worry about readers making comparisons. Except for other journalists checking the competition, no reader had the resources or the patience to do it. They might not have intended to produce a duplicate, but in practice they often did and still often do.

Khrishna Bharat, the founder of Google News, has probably sifted more news from more sources across the world than anyone alive at the moment (he says that he would have been a journalist had he not become a software engineer). He made one of his first appearances outside the United States on behalf of Google at a conference of editors in Seoul in 2005; Google News had launched three years earlier. I remember his polite wonder and bemusement at the lack of interest the journalists showed in his gentle hint that the power of comparison was gradually going to enforce big changes in what editors did. This was Bharat's insight:

> Usually, you see essentially the same approach taken by a thousand publications at the same time... Once something has been observed, nearly everyone says approximately the same thing... It makes you wonder, is there a better way? Why is it that a thousand people come up with approximately the same reading of matters?
>
>   Why couldn't there be five readings? And meanwhile use that energy to observe something else, equally important, that is currently being neglected... I believe the news industry is finding that it will not be able to sustain producing highly similar articles.[15]

News-hungry consumers have spotted that established media have managed for a long time to hide their drift into a high degree of sameness, duplication and oversupply. This slow convergence happened because of pressures on reporting resources, laziness and the common herd instinct to imitate success. But most of all it happened because it could; readers didn't know or care about the diminishing differences between news media because they never compared one with another. Few ordinary readers conduct systematic surveys now, but many now know that originality of approach or reporting is not always present and has to be sought. For example, Jonathan Stray chose a story reported by the *New York Times* tracing the responsibility for hacking American company computers to two technical schools in China. He analysed 121 separate versions of the story; seven of them (6 per cent) were based on original reporting and the rest were rewrites involving paid effort but with little or no value added.[16]

Software that is similar to, and developed from, programmes designed to spot students plagiarizing published work can be used to spot 'churnalism', the lazy rewriting of press releases or other PR material in reporting.[17] The software is in its infancy and has difficulty distinguishing between useful facts being transmitted from a written source and lazy copying, but it will improve. Google News has already built criteria into its algorithms that rank stories that it lists. A filing updating the patent for Google News revealed 13 measurements that include the length of articles, 'human opinion of the news source' (opinion research conducted by Google), the size of the newsroom, the number of news bureaus outside headquarters, the breadth and global reach of the news organization and the score of 'original named entities'. This last item seems to count the occurrence of names in a story and to assume that a higher name count means that it is more likely to be original reporting.[18]

But the much wider range of routes by which information can be acquired or sent also has hidden risks and costs. The next few sections look at these.

The downside risks of choice

Trust in journalism fell in most developed societies over the past 30 years, but trust in many social institutions – government, political parties and politicians, churches, companies – fell at the same time. Media scholar Michael Schudson believes that the important change was the protests and debates of the 1960s: 'What the sixties taught many Americans and many others around the world was not just that government cannot be trusted but that it is safe, perhaps admirable, and surely fashionable to say so.' Schudson also observes that falls in trust in news in media-literate societies are signs that something has gone right, not wrong. Scepticism about news is healthy.[19]

Add the cumulative worries about the cultural and psychological effects of television, and then the colossal proliferation of sources provided by the internet, and people begin to worry that the process has gone too far. Truth in the digital era is too rootless and malleable to be sure of, as a character in Daniel Kehlmann's novel *Fame* complains:

> How strange that technology has brought us into a world where there are no fixed places any more. You speak out of nowhere, you can be anywhere, and because nothing can be checked, anything you choose to imagine is, at bottom, true. If no one can prove to me where I am, if I myself am not absolutely certain, where is the court that can adjudicate these things?[20]

There is no guarantee that more information makes the world better. For the past few centuries, most change has been in the direction of circulating more information in free societies. The risk and conflict provoked by disclosure has generally been considered worthwhile. But information now circulates at such speed, with such ease and in such quantities that the question has changed. Does news and information meet the need? Freedom can hurt the interests of those who enjoy its increase. 'The internet will not automatically preserve – never mind improve – the health of democratic politics', Evgeny Morozov writes. 'Yes, a wired future might look good for democracy if some of the social functions currently performed by traditional media are taken up by the new internet projects. But that outcome needs to be demonstrated – perhaps constructively aimed at – rather than assumed.'[21]

Much unreflective hype dazzled by technological opportunities skates past questions of social, cultural or political effects. Most of the radical changes in the means to transmit and distribute information in history have been followed by irrational optimism, then doubts, debate and eventually a more balanced use. The net outcome has always been a gain, even if some technology fads fail to deliver their initial promise. But that gain has to be consciously designed and worked for. We currently know very little about what information travels around new networks, and how, let alone what effect and influence it might have as it goes. We do know that there is no alternative to facing the challenge, since the profusion of digitally driven information is not something that can be reversed.

So, as journalism tries to redefine its role in the new information economy, the nature of experiment in journalism matters a great deal. Journalism makes a contribution, along with other actors and organizations in civil society, to the quality of public reason. Unless there is a benchmark to help ascertain and judge what is true, journalism's most basic work is undermined. That means that the quality, not just the quantity, of experiments in sustainable journalism is significant. Those experimenting have to take a social or democratic function into account as well as a commercial one.

Authority

Intellectual discoveries and decisions of lasting importance tend to be made by shifting combinations of individuals and groups. The criminal justice system balances the sole power of a judge with a jury. Academics cannot publish in the best journals without the permission of a small jury of their peers; the standing of what they have written is then informally voted on by more experts who can cite it as an authority or ignore it. The pace of scientific discovery in the 18th century increased as the interested parties built up the habit of printing and distributing accounts of breakthroughs across borders. But many key contributions to human history have been the product of a single mind or hand.

Digital communications has grown and, by a massive order of magnitude, the number of consultations, votes, opinions and sources that can be brought to bear on many choices. The opening of this opportunity for journalism generated many claims that news reporting would now be 'crowd-sourced' and would be richer and more accurate as a result. Some went further and anticipated a complete reconstruction of 'news' because the power to define it and process it would be distributed among many more actors. Individual expertise, argued some, would be superseded by 'algorithmic authority'.[22] In practice, news organizations began to adapt but they did not reconstruct themselves entirely.

Broadcast news channels began using 'user-generated' video almost immediately and now do so routinely. Raw information can reach news organizations by more routes and from more sources. This is not an unqualified advantage. Clearly 'users' or 'citizen journalists' can provide eye-witness accounts especially by uploading pictures or video; a breaking news event will be reported more fully more quickly with social platforms such as Twitter, Facebook or Wikinews, which group different fragments of the same narrative in the same place or stream. It is easier for alternative perspectives to be made available: sites such as Global Voices Online exist to amplify grassroots observation and comment that might be ignored by mass media.

But the increase in the quantity of information does not alter – or surely should not – the requirement to verify the accuracy of the information. In news organizations under pressure from lower income or resources and the higher speed of the news cycle, the need to verify or check large amounts of material of unknown origin can, and has, led to embarrassing mistakes. Newsrooms have often only adapted their workflows slowly to cope with this new element. This is something that journalism has done before. The arrival of the telegraph in the 19th century had increased the quantity and scope of information being handled and meant that news could, for the first time, be treated as something that evolved continuously and could be updated more often. Workflow adapted. In exactly the same way, some of the most important testing of new ideas is now happening on news sites that specialize in grassroots (or citizen) stories or pictures, but which have accepted the responsibility to develop better disciplines and means of verification. This was the impulse behind Mark Little's foundation of Storyful,[23] and can be seen at work in the SwiftRiver platform built for the African crowdsource news site Ushahidi.[24]

The key to the use of what has become known by the ugly formulation 'UGC' (user-generated content) lies in the integration of new material into old processes and criteria used to evaluate and sift it. Information is mostly useful if it can be shown to be reliable. Sites that consist of nothing but unsorted information tend to be incoherent and hard to assess. The ability to sift, edit and give meaning to the contributions and responses of readers turns out to have a value that people appreciate.

Newspapers that once confined readers contributions to 'Letters to the Editor' opened their online stories to comments from readers. But this has not been the enriching experience that many news websites expected. In common with the pattern of much interaction on the web, a very small number of commenters write a high proportion of the comments.[25] And a high proportion of 'commentary' is moronic abuse, even on sites whose journalism does not fit that description. In private, many editors despair of the standard of comments threads on their sites. Debates have begun about how to develop comment practice and software so as to raise the quality of comments: how to sift the best to the most prominent position,[26] how to make individual conversations easier to follow. No newsroom has the resources to edit comment streams, so a long string of thousands of comments may contain 10 interventions of real value to the site's readership. Automatic filtering software can weed out abuse or obscenity. Anonymous comments are starting to go out of fashion. In the future, quality news websites may well insist on commenters identifying themselves.

The Guardian, which invested heavily and early in its website, advertised 'open' journalism and its editor talked of the 'mutualisation' of reporting.[27] But the newspaper's reporters still sift information (as they have always done) and editors still edit, taking decisions about accuracy, reliability, inclusion and exclusion. The newspapers that published extracts from the hundreds of thousands of American military and diplomatic documents given to WikiLeaks still sifted the material through their own editorial processes.

As *The Guardian*'s dealings with WikiLeaks and its exotic, eccentric founder Julian Assange illustrated,[28] new information flows create new relationships and dilemmas. But at the end of the day, the authority of the publication rests with a single individual, or a very small group of them, charged with maintaining its reputation. The work between WikiLeaks and a small consortium of newspapers across the world was unusual but the newspapers decided that they would treat Assange as a source or supplier and not as a co-editor. A source of information on an unprecedented scale, but a source all the same.

The boundaries around journalism – and who is a journalist – may have blurred, but that does not reduce the need to sift for truth. One *Guardian* journalist who has been unusually adept at using social media to inform his reporting has also become a prominent voice reminding journalists that the more material you gather from strangers, the more important is checking and verification. Paul Lewis had only joined Twitter two days before protests at the G20 summit in London in April 2009. After a man died after being struck by a policeman, Lewis posted a request on Twitter for eyewitnesses, and gradually gathered evidence, including mobile-phone video, which undermined the official account of what had happened. But Lewis stresses that this is a new research method and, while very effective for consulting a large number of people who might have witnessed something important, it is not a substitute for assessing the truth of what a reporter is told. It is highly likely, he says, that unscrupulous governments with an interest in manipulating news – without appearing to do so – will embed their operatives in social media networks under plausible identities.[29] There are already clear indications that countries ranging from China, America, Syria and Iran have looked into this.[30]

Manipulation

Governments enjoy legal and material advantages in grappling with the complex new public sphere that blogs and social networks create. But there are many persuaders who have a stake in exploiting new media's weaknesses. The possibility of immediate publication almost immediately altered attitudes to certainty. News agencies, whose reporters were under the fiercest pressure to be fast, wrote extensive rules to try to ensure that the mistakes made at speed were as rare as possible. Broadcasters, in their turn, followed their example. But these organizations were small in number and their journalists worked under contracts and codes of conduct: the rules stood a good chance of being observed and enforced.

None of this applies to blogs and online sites. A blogger who aims to build an audience large enough to make some money from the site must update and provide new material very frequently in order to be noticed by the layer of aggregators and networks that may well determine how many people see a post. At the sharp end of competition in a specialist area, a matter of seconds can make a difference of thousands of users clicking on one site or another.

More important still is the effect of running an online news site on the economic principles that worked for freelance journalists. The few online news sites that have broken through financially have built working methods that stress impact, pace and productiveness as measured by hits and the frequency of new stories and updates. Gawker, the most successful of the gossip-based sites with global ambitions, is produced from a New York office dominated by a big screen, which lists the 10 stories most read by new readers in the previous hour. Gawker's founder, Nick Denton, says that the 'Big Board' is to encourage competition: 'Sometimes one sees writers just standing before it, like early hominids in front of a monolith.'[31]

This leaves such sites open to manipulation, since the need for speed will trump all other considerations. Very few people whose business is to manipulate are going to talk about it openly, and their claims aren't easy to verify, but one fashion business PR man, Ryan Holiday, has written about the tricks he used. He concentrated his efforts on rag-trade bloggers who were paid by results, by the hit rates of their individual stories. Holiday writes that 'conflict of interest' should be seen differently for bloggers:

> In the pay-per-pageview model, every post is a conflict of interest. It's why I've never bought influence directly. I've never had to. Bloggers have a direct incentive to write bigger, to write simpler, to write more controversially or, conversely, more favourably, to write without having to do any work, to write more often than is warranted. Their paycheck depends on it.

Holiday even framed a rule of thumb for marketers: if a random blog is half as reliable as a *New York Times* article that was fact checked, edited and reviewed by multiple editors, it is twice as easy to get coverage on. Persuade enough unreliable blogs to form enough of a critical mass of rumour and there is a good chance it will be taken up by more serious media afraid of missing out on hot news. For people who were finding their cause unappreciated or their message hard to get across, he advised them to look at the playbooks of the past: 'Look at media hoaxes from before your grandparents were born. The same things will play.'[32]

These risks, which almost by definition cannot be measured with any accuracy, should make us cautious about linkage. News media have been advised, in what has become a well-known slogan, to 'do what you do best and link to the rest'.[33] This only begs the question of how to filter 'the rest' so that it matches the standards of the site doing the linking. Many hundreds of thousands of hours have been spent on online new sites trying to automate linkages for any given content – and some progress has been made. Does newspaper A only allow its system to generate links to papers B, C and D because it thinks they operate the same editorial standards? Or does it allow the software robot to search the entire web for relevant content? It is not impossible to imagine that software could be written to sift news articles for quality, but in practice even Google has found this hard.

But not impossible. Google News scans 50,000 sources in 30 languages and claims to connect 1 billion users per week to news stories. We know something of how the Google algorithm chooses which article to prefer on a given topic, because Google's patent filings list the metrics that are applied to which stories to put at the top of the stack that the user sees.[34] Some of these filters might be described as 'hygiene' checks: the volume of production from a news source, writing style (checked against 'spelling corrections, grammar and reading levels'), length of articles, global reach, audience and traffic. Some reflect the (so far unsuccessful) aim to make Google News an advertising platform. But others are more qualitative and more interesting. They include:

- The 'Breaking News Score', which awards a higher value the quicker a story is published after an event.

- Usage patterns: well-known sites score higher.

- 'Human opinion of the news source': users may be polled or their preferences measured.

- Staff size, the number of news bureaus, number of topics covered.

- 'Original named entities': the number of names in a story not duplicated elsewhere, taken as an indicator of original reporting capacity.

Objectivity under strain

The idea that journalists should bind themselves to rules about factual accuracy, fairness and impartiality did not take hold until journalism was being bought by mass readerships composed of many varieties of belief and origin. Selling newspapers by subscription, which became the norm in many parts of the world in the late 19th century (except in Britain), also drove down inaccuracy and invention: a cancelled subscription was a relatively high penalty to pay and owners began to encourage editors to raise standards. News agencies such as the Press Association (Britain, founded 1868) and the Associated Press (USA, 1846) began to supply news that was styled to be suitable for a huge variety of outlets: a straight, factual style was essential. Broadcasting – founded on scarce, government-controlled spectrum and seen as uniquely powerful – adopted impartiality as a guiding principle and built solid internal regulations to ensure it. The current edition of the BBC Editorial Guidelines, although they extend beyond both news and impartiality, runs to 367 pages.

The attractions of doctrines of objectivity or impartiality were a function of a limited number of news outlets serving mass audiences. Patterns of distribution have become more complex and shifted from 'one-to-many' to 'many-to-many'. It is not surprising that the assumptions behind valuing news for objectivity before all else, after accuracy, should have come under attack and are being rethought.

There are now just so many points of view available to everyone if they choose to consult them. A certain simplicity to public life and the public sphere has gone. It is increasingly unrealistic for accounts of public debates to pretend that there are only two interesting points of view; the artificiality of such oversimplification is obvious more quickly to more people with the information at their fingertips to falsify it. The speed and variety of internet-borne information drives informality of style and tends to prefer the personal to the impersonal or institutional. BBC reporters, once highly constrained in the expression of personal opinions, now become bloggers; there are limits to their opinions, but the limits on what they can say and write have to be renegotiated afresh. The internet is completing a process that had begun with the proliferation of broadcast channels created first by technical advances and consolidated by the deregulation of the Thatcher–Reagan era in the 1980s. The cumulative effect of these changes has been to strip broadcasting of the institutional protection for its authority.

An institution like the BBC retains a legacy of trust and respect from the past, but now has to maintain its reputation by different means. This led a recent Director-General of the BBC, Mark Thompson, to think the unthinkable about opinion relating to television, and to suggest that the rules covering all broadcasters might be out of date because the distinction between the internet and television was collapsing. BBC News, Thompson said, should continue to be impartial, but why should opinionated newspapers be able to run their own television channels and not be bound by the rules on balance?[35]

The dilemma that this rethinking posed for journalists lay in nervousness inside news organizations about abandoning the safe territory covered by the ideas 'impartial', 'balanced' or 'unbiased'. Even among print or online publications that are under no legal obligation to follow these principles, admitting that journalism involves judgements, or even selection, comes hard. It is always easier to mount a defence based on facts rather than making judgements based on the facts. But over time, the requirements of balance have become mannered, not to say misleading. In the worst cases, it can lead to distortion with bad consequences.[36]

Critics of formal balance such as Jay Rosen argue that the imposition of such a template for reporters is intellectually debilitating. 'My primary objection to this safe, cozy and ultra-simplified view was that it imposed certain intellectual costs on journalists', Rosen wrote, arguing that the cost lay in hiding the individual judgements made to decide what the news is, or so-called 'framing decisions'. They cannot be scientifically balanced or objective and should be seen for the opinions and judgements that they are.[37]

Curious news users can now see online sites that do not subscribe to rules about balance. They can compare and choose. Journalists in the future can rely on two rules of thumb that are better than balance: one new, one timeless. First, online reporting makes journalism much more transparent by natural means. Not all sources can be declared, but raw material, documents, interview transcripts and data can all be linked in a text. In effect, serious reporters interested in building trust in their work will have to be in the habit of tying what would once have been called footnotes into their work.[38] Second, and following on from greater transparency, journalists are better advised to apply a 'fair to the truth' test. This is the test that a viewer, listener or reader applies to journalism: if I were there, would I have described it like that? No such test can be an exact science and it is easy to cheat. But no test that has to balance the requirements of getting as close as possible to the truth, while also being fair, can ever be scientifically precise. But there is nothing to stop news organizations being more open about how they do things and the human element in the decision, dissolving the pretence that selecting news is a branch of mechanical engineering.

The advantages and drawbacks of institutions

To an important extent, difficult journalism in the public interest – either requiring large resources or resilience against attack – depends on strong institutions. Large companies that can cross-subsidize news operations can have been able to afford not only reporting staff but lawyers. Reportage that has entered legend – the exposure of MP Jonathan Aitken,[39] or the campaign over the drug Thalidomide – has often done so as legal battles. Such fights are usually expensive, even if they do not reach court. Insurance policies, expensive in themselves, do not always cover costs. A major newspaper will also face threats of withdrawal of advertising. In Britain, it is very rare for these threats to be made and still less for them to be carried out, but it does happen. An emblematic sequence in the documentary *Page One* devoted to the *New York Times*[40] sees the newspaper's media writer David Carr deliver to his editors a long piece that is not going to go down well with the company he has been writing about. 'This is where the institutional muscle kicks in', Carr mutters as he leaves the editor's office, confident that he will be defended against complaint. Counter-attacks on Carr's draft article are duly seen off by his editors.

In a world that promises so much choice of information, the habits and loyalties that held audiences and readerships stable are not likely to continue. Reputation and trust in a news brand, already important, play an even more important role. This will be even more true if the 'bundle' of a newspaper ceases to be seen as a package and is only accessed as a store of individual items. When newspapers first went on the web, half or more of their traffic entered at the home (or front) page of the site. By 2012, the head of Google News, Richard Gingras, was reporting that only 25 per cent of inbound traffic to websites was starting at the home page. Three-quarters of users arriving via a search engine are looking for a particular story, just one fragment of the jigsaw.

Consumers of news journalism routinely moan about the inaccuracy, bias or ineptitude of the newspapers and television programmes that they see regularly. The complaints often coexist with basic, taken-for-granted trust operating at some other level. To see this ambiguity at work, look at the first phase of the life of WikiLeaks.

WikiLeaks was built as a technically secure digital platform that would allow whistleblowers and leakers to post secret documents where they could be read without their exact origin being revealed or the platform being taken down. This extraordinary technical strength was also a weakness. Before it became world famous for the huge leak of American military and diplomatic documents in 2010, WikiLeaks had made available many other secrets dealing with tax avoidance in a Swiss bank, corruption in Kenya, the prison regime at Guantanamo and a British National Party membership list. But the material was presented raw, stripped clean of commentary and explanation – or indeed of any account of how it got there. Many of the documents were so dense and technical that they were incomprehensible to all intents and purposes. They were disclosed that way partly for reasons of security and partly because the two hackers running WikiLeaks, Julian Assange and Daniel Domscheit-Berg, believed at the time that information spoke most powerfully if not mediated by journalists liable to be corrupted by their proximity to power.

In the event, their information hardly spoke at all. Both Wikileakers were surprised and disappointed. Besides the fact that neither man at that stage had grasped how to market WikiLeaks's extraordinary information globally (Assange later became very good at this), no one finding the documents could have any clue as to whether they were genuine or not. Mass media, whatever its defects, will usually distil, put into context and explain; it will have a track record that people can know. In its first phase of life, WikiLeaks had none of this context that could signal trustworthiness (or otherwise). Their disclosures only reached an audience of any size when picked up by mainstream media. In the next phase, Assange systematically partnered with well-known newspapers; his scoops were better projected as a result, underpinned by the history and reputation of the newspapers involved.[41]

But fear about the erosion of journalism's institutions can prevent journalists from seeing clearly the disadvantages of the same institutions. In periods of rapid change, institutions are not agile. When American newspapers were threatened with the loss of much of their classified revenue by the appearance of Craigslist, agility might have helped. But companies with shareholders cannot take large risks with apparently solid revenue streams without risking shares being sold or shareholders rebelling. Above all, large institutions acquire fixed ways of doing things: organizations exist to reduce and simplify choices by using accumulated wisdom to avoid making every decision from scratch. Large newsrooms risk becoming bureaucratically rigid and overattached to familiar process, as will happen in any large organization. Rigidity is less dangerous when things are stable, but its cost increases in moments of turbulent change.

But large journalism institutions are not going to vanish. Some may fail, some become smaller. Journalism is now being carried out across a vastly wider range of types and sizes of organization. The complex interplay between the different powers of old and new emerged after the fall from grace of the cycling star Lance Armstrong. Following a classic pattern, the truth that Armstrong took performance-enhancing drugs was finally established by an expert report after many years of rumours, lawsuits and a myth of innocence maintained by ruthless manipulation by Armstrong and his colleagues. But that report would not have been commissioned if doubts about Armstrong had not been planted and kept alive by a combination of reporters working in established institutions (the *Sunday Times* in London and the *New York Times*) and a small specialist cycling blog, NY Velocity. The reporters from the institutions took the risks, could suffer the hostility of the Armstrong camp because they were shielded by big newspapers, and were sued. NY Velocity kept the doubts alive when larger media lost interest – and published long dense scripts that reached fewer readers but had an effect by being in the public domain and circulated among the knowledgeable. The heroes of the final fall of the cycling star were not either old or new media: the two were interdependent.

The management of abundance

Each surge in the quantity of news information available provokes new ways of distilling it for busy people hungry to know. In 1923 Henry Luce founded *Time* magazine on the principle that would now be known as 'curation' and 'aggregation', by simply summarizing – in 28 black-and-white pages – the best bits from publications ranging from *Atlantic Monthly* or *Christian Science Monitor* to *New York World*. Seven decades later, a similar magazine using the same technique with added irreverent attitude began in London called *The Week*. The information now available to the world's wired populations is so rich, ever-expanding and wide that journalism's context is radically changed once again. Journalists have to adjust to new tasks. Processing material at speed has a long tradition, but that is now combined with unprecedented quantities of possible information. The result is new ways of organizing collective editorial intelligence.

The most striking attempts to do that involve artificial intelligence. Look up the company results section of the Forbes.com website and the short summaries of company results are produced by Narrative Science, which describes itself like this:

> Narrative Science, an innovative technology company, turns data into stories. Narrative Science has developed a technology solution that creates rich

narrative content from data. Narratives are seamlessly created from structured data sources and can be fully customized to fit a customer's voice, style and tone. Multiple versions of the same story can be created to customise the content for each audience's specific needs.[42]

In short, no human writers or editors are involved. Forbes is a well-edited magazine and one can well imagine that the appearance of these slightly eerie snippets was preceded by some trial and error before they were put up on the site. While the writing of the company results bulletins is hardly exciting, it is plain and fluent as far as it goes.

There are, however, tasks that cannot be automated. Pictures need to be chosen for websites, results from algorithms need to be sanity checked, automatically generated material needs to be proofread. One way to have this work done at one of the lowest rates available is to turn to the Mechanical Turkers. The name is taken from an 18th-century chess-playing 'automaton' called the Turk, later revealed to be a human chess master hidden inside the 'machine'. Wikipedia's introduction to this service from Amazon could come straight from a science-fiction novel:

> The Amazon Mechanical Turk is a crowdsourcing internet marketplace that enables computer programmers (known as *Requesters*) to co-ordinate the use of human intelligence to perform tasks that computers are currently unable to do... The Requesters are able to post tasks known as HITs (Human Intelligence Tasks... *Workers* (called *Providers* in Mechanical Turk's Terms of Service, or, more colloquially, *Turkers*) can then browse among existing tasks and complete them for a monetary payment set by the Requester.[43]

One study concluded that a large segment of the work done by the Mechanical Turkers was the generation of spam.[44] Twitter engineers described how they were using Mechanical Turkers to check, help and refine search software that was being developed to enrich the delivery of tweets, which are suddenly trending to attach suitable advertisements to them.[45] One of the programmes is called Clockwork Raven.

These are examples of what is happening at the junction of media, anthropology and software as experimenting new businesses rewrite information infrastructure and struggle to find business models in them as they go. The driver of this search is unprecedented abundance.

In time this will change the mix of skills in a newsroom and has already done so. For the past decade or so, forward-thinking editors all over the world have been striving to get software geeks to feel at home among reporters. The majority of new tools coming into use to manage abundant information have not been invented in buildings occupied by journalists.

Journalists have often made new breakthroughs, but they have had to leave their buildings first in order to put the innovation together. Burt Herman, one of the founders of Storify.com, began his career as an Associated Press reporter. Several years ago he decided that journalists needed better tools to deal with huge volumes of eye-witness information, which were too large and chaotic to make much sense. He teamed up with a software developer and Storify was the result. The platform draws together blogposts, tweets, images and tries to make the most useful sequence out of them. Again, this was not either exclusively new or old: the result would not have been the same if Herman hadn't had conventional journalism experience.

People who want news want the flow to reach them in ways that fit into their devices and at times in their daily lives when they have time to check what's happening. Breakthroughs in improving that experience are as likely to come from information architects and developers as from journalists. Twitter is one example of a response to this need. Ben Huh, after graduating from a university journalism degree, founded the first network of sites to create a platform for the posting and swapping of cute cat pictures. The money he made out of cats has given him the leisure and freedom to tackle a more serious issue. Huh has recently focused on breaking down news information into what he calls 'sub-atomic particles' and making it easy to use on mobile devices.[46] The release of the first version of his app for mobiles earned him a sneering column in the *Washington Post* from a commentator who had not grasped that innovations in news have often come from unusual sources.[47]

Journalists are beginning to specialize in 'curating' huge feeds of moving information that arrives broken into small fragments of varying accuracy.[48] One writer speaks of journalists shifting from being 'gatekeepers' to being 'gatewatchers'. Major events from sport to politics are 'live-blogged' in frequently updated pieces of writing, audio or video that act as a running commentary; the same process, with smaller fragments of words, can be done with Twitter or any of its equivalents across the world. Like many new techniques, live-blogging tended to go down best with users when practised by journalists trained in old techniques: writing clearly, concisely and trained to spot the most interesting details when working at speed.[49]

News organizations wrestle with the dilemmas that these 'quasi-live' reporting methods generate. Working at speed and with information that cannot be immediately confirmed, reporters have tended to be very careful in attributing sources where they might not have bothered to do so before, and to make explicitly clear when they are relaying unconfirmed information. I suspect that as further adaptations to abundance appear, anybody (whether calling themselves a journalist or not) who is handling information as an intermediary, will get used to labelling and ranking it. We can only hope to understand large quantities of new information by being able to locate it in a hierarchy that indicates its value. Media organizations often label 'commentary' and 'analysis' to distinguish it from news. In the future, information consumers may want to know whether information is sourced and perhaps whether the source is considered reliable, whether it has been copied from elsewhere, whether it has been confirmed, denied, corrected or updated. All of these pieces of information can be carried by media now, albeit in lengthy forms. Because more and more news information will not reach people in packaged bundles (such as newspapers or news programmes) that lend credence to all the items under their 'brand', it will be even more important for individual items to carry indications that allow a user to value them accurately.

British media analyst and activist Martin Moore speculated on a new hierarchy of the kinds of journalists who might emerge from these changes. He began with the 'Uber-Brand', the individual star journalist who is famous and magnetic enough to pull in traffic merely with their name. He cites Jeremy Clarkson, Stephen Fry, Caitlin Moran or Charlie Brooker as examples. Internal estimates at *The Times/Sunday Times* reckoned that Clarkson was responsible for 25 per cent of the site's pre-paywall traffic.[50] Moore's light-hearted list of future archetypes goes on through hamsters (frantically producing too much in a hurry), through 'portfolio-istas' (freelancers) and geeks. As Moore notes, only two of his seven categories would be full-time employees of news organizations.[51]

One category not on Moore's list is a data specialist. Digital storage of information means that the quantities of data reaching many communities of interest are going to get larger. Journalism organizations may get data sets because public or private bodies release them, or they may be leaked. The city of Chicago was releasing five gigabytes of data per month in 2010; by 2013, the authorities were releasing six times as much.[52] Either way, they will need specialists in evaluation, data storage applications, interpretation and visual display. Teams of data specialists are already appearing in the richer and more advanced newsrooms. The skills and results are evolving at astonishing speed and the techniques being developed will be needed for a long time to come.

Some of the data that gives big legacy media organizations some of the biggest headaches is their own data. News organizations used to think of their 'product' as their daily output. With digital storage, the organization's archive is a store of news and analysis that grows. Think of a newspaper as a mountain of data with fresh topsoil added every day. The accessibility of a new archive is changing the nature of news organizations and their relationship with the audience. Previously, a researcher could search a newspaper library or, less often, consult the film, video or sound archives of a broadcaster. But it was a laborious and time-consuming business. Those archives are now often available for free or small fees (broadcast news archives remain relatively costly). Robert Cottrell, of the much-read aggregation site Browser.com, argues that the wisest new hire for established newspapers and magazines would be a 'smart, disruptive' archive editor. 'Why just sit on a mountain of classic content when you could be digging into it and finding buried treasure?'[53]

Yet because this material was written for the specific needs of a particular day, its use as background history has so far been limited. 'Topic pages', which aim to arrange past coverage into strands that cover major subjects in an accumulating encyclopaedia,[54] involve a lot of irritating repetition, particularly if, as in most cases, they are automated. These obstacles will be overcome as established news organizations see a higher premium in demonstrating the depth of their knowledge and understanding.

New media and change: a case study

Journalism is inseparable from politics. One of the claims made for new media are that they are inherently more democratic because of the ease with which uncensored information can be spread. Power in totalitarian or authoritarian societies always depends to some extent on control of information. When news was controlled by publishers and broadcasters, control was relatively easy. In the era of the smartphone, a government would have to isolate its population from the internet – or erect an enormous apparatus to filter content. And in the latter case of trying to monitor peer-to-peer communication, no control system is complete or without leakage, as the Chinese authorities have found out.

With the consumer internet approaching its 20th birthday in 2011, a series of insurgencies erupted in the Arab world in which information control played a significant part. Just how significant that role was is still being disputed and researched in detail. Five anti-government movements began in the spring of 2011. In Tunisia, a dictatorial regime collapsed completely. In Egypt, a dictator was toppled and his regime partly disabled. In Syria, an armed rebellion became a bitter and protracted civil war largely shaped by religious-tribal divisions. In Libya, an eccentric and vicious regime lost power after a short civil war decided by outside help. In the tiny Gulf kingdom of Bahrain, demonstrations were put down by force without many concessions by the ruling family.

Although the outcomes were very different in all five cases, the cracks in previous stability were made more likely by the awareness that change was more possible than previously appeared. One contributory factor was a dawning realization that there was a different public sphere from the official one. Non-democratic regimes may have plural sources of information (newspapers with different editorial characters appealing to different demographic groups, more than one television channel) but they take care to set strict, known limits beyond which news media cannot publish. Within these five countries, insiders may gossip, journalists may learn more than they can reveal and educated people may be cynical about what appears in semi-official media, but this gossip and dissent is kept to a small circle. Different versions of what may be happening are not available. With local variations, this describes the news culture of all five of these countries.

The first dilution of the control of news had nothing to do with Facebook or Twitter; neither had been dreamt of when it occurred. Satellite television altered the politics of the Middle East in slow but profound ways. Satellites do not respect borders. When satellite channels first became available in Arab states in the 1980s, this caused little worry: it was widely assumed that satellite channels were not being set up for news. They were ideal for soap operas. Besides, there was an informal, unwritten understanding between governments in the region that media under their domestic control would not cause harm or offence in a neighbouring state with which relations were friendly.

Someone in Qatar persuaded the Emir of that small but affluent state that satellite television was an opportunity for him to invest in some influence beyond his own borders. So began Al-Jazeera, a still-growing network funded by Qatari money. The Arabic station's reporting on Qatar was careful not to tread on the toes of the ruling family. But both the Arabic and the English-speaking channel that quickly followed were uninhibited about neighbouring countries. Money was available for new developments, and bright talents literate in new technologies arrived to set up a high-grade website linked into social media, which was taking off rapidly in Arabic. Mobile-phone ownership rose fast in the Middle East in the first decade of the new century.[55] The resources and skills needed to create and distribute uncensored information were not available to all but a significant minority. Egypt had an active blogging community in the years before 2011, divided between 'secular reformist bloggers' and Muslim Brotherhood bloggers.

Both groups had contributed to chronicling human rights violations, including building 'Pigopedia', a decentralized online database of pictures of police alleged to have been involved in torture. When all these developments interacted, a new and separate public sphere was created in several Arab states.[56]

This is not to say that the insurgencies were created by media influence, let alone by new media and still less by Facebook or Twitter. Protests are made by people deciding to take risks that they have not taken before. The underlying causes of the timing of the Arab revolts ranged from rising food prices caused by commodity market movements, long-standing tribal resentments and religious objections to secular regimes. But new media can raise the pulse rate of protest by creating a real-time sphere of exchange and discussion that is completely decoupled from the restricted official media. By the time of rebellion in Tunisia in January 2011, there were effectively two public spheres: the formal, official one and the informal, digital one. The government had lost control of what people knew. Not only could they not write the public agenda, they could not set limits to it – as they had lost their information monopoly long before.

If the informal sphere had been confined to personal exchanges inside the Tunisian smartphone intelligentsia, it might not have been much of a threat. But Al-Jazeera correspondents and editors were not only reporting from the streets but were taking material from Tunisians who uploaded footage to Al-Jazeera's servers in Doha. The video of Mohammed Bouazizi – the street vendor whose suicide triggered the Tunisian protests – setting himself on fire was seen by a Tunisian-born blogger working outside the country. Sami Ben Gharbia put it on his blog, nawaat.org. The video was picked up by Al-Jazeera and played back into Tunisia to a much bigger audience.

Al-Jazeera energetically reported the WikiLeaks disclosures about the corruption and self-indulgence of the Tunisian ruling family, lending authority to what might previously only have been rumours.[57] Those who did not have access to Al-Jazeera by satellite could always get at least some coverage on a PC, laptop or smartphone. In their turn, the Egyptian authorities tried to bolt the stable door long after the horse had bolted. As the Tahrir Square protest against President Hosni Mubarak grew, the generals cut off Egypt from the internet and then from international mobile phone networks. Neither step worked: hackers and geeks all over the world collaborated to provide workarounds. The autocrats were paying new communications and media an unintended compliment by admitting the power of newly knitted networks.[58]

But such networks cannot unseat tyrants merely by their existence. The balance of military and paramilitary forces, population demographics, the manipulation and surveillance skills that the authorities have taught themselves or bought and the willingness of a regime to shed blood in its own defence – all these factors meant that the revolution was only partly successful in Egypt, fought to a standstill for months in Syria and put down in Bahrain. The importance of social and new media was much trumpeted by journalists covering these events, not least because they relied heavily on the information carried by these media. What very few journalists saw was that the mobilization that social media helped was not necessarily towards open, plural democracy on the Western model. Long before the internet, scholars of Islam had mourned the fact that modern means of transport had improved the means with which journalists could reach troublespots – and that very speed of movement meant that they were less familiar with the details of the cultures, religions and societies on which they alighted.[59] New media can accentuate this problem of superficial understanding. The euphoric crowd-sourced conclusion of the journalistic herd in Tahrir Square wasn't better than the warnings of a few experts.[60] And at least one expert now worries that the habits of exaggeration, hyperbole and abuse made easy by social media are harming the rapidly changing political cultures of countries such as Egypt.[61]

Conclusion

It cannot be repeated too often that the indications of changes in journalism wrought by digital technology set out in this chapter capture only a first phase. Technology evolves by trial and error; the social use of innovations teaches technologists that software and devices won't be used quite as they expected – and they think again. Successive rolling waves of discovery, experiment and adaptation will rewrite the story at regular intervals. In the years of the consumer internet, we have already come a very long way. It was only in 1999 that an American writer on technology and hacking, Mark Frauenfelder, wrote a piece for the magazine *The Industry Standard*, explaining the attractions of the new web tools for something called 'blogging'. His editors decided that blogging wasn't such a big deal and didn't publish it. Frauenfelder went on to start the eclectic blog Boing Boing, now one of the most popular in the English-speaking world.[62] Marshall McLuhan said that 'every new medium begins as a container for the old'. We should expect that new technologies will be put to old purposes at first, but we should expect that to change.

It is very easy to be swept up in a bubble of techno-optimism and fail to ask the questions that any informed democracy should be asking itself. Two questions are worth bearing in mind throughout the long cycle of changes to come: are journalists prepared to be judged by a standard of truth? And is journalism doing something of public value? The dispersal of the ability to publish from a small number of capital-intensive businesses to millions of digital voices endows many individuals with a means to self-expression they never previously possessed. But this may have unintended effects on the quality of public reason and debate.[63] There is already an extensive literature on the effects of internet-borne knowledge on peoples' ability to only read what they will find congenial and affirming to their existing beliefs and the consequence of a rise in beliefs that defy reason. One writer claimed that we are now living in a 'post-fact' society. Many people do not mourn the mainstream media's loss of dominance over the public agenda but worry at the same time that it seems increasingly easy to hijack the agenda, even if only for very short intervals. These anxieties are of course not caused by technology-driven change alone: many societies are more plural and diverse than they were, elites do not shape education or culture as they once did.

There is a widely argued belief that media which carry both news and opinion, in any mixture, should not be required to be 'responsible', but to provide their greatest service by being chaotic, irreverent, sceptical, competitive, plural and open to new ideas. But societies cannot organize themselves without values and beliefs. If journalism involves the effort, however inadequately and iteratively, to establish the truth of what matters in real time then some standard by which truth can be measured must be used. Media must therefore sometimes ask if their activities contribute to any decay of public reason and they must expect societies to ask the same question.

A third question has been bitterly and inconclusively debated: does digital strengthen or weaken the media's ability to hold power to account? Those anxious on this account cite the weakening of strong journalism institutions. They point to the fact that a larger population of blogging commentators is not the same as preserving the ability to report first-hand. In one sense, this is an unreal clash of opinions. The power of digital technology to alter the business models of media of the previous era can't be reversed or cancelled. The fall in advertising income reaching established media, the largest single cause of decline, was not caused by bloggers, but by the defection of readers and viewers. I will return to this issue in Chapters 9 and 10, but the key must lie in media's ability to put what is of timeless value to work in new circumstances. The question that should never be far from our minds is: are we tying innovation to worthwhile purpose?

Notes

1   *Wired* is the California-based website and magazine that has come to be an emblem of the news media revolution.

2   comScore MMX Worldwide, October 2012.

3   MailOnline claims to be profitable but this is more technical than real. The company's accounts and disclosures do not indicate what costs are allocated to this part of the business. **http://arifdurrani.mediaweek.co.uk/2012/07/25/ how-did-the-mail-online-become-a-profitable-newspaper-site/** (accessed 7.1.12).

4   **http://www.shirky.com/writings/herecomeseverybody/powerlaw_weblog.html** (accessed 7.1.12).

5   Quoted in Nate Silver (2012) *The Signal and the Noise*, Penguin, New York.

6   **http://thesocialskinny.com/100-more-social-media-statistics-for-2012/** (accessed 7.1.12).

7   **http://mediadecoder.blogs.nytimes.com/2012/02/06/a-super-bowl-where- viewers-let-their-fingers-do-the-talking/** (accessed 7.1.12).

8   **http://www.guardian.co.uk/technology/2011/jan/04/faceboook-mark- zuckerberg-google** (accessed 7.1.12).

9   News Corporation's British subsidiary News International, owners of *The Times*, for which I worked.

10 Naughton, J (2012) *From Gutenberg to Zuckerberg: What You Really Need To Know About the Internet*, Quercus, London.

11 These issues are discussed in more detail in Chapters 6, 9 and 10.

12 Hal Varian, chief economist of Google, quoted in Fallows, J (2010) 'How To Save the News' *The Atlantic*, June.

13 One prominent example would be Politico, the Washington political journalism organization that began online and now distributes a free print edition of around 30,000 copies daily in the city.

14 Baldwin, T, McVoy, D and Steinfield, C (1996) *Convergence: Integrating Media, Information and Communication*, Sage, Thousand Oaks, CA. (cited in Pablo J. Boczkowski (2005) *Digitizing the News*, MIT Press, Cambridge, Mass.).

15 Quoted in *The Atlantic*, May 2010.

16 **http://www.niemanlab.org/2010/02/the-googlechina-hacking-case-how-many- news-outlets-do-the-original-reporting-on-a-big-story/** (accessed 20.5.13).

17 See **www.churnalism.com**.

18 http://www.mondaynote.com/2013/02/24/google-news-the-secret-sauce/ (accessed 9.3.13).

19 See Michael Schudson in Peters, M and Broersma, M (2013) *Rethinking Journalism: Trust and Participation in a Transformed News Landscape*, Routledge, Abingdon.

20 Kehlmann, D (2011) *Fame*, Quercus, London.

21 Boston Review, July/August 2010 http://bostonreview.net/BR35.4/morozov.php (accessed 20.5.13).

22 See http://georgebrock.net/algorithmic-authority/ (accessed 20.5.13).

23 http://www.nieman.harvard.edu/reports/article/102766/Finding-the-Wisdom-in-the-Crowd.aspx (accessed 12.2.13).

24 www.ushahidi.com (accessed 20.5.13).

25 http://www.themediabriefing.com/article/2013-02-11/its-tough-below-the-line-the-paradox-of-reader-comments (accessed 11.3.13).

26 http://www.niemanlab.org/2012/06/pay-attention-to-what-nick-denton-is-doing-with-comments/ (accessed 11.3.13).

27 http://www.guardian.co.uk/sustainability/report-mutualisation-citizen-journalism (accessed 11.3.13).

28 Leigh, D and Harding, L (2011) *WikiLeaks: Inside Julian Assange's War on Secrecy*, Guardian Books, London.

29 http://mediastandardstrust.org/blog/crowdsourcing-verification-and-%E2%80%98alpha-users%E2%80%99/ (accessed 20.5.13).

30 See http://www.aljazeera.com/indepth/opinion/2011/08/201183171859264925.html
http://www.guardian.co.uk/technology/2011/mar/17/us-spy-operation-social-networks
http://online.wsj.com/article/SB10001424052748703610604576158290935677316.html (accessed 20.5.13).

31 http://www.newyorker.com/reporting/2010/10/18/101018fa_fact_mcgrath (accessed 20.5.13).

32 Holiday, R (2012) *Trust Me, I'm Lying: Confessions of a Media Manipulator*, Portfolio Penguin, New York.

33 The phrase was first coined by Jeff Jarvis, who blogs at buzzmachine.com

34 http://www.mondaynote.com/2013/02/24/google-news-the-secret-sauce/ (accessed 20.5.13)

35 http://www.guardian.co.uk/media/2010/dec/17/mark-thompson-bbc-fox-news (accessed 20.5.13).

36 See Chapters 6 and 7.

37 http://pressthink.org/2013/01/mounting-costs-for-the-default-model-of-trust-production-in-american-newsrooms/ (accessed 11.3.13).

38 http://georgebrock.net/support-for-the-footnotes-campaign/ (accessed 20.5.13).

39 http://www.guardian.co.uk/politics/1999/jun/08/uk (accessed 20.5.13).

40 http://www.imdb.co.uk/title/tt1787777/ (accessed 20.5.13).

41 Daniel Domscheit-Berg, D (2011) *Inside WikiLeaks*, Jonathan Cape, London. See also *The Times*, Saturday Review, 12 February 2011, London.

42 http://blogs.forbes.com/narrativescience/ (accessed 20.5.13).

43 http://en.wikipedia.org/wiki/Amazon_Mechanical_Turk (accessed 20.5.13).

44 http://www.fastcompany.com/1711157/mechanical-turks-unsavory-side-effect-massive-spam-generation-updated-amazon-comments (accessed 20.5.13).

45 http://engineering.twitter.com/2013/01/improving-twitter-search-with-real-time.html?m=1 (accessed 20.5.13).

46 http://gigaom.com/2012/10/15/circa-wants-to-rethink-the-news-at-a-sub-atomic-level/ (accessed 4.11.12).

47 http://www.washingtonpost.com/lifestyle/magazine/gene-weingarten-modern-journalism-and-cat-pictures/2011/10/10/gIQAfgbUMM_story.html (accessed 27.2.13).

48 The poster boy for this new function is Andy Carvin of National Public Radio in the United States who sifted for signals in the noise of live information coming out of the disturbances in Cairo in spring 2011.

49 Thurman, Neil J and Walters, Anna (2012) 'Live Blogging – Digital Journalism's Pivotal Platform? A Case Study of the Production, Consumption, and Form of Live Blogs at Guardian.co.uk, *Digital Journalism* 1.1. Available at: http://works.bepress.com/neil_thurman/12 (accessed 20.5.13).

50 http://www.vanityfair.com/business/features/2009/11/michael-wolff-200911?printable=true (accessed 20.5.13).

51 http://martinjemoore.com/the-journalist-of-the-future-7-or-8-archetypes/

52 *The Economist*, 27 April 2013.

53 http://www.ft.com/cms/s/2/009050e4-75ea-11e2-9891-00144feabdc0.html#axzz2RehWjNYP (accessed 18.2.13).

54 The most ambitious exercise of this kind I know of is at the *New York Times*. See http://www.nytimes.com/pages/topics/index.html (accessed 20.5.13).

55 AudienceScapes mobile phone research brief, June 2011.

56 Nanabhay, M and Farmanfarmaian, R (2011) 'From spectacle to spectacular: how physical space, social media and mainstream broadcast amplified the public sphere in Egypt's "revolution"', *Journal of North African Studies*, vol 16. no 4, Dec.

57 http://georgebrock.net/wikileaks-and-tunisia/ (accessed 20.5.13).

58 http://georgebrock.net/egypt-what-the-autocrats-didnt-quite-get/ (accessed 20.5.13).

59 Kedourie, Elie (1989) ' Reporting Islam', *Encounter*, February.

60 http://georgebrock.net/journalists-and-the-perils-of-the-optimistic-herd/

61 http://www.foreignpolicy.com/articles/2013/02/07/twitter_devolutions_arab_spring_social_media?page=0,0 (accessed 11.3.13).

62 http://www.fastcompany.com/1702167/inside-wild-wacky-profitable-world-boing-boing (accessed 20.5.13).

63 'Public reason' has a specific meaning to legal and political philosophers discussing the ideas of Immanuel Kant and John Rawls; I am using it here in its non-technical sense.

The business model crumbles

06

> *The Internet will strut its hour upon the stage and then take its place in the ranks of lesser media.*
>
> **SIMON JENKINS, *THE TIMES*, 1997**

> *Institutions will try to preserve the problem to which they are the solution.*
>
> **CLAY SHIRKY, *SXSW* CONFERENCE, 2010**

In the late 1990s, the massive Turkish daily *Milliyet* occupied modern offices on the outskirts of Istanbul next to the newspaper's printing plant. Offices on one side of the editorial floor had one wall of glass. These spacious windows looked straight on to the lines of presses, as if to remind the columnists and editors that they too were part of a manufacturing operation.

At the start of the 21st century, mainstream journalism still retained its familiar outward shape as it went about its business: television news bulletins still attracted large audiences, newspapers appeared each morning. Over the previous two centuries the process of news, explanation and opinion had matured and brought an industrial logic to public information. There was rolling 24-hour news, more radio stations than ever and magazines were in good health. There were hints of trouble from experts familiar with the figures and cyber-gurus predicting a nuclear winter for newspapers. But many journalists thought that nothing very dramatic had happened in the first years of the internet age in the 1990s and that prophecies of doom were overdone.

In fact, by 2000, print news publishing had slipped into far deeper trouble than was obvious. Looking back, it would have been very odd indeed if news media had turned out to be immune to the law of creative destruction that operates in all democratic market systems. Journalism and news are being deindustrialized. Print will be only a relatively small part of the news system of developed societies; terrestrial television may no longer dominate the airwaves. The companies and organizations that governed the world's news output in the past half century are losing control of that space. Whether they will be replaced by equally large rivals or a larger collection of smaller news producers, aggregators, filters and networks is not yet clear. But power has shifted away from production and towards distribution.

Advertising revenues had been kind in the long boom of the 1980s and 1990s, masking the slow deterioration of the economics of print. The growing quantity of information and the choice it provided to its users had started an irreversible momentum towards unpredictable and dangerous change. Change that had been reassuringly gradual in the 1990s accelerated at alarming speed in the new century. Too many people in positions of influence in the media thought that they could adapt. In fact transformative change was needed. What had been a simmering, bubbling problem of gentle declines from very high audiences, readerships and revenues became a full-scale emergency.

Over a cliff

Print advertising revenue, which in some parts of the world had appeared immune to attack by new media, began to reflect what was happening. In 1950, total advertising income for US newspapers was $20 billion. In 2000, it had reached $63.5 billion. By 2012, in almost perfect symmetry, the figure was $19 billion.[1] Although revenue had not peaked until 2000, there had been a clue to underlying weakness in the previous 10 years: growth had stopped keeping up with GDP growth since the end of the 1980s. In French newspapers, the ad sales revenue per copy had stopped rising at the same rate as GDP in the late 1980s and gone into decline in 1999.[2] These were not the signs that people in the print industry wanted to see. 'Newspaper industry regains health', chirruped a *New York Times* headline in 1998.[3] Between 2001 and 2011, total employment in the US newspaper industry fell by 44 per cent from 414,000 to 246,000. One study of trade balance figures between 1995 and 2007 in the EU newspaper industry revealed income shrinking ('negative growth rate') by 10.6% per year.[4]

The 'delay' before the full effects of the internet were seen on printed newspapers was not surprising. Wide adoption of new technology is rarely as fast as hype suggests. People, rationally, wait till technology has bedded down, been tested and become more user-friendly than launch versions often are. They wait to see if the performance promised actually happens and that it has no hidden catch. Newspaper buyers gradually discovered that they genuinely did have a wide range of news sources that were free and that they could access at any time. In the 1990s, PCs appeared on most desks at work. After 2000, the internet went mobile, courtesy of wireless networks.

Michael Crichton, writer of the novel *Jurassic Park* (1990), infuriated the news business with a 1993 article in *Wired* headlined 'Mediasaurus' in which he warned that the news media would not last another 10 years, and did not deserve to.[5] His timing was out, but his understanding of the danger to established media was not. Andy Grove, the founder of chip-maker Intel, made similar premature prophecies.[6] So much investment, habit and vested interest was locked into the advertising business model that those operating it were reluctant to even acknowledge that much was wrong until the evidence was inescapable. Salespersons of advertising space had, in many news publishing companies, become farmers cultivating predictable revenue and custom rather than the hunter-gatherers they needed to be.

Companies were slow to adapt, partly – and paradoxically – because they were so efficient. Cost-efficiency built the foundations of Rupert Murdoch's News Corporation. A newspaper could be marketed by eye-catching journalism without the need for expensive marketing departments; press lines could be operated with fewer people; a better deal could be cut for the bulk buying of newsprint. Even if revenue was flat, costs came down and a higher return on investment was restored. Whatever else politicians and pundits might say about the company's owner, stock market analysts could see that News Corp companies did this better than most.

But cost-efficiency competition had a long-term cost that wasn't measured in money. Newspapers changed their editors, their editorial personality, even their readers, quite regularly. By 1990 the basic economics and logistics of newspaper manufacturing and distribution had changed little in a century. This extraordinary degree of stability turned the publishing side of newspaper companies into conservative and hidebound organizations. They were operations-dominated because the logistics of getting out daily newspapers is hard. But they had often shed or allowed to atrophy the capacities to innovate or to react to new conditions.

The early indicators of shifts away from print were the defections of classified advertising and young readers. In Britain in 2002, the internet only held a 4 per cent share of classified advertising, print retained 96 per cent. These shares converged as print's grip on classified loosened and the internet became the dominant player. But the internet did not actually overtake print as a classified medium until 2008. By 2015, the shares will be almost reversed: one estimate says 83 per cent for the internet and 17 per cent for print.[7] The threat, and some damage, to print classified income had been evident since the mid-1990s; it took more than 10 years for that to be visible as writing on the wall. Classified advertising was once half (51 per cent) of the income of regional newspapers while only 12 per cent for nationals. When people speak of the economic crisis that threatens news, they usually speak of famous, national titles. The threat to local papers is larger and more immediate.

Around 5 million British readers between the ages of 15 and 34 had dropped out of daily newspaper reading between 1990 and 2002.[8] By 2010 people aged 16–24 were spending only 4 per cent of their 'media consumption' time on print; adults spent almost twice as much at 7 per cent. Sweden's newspaper readers in the older age groups held more or less steady until 2008. But the three youngest groups, from 15 to 29, started declining in 2000 and went into a steep dive in 2007.[9]

In Britain until 2005, the total circulation volumes for quality national newspapers and consumer magazines had held just about steady; popular nationals and regional papers were sliding downwards. From 2005 onwards, all four categories began to fall (see Figure 6.1).[10] Change most probably speeded up because of the sudden popularity of broadband and its widening availability. In 2005, one British household in three had broadband: 34 per cent. By 2010, that had doubled to 68 per cent. This was the tipping point at which many habits changed. Light, user-friendly tablets such as the iPad also drove the change.

These consumption trends had been slow to alter but accelerated as the century's first decade ended. Access to the internet by mobile devices doubled between 2010 and 2012. The use of online for news and newspapers went from 20 per cent of users to 47 per cent between 2007 and 2012.[11]

The worldwide recession that began in 2007–08 made the situation worse for print, but did not start the fall. Weekday print circulation at the top 25 American papers fell 41.6 per cent between 2005 and 2013; March 2005 was the month of the industry's all-time advertising sales peak.[12] An OECD survey of news in more than 20 countries concluded that the global newspaper market slowed down from 2004 onwards, well before the first tremors of the global financial crisis. The flight from print as a medium did not occur at the same time or at the same rate in any two places. The impact could be seen as early as 2000 in Denmark, France, the United States, the Netherlands and the UK, but was not visible in Canada, Finland, Spain or

FIGURE 6.1 Print circulation decline accelerated after 2005

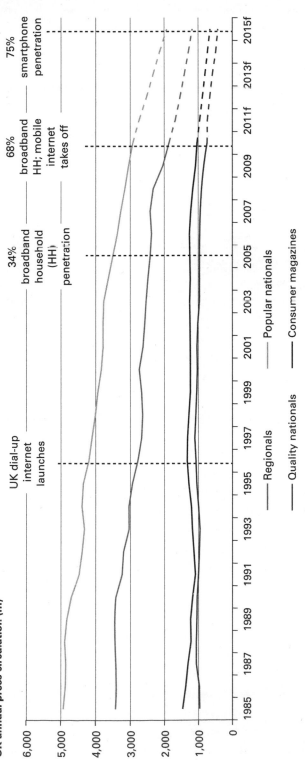

UK annual press circulation (m)

UK dial-up internet launches	34% broadband household (HH) penetration	68% broadband HH; mobile internet takes off	75% smartphone penetration

—— Regionals —— Popular nationals

—— Quality nationals —— Consumer magazines

SOURCE: Enders Analysis based on ABC and Newspaper Society

Italy until 2007.[13] The recession shrank the newspaper publishing market in every OECD country between 2007–09 and by more than 10 per cent in 12 of them, including the UK (21 per cent) and the United States (30 per cent). When the world recovers from one of the deepest slowdowns in modern history, print publishing will recover a little of the ground that was lost when a cyclical recession exacerbated a structural decline. But the long-term erosion of print will not reverse. It has further to go as advertising follows changes in what people do. As of 2011, one leading US analyst reckons that newspapers in the United States account for around 7 per cent of the total time that Americans spend with media, but draw 25 per cent of all advertising. The gap can only reduce.

Print is not dead

This does not mean that 'print' will die. It means that the business model for daily newspapers is in trouble and that trouble is most acute for general-interest newspapers. What applies to the time-sensitive, advertising-dependent economics of newspapers does not automatically apply to books, directories or magazines. All supply different demands in different ways.

In more than one continent, not even that is obvious from the statistics. Over five years to 2012 newspaper circulations in Asia have grown by 16 per cent, while those in Western Europe and North America have fallen by 17 per cent.[14] Circulations have risen in India, Brazil and China. In India, literacy and purchasing power (newspapers are very cheap) are on the increase. In China, the nervous authorities have been conducting cautious experiments in allowing new publications not under direct state control. There are signs that the rapid growth of print in both China and India may now have slowed.[15] The healthy growth of print in India is pushed by the very slow development of the internet there,[16] and particularly of broadband. Alternative new media will develop, suited to Indian conditions, but will be based around mobile telephones and tablets (or merged versions, becoming known by the ugly term 'phablets'). The adoption of mobile devices grows five times faster worldwide than the adoption of the internet.[17] Google engineers design new products first for mobile use and only afterwards for PCs.

India will watch newspaper growth at the same time as experiments in moving information by new routes. In the four years to 2009, the number of India's paid-for daily newspapers grew by 44 per cent. In 2008, India overtook China as the country with the world's largest paid-for total circulation

(110 million copies). Before the recession, newspaper and magazine advertising in India was growing at more than 20 per cent per year. Nearly 100 satellite news channels have been launched in the country in the last 20 years, rattling through stories at a speed that make their European or US equivalents look positively sleepy. But even with this current growth in print, India will experience the same basic change that has already hit other parts of the world.

Experiments with new possibilities have begun sooner. In a village in Uttar Pradesh, 50 miles from Lucknow, any attempt to invent local news must work with the grain of local conditions. Neither radio, television nor newspapers take any interest in the poor rural village of Rampur-Mathura, where the local language is Avadhi. Few villagers would have access to radio or television. But most have at least a low-end mobile phone. In a small pilot project called Gaon Ki Awaaz ('local news') conducted by the International Media Institute of India, a couple of people in each village were chosen as reporters and gathered local stories – thefts, fires, holes in the road, floods, births, deaths, official information or prayer meetings. They recorded the stories in the local dialect and sent them to an editor, who filtered them and perhaps added in region-wide information on crop prices, weather forecasts or even advice on sanitation or childcare. The selection was then turned into a voice call and sent back twice a day to subscribers of what was a small service with 500 paying subscribers paying a modest monthly fee.[18] The pilot only lasted a few years, but if it turns out to be a model, it will be because old practice (there is an editor, filtering) is blended with mobiles and laptops.

Journalism in most places in the world will be on a mixture of digital, broadcast and print; the proportions on each platform and the relationship between them will depend on culture, history, wealth, law, governance and technology infrastructure. In China, where 38 per cent of the population were internet users by 2011,[19] the change in the public sphere will be the function of the clash between those more knowledgeable users, the digital intelligentsia and the authorities.

In China, the freedom to experiment is highly constrained by the control of ideas and debate held by the Communist Party. Many predictions that new technologies such as satellite television or the internet will loosen the party's grip have failed to come true. The Chinese state spends a colossal but unknown sum on the surveillance and control of internet-borne conversation. But the size of the Chinese internet population itself has nevertheless altered the public sphere in China, even if the country's power structure remains in place. One internet user in five in the world is now Chinese; the connected population in the Peoples' Republic is now larger than all the inhabitants of the EU.[20]

In 1989, a crackdown at a newspaper in Shanghai helped to bring protesting students to Beijing's Tiananmen Square for what turned into weeks of occupation before several hundred of the demonstrators were killed when the army cleared the square. But that was before the internet, the authorities' attempt to shut out undesirable websites (by means of what has been called the 'Great Firewall') and a hugely popular Chinese version of the micro-blogging platform Twitter called Weibo. China scholar Perry Link explained what the internet has changed:

> The largest difference between 1989 and now, in my view, is that the popular understanding of what a free press can do is more mature now... Now, thanks mostly to the internet, journalists, netizens, and the public have a much more detailed grasp of what they can do, and want to do, with a free press. They know better how to use journalism to expose corruption, highlight injustice, organize public opinion to bring pressure, and so on. The threat to authoritarian power is greater now.[21]

The Chinese government has evidently decided that they will use digital weapons against new threats. For several months at the end of 2012 hackers using methods associated with the Chinese military tried to break into the *New York Times* computer system. Routing the infiltration through US university networks, the hackers appeared to be trying to find the sources for – or to simply take revenge against – the newspaper's recent investigation into the massive private wealth built up by China's prime minister Wen Jiabao. Fifty-three accounts were broken into, but the newspaper said that no sensitive data or customer information was stolen.[22]

The long trends can be seen best in countries that appear at first to be outliers or exceptions. German news media seemed for some years to be immune to the forces that had begun to affect newspapers even in neighbouring countries, let alone further afield. In 2010, the Axel Springer group was reporting profit margins of 27 per cent on its national newspapers, *Bild* and *Die Welt*.[23] But popular newspapers, such as *Bild*, have built up such large profit margins in the past that they have a cushion protecting them for a time against new trends. Germany is beginning to experience print decline: the slide just began later than in Britain or America. Germans have taken only slowly to the internet, and their media companies have survived better than their counterparts elsewhere. But, in 2012, a German news agency and a newspaper, the *Frankfurter Rundschau*, both filed for bankruptcy; the *Financial Times Deutschland* closed. In 2011, Springer's head of strategy said that the group expected to lose an average of 5 per cent of circulation each year for the next five years. The business crisis of print has also arrived late and slow in Japan and Finland.

Palliative care for print

Newspapers have not been passive as the pressures have accumulated. But nor have they solved their problems. Unable or unwilling to cut back their costs, newspapers tried to broaden their offering and their readerships in order to counteract the long decline.

In Britain, the riches of the long advertising boom flowed first into Saturday editions, those editions of national papers that had long been poor relations of the weekdays, with lower circulations. Starting with a revamped and expanded Saturday *Daily Telegraph* in 1987, the quality papers followed suit. Lifestyle coverage had expanded in all newspapers in the 1980s as the drift away from hard news gathered pace and as a long economic boom increased consumer appetite and advertising. Newspapers wanted more rounded, empathetic editorial personalities to appeal to and hold the loyalty of extra readers. Until that point it had been assumed that all the available advertising and coverage needed or wanted for travel, food and wine, cars and health was supplied by extremely fat and lucrative Sunday papers.

But advertisers who were ready to pay could not find colour advertising: existing editions were jammed. A rush to create new supplements and titles on both days of the weekend was the result. As with the start-ups that began after the defeat of the printing trade unions at Wapping in 1986–87, by no means all succeeded. Two new upmarket Sunday titles joined the fast-expanding Saturday sections of the established titles in the scramble for advertising revenue not already mopped up by others. The hapless *Sunday Correspondent* began in 1989 and lasted just over a year; *The Independent*, then enjoying heady success, started *Independent on Sunday* in 1990. The latter was immediately a commercial disappointment, partly because the failing *Correspondent* was crowding the market, and the Sunday edition did permanent damage to the daily *Independent*'s finances. The Saturday sections lasted better, but shrank as advertising began to desert print 15 years later.

Take the whole UK national newspaper market or divide it into popular, mid-market and upmarket: however it is split up, any part of it is always overcrowded. Even now, the wish to own a newspaper for access, prestige and influence trumps commercial considerations. Where a rational economist would find room for four daily quality papers, there are five. Several may be uneconomic at one time; one is usually the weakest and the closest to going under.

The Independent was in this position when it changed format to tabloid in late 2003. It was quickly followed by *The Times* and subsequently by *The Guardian*, which went into a hybrid 'Berliner' size between tabloid and broadsheet. The changes gave the newspapers temporary appeal to new readers, particularly those who had abandoned them because broadsheet papers are hard to read on crowded public transport. Around two-thirds of the sale of 'national' quality papers is in and around London, meaning that significant numbers of their readers buy the paper on their way to work in the centre of the capital. But once the effect of the novelty had worn off, the deeper trends reasserted themselves and the circulation declines continued.

Business papers such as the *Financial Times* and *Wall Street Journal* set up satellite printing plants for foreign editions. They were successful as marketing for these titles, if usually internally controversial because of the high costs involved. But developments were against them. In 2012, a German-language version of the *Financial Times*, produced in small format, was shuttered after 13 years of losses. General-interest printed newspapers secured only small international readerships until the internet made distribution of their journalism possible at very low cost. Another option was to put Sunday papers on diets so severe that they really no longer were separate papers but seventh-day editions of the main paper. Both the *Sunday Telegraph* and *Independent on Sunday* went through this slimming. *The Guardian* considered shutting *The Observer* as a distinct title in 2009 and restarting with a *Sunday Guardian*, but backed off after protests.

The most successful single attempt to revive the fortunes of print was a complete change of business model: giving away newspapers for free. Across Europe, multi-country chains began short, snappy newspapers with low overheads in cities from Paris to Prague, which were thrust into the hands of commuters for a quick read while on their way somewhere. A chain of *Metro* newspapers in continental Europe did well initially, but circulations flagged as smartphones widened online use on the move; a London give-away with the same name, owned by Associated Newspapers, also flourished on a tightly managed formula of convenience, low-cost advertisement space and well-packaged, low-cost editorial. In many places, including London, the key assets held by the newspapers were not equipment or journalists but the rights they had bought to distribute on the underground and overground rail systems. One of the most spectacular turnarounds was the decision to turn the long-established London *Evening Standard* into a free newspaper in 2009. Three years later, the *Evening Standard*, which had been on course to lose £30 million in a year, turned in a £1 million profit.[24] The paper was able to demonstrate to advertisers that they could reach a much bigger readership by saving them the trouble of stopping to fiddle around with money to buy a paper. To pick up an *Evening Standard* on a homeward journey, all the reader has to do is lean down and pick one up from a dumpbin, without breaking step. Free newspapers, in the right place at the right time, represent useful value to readers who might not otherwise stop or pay for news.

Some continental European governments, lobbied by the industry and scared of presiding over closures, maintained – and in rare cases increased – public subsidies to print. Some of this support, in countries such as Italy, Sweden or France, were long-standing. The snag of taxpayer-funded subsidy is that it preserves the problem without solving it, and the costs rise as the crisis gets worse. Italy cut back press subsidies in 2011 as its government hit financial trouble. A similar cutback must be likely in France, where support was boosted in 2008. One analyst reckoned that the total support to all newspapers in all forms amounted to €1.4 billion, in an industry with a turnover of only €10 billion.[25]

The booming Indian newspaper market has been the scene of one of the most bizarre and cynical strategies pursued anywhere to deal with competition in print and from other media. The venerable *Times of India* is owned by the Jain family and is a money-making machine of feared and respected power in that market. At a daily circulation of 4.3 million, it has the world's largest English-language daily sale. I spoke on a conference panel a few years ago alongside a senior executive from the *Times of India*. A member of the audience accused the newspaper of taking money from companies and celebrities for coverage in the paper's news and gossip pages. The executive gave an affable but vague answer that, I was surprised to hear, included no denial that this practice took place. In fact, the newspaper encouraged it and institutionalized it. The two generations of Jains who run the newspaper came to a simple conclusion: that the ambiguity at most newspapers between commercial and social imperatives were confusing and wrong. A newspaper is a platform whose space is on offer to advertisers. The Jains thus began, discreetly at first, to demolish the wall that is supposed to separate commercial from editorial activities. Editorial would still look like editorial; advertisements would sell a product or brand directly in the normal way. But advertising would also be sold in more oblique ways.

The *Times of India*'s second section is marked in small type under the masthead as 'advertorial, entertainment promotional feature'. This is the only oblique warning that the celebrity gossip is written by the paper's staff but paid for by the stars or by their publicists. The Jain brothers claim that this is 'advertorial' and a common worldwide practice. 'We are not in the newspaper business,' Vineet Jain told an interviewer, 'we are in the advertising business.' They also defend the organized sale of editorial space as preferable to the alternative, the buying of favourable coverage with cash handed out in plain envelopes by PR people. The *Times of India* also sells advertising in exchange for stakes in the company taking the space. Other newspapers do barter deals for advertising, but the *Times*'s rivals say that the paper will favour advertisers in editorial coverage. In 2010 a report compiled by India's Press Council concluded that the *Times*'s advertising practices had encouraged an 'epidemic' of paid coverage in print and on TV. Many rural papers sold coverage to political candidates on a tariff: varying amounts for varying number of days' helpful coverage and an extra payment for hostile stories about an opponent. Several papers – *The Hindu*, the *Indian Express*, *Malayala Manorama* – say that they outlaw these deals. 'Every competitor at first agitates over it, gets angry about it, and then quietly apes it,' a magazine editor and blogger said of the cumulative effect of the Jains' policies: 'Each player in the Indian market, whatever the language, is left with very few options. And newspapers who say they are not doing it are basically lying.'[26]

Flipping to digital

Many of the attempts to improve the performance of print actually worked, up to a point. But the successes and failures all had one thing in common: the long, deep changes in the way that people get and use information were against them. Some commentators hold journalists, with rigidly fixed ideas about how journalism should be done, as at least as responsible as managers for this failure fully to adapt. Professor Robert Picard thinks that journalists don't focus on whether or not they are creating work that people might value:

> If one conscientiously reviews changes made in news organizations in recent decades, it seems clear that the changes introduced have been highly limited, cosmetic, and weak efforts to preserve a gilded age of journalism or have been designed to soothe investors and give the impression of active managerial responses to the changing environment.[27]

Because it is now so clear that these sticking-plaster solutions have at best only alleviated problems and not eliminated them, large changes are now under discussion in newspaper boardrooms. Plunging circulations and revenues are on the edge of forcing big decisions. The difficulties of the US press give a cue to the options most probably under consideration. So far only one major newspaper in the United States has switched off its print version completely: the venerable *Christian Science Monitor* is now digital-only. A handful of other papers have reduced their frequency to two or three days per week.[28]

The sensitive topic of an iconic British newspaper either reducing its print frequency or – less likely – cutting it altogether barely ever surfaces in public discussion. That does not mean that plans and calculations are not being made. The editors of *The Guardian* and the *Sunday Times* were asked in 2010 when their papers might stop being printed. Neither answered the question directly, but both said that they thought their papers had bought their last printing presses. That answer assumed that neither newspaper would be appearing on paper between 20 and 30 years from that date. But that conversation was held before circulations began to slide faster (see Figure 6.2). Shrinking or switching off print is far more likely to be a real choice for some newspapers in the next 5 to 10 years. What was once unthinkable is now not shocking. The chief executive of the troubled Australian publisher Fairfax Media said that printed papers in the future will become 'expensive, bespoke and narrowly distributed' and that his

FIGURE 6.2   UK national newspapers: the accelerating rate of fall

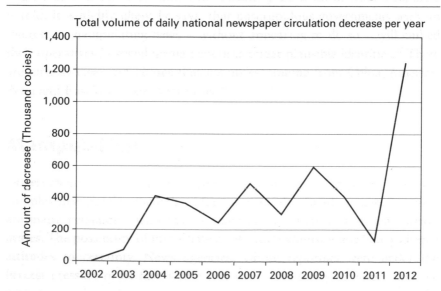

SOURCE: http://en.wikipedia.org/wiki/List_of_newspapers_in_the_United_Kingdom_by_circulation

company could stop printing in 'three, five or ten years'.[29] Tablets are optically easy to read and newspapers quickly adapted to the smaller screens. Touch screens and flat-rate broadband subscriptions help to drive up the number of people reading news on the move.

At present, the major British newspapers are edging sideways towards the digital tipping point. Print staffs and print supplements are being cut back and people and resources shifted into digital. Digital is people-intensive because the range of potential experiments is so wide. Any national newspaper with the usual wide range of subject matter is currently considering: whether it has the right kind of paywall (or whether and how it might have one if it doesn't have one); optimizing digital content for a proliferating range of mobile screens and operating systems; the management of its interactivity with users and commenters; extracting journalism from massive sets of raw data and how to make the best use of the newspaper's archive. That list is nowhere near exhaustive, but it illustrates one of the dilemmas of a world in which the best business model is not obvious. Many bets have to be laid; most will not pay off.

Some of the American newspapers that have retreated from print have done so because their managements thought they had no other choice in the face of overwhelming losses. A number that have folded or been sold hit trouble because, while the business may trade at a profit, the margin is not high enough to support heavy borrowing. At the turn of the 21st century, most US newspaper chains made profits of 20 per cent or more. By 2012 the average media company profit had fallen to 5 per cent. British newspapers, not yet under this kind of pressure, are hoping that they can delay tilting from print to digital until the business prospects for digital are better. Estimated digital revenue for the big British newspaper groups in 2009 was highest at the *Financial Times* (at 36.3 per cent of its income) but the next highest was Guardian News & Media at 16.9 per cent. These proportions are the inhibition against tilting too early: no company can know what proportion of its print income can be converted to digital if it were to force its advertisers to change platform.

But the rate of losses does not allow these newspapers to wait indefinitely. Even if some slightly better financial performance can be assumed if the recession fades, none of these papers have the resources to continue losing money for more than a few years each. News International, owners of *The Times* and the *Sunday Times*, has clearly been contemplating reducing the total costs of both papers by making them share more facilities and resources. Even considering this triggered a stand-off between the management and the independent directors of *The Times*. Any sort of merger raises esoteric legal problems, since Rupert Murdoch gave a formal undertaking when buying both newspapers to keep them separate. *The Guardian* has made large investments in digital and in 2012 earned £40 million of online income; income per user is rising faster than the number of visitors.[30] But in 2011–12, *The Guardian* group lost £44.2 million, having lost £37 million and £38 million respectively in the previous two years; the losses run at close to £100,000 per day. By way of comparison, the losses for the same three years for *The Times* and the *Sunday Times* were £88 million, £45 million and £12 million. There is no obvious business model for *The Times*, and the *Sunday Times* is not the cash cow it once was.

The Guardian has money in the bank, can expect the advertising market to improve and its losses have often been covered in the past by the used-car magazine and website *Auto Trader*. But it has lost £40 million of classified advertisement income from a turnover of £230 million and little has yet replaced it. *The Guardian*'s chief executive has warned that, at the current rate of loss, the reserves would only last 'three to five years'.[31] It is not far-fetched to imagine that *The Guardian*'s future might be as a news and opinion global website, which publishes no daily paper edition but an upmarket weekly magazine of essays and reportage on current affairs in the manner of the *New Yorker* or Germany's *Die Zeit*.[32]

Making people pay: walls and meters

The internet, at a structural level, creates two difficulties for news publishers. For many, but not all, newspapers it has weakened or destroyed cross-subsidy of news reporting by making money from selling advertising space. Having done so, it works against the logic of bundling a varied collection of content for delivery to the reader. The internet splits users and their tastes, allowing them to go straight to the material they want without passing through the rest of the package.

The first response by the publishing companies lay in amending the pattern of the past. If advertising revenue was falling, then circulation income would have to rise to compensate. It was not that simple. The instinct to charge for digital news inaugurated a debate about 'paywalls', which has produced no settled result. The debate will continue for many years because no clear business model has emerged from experiments so far. Collecting subscriptions and excluding those who don't pay has an effect on what can be shared and how it is exchanged. A subscription paywall collects revenue from the user but inhibits the sharing of stories, which comes so naturally with the internet. A paywall can also cut writers off from interaction with readers. Some may not need or want this interaction, but most do. The *New York Times*'s first experiment with a paywall around all its output in 2009 was brought to an end by a mutiny among the paper's most famous columnists, who objected to being isolated from their audience and the reactions on which they had come to rely.

Every experiment in paywalls is useful – including the ones that fail. Each tryout generates information that other people can use. In a digital world in which information is so quickly shared, failure in business can be a form of public good (but success is better). Bearing in mind that these experiments are in full swing and that new discoveries and trends will appear all the time, the following points are worth making about charging for news content:

- It makes no more sense to say that 'information wants to be free' than it does to say that 'information wants to be expensive'. But reliable news is expensive to produce and remains so despite the pressures that reduce – often to zero – the price of internet information. As the American businessman Warren Buffet remarked, the internet is much better for consumers than it is for producers. Making money from any activity that relies on the internet looks so hard that many have concluded that it is impossible. I would argue that the disruption of traditional ways of thinking and doing news has been so drastic that it has taken years for news producers, old and new, to start to think their way round the problem of reconciling the value of news with what people are prepared to pay for it.

- Experiments conducted in a disruption are inherently unpredictable. But one reliable test can be applied to paywall experiments: does the charge levied fit with the technology and the audience? Is it easy to use? In an era when information travelled only down gossip networks and official proclamations, newspaper must have seemed almost miraculously useful and easy to use. Hard information, lots of it, in a compact, portable bundle that you could use more than once. Today, any company selling anything on the web, including information, will be judged against global winners. Is this as easy as buying something from Apple or Amazon? Does the paywall stop users sharing its product? News has always been something that disperses beyond the purchaser. In the high modern period of newspapers in the late 20th century, between two and three people saw each copy of a daily newspaper. In limited cases, a publisher may be able to charge money and confine the information to a single reader where the reader's need for the information is strong enough. Peoples' need for cricket or baseball statistics might be so strong as to persuade them to pay without being able to share. This does not seem to apply to all information.

- When it came to make its second attempt at a paywall, the *New York Times* built it with gaps that allow its links to be shared without attracting a charge (see Figure 6.3). Several factors might explain the difference in performance, but the fact that the *New York Times* paywall is porous and *The* (London) *Times* is not must be among them. The internet gives people opportunity and permission to do things they were not able to do before. From swapping a link on a social network to an interesting dispatch from Burma, a recipe or a titbit of gossip is so easy that it has become natural for millions. Paywalls that interfere with this are unlikely to work. Charges based on moral, democratic obligation – 'people should pay for news' – are even less likely to do so.

FIGURE 6.3   *New York Times* vs *The Times* (London)

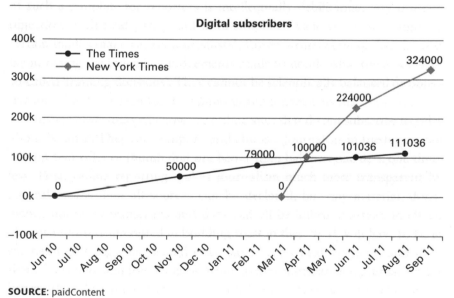

SOURCE: paidContent

- Paywall experiments at mainstream newspapers have had results ranging between ambiguous and discouraging. But the trials have almost always delivered information that has allowed better tailoring second time round, if a new experiment is mounted. The most important lesson has been that the relative advantages of mass and niche have altered. Any producer of information must now study the demographics and anthropology of the different needs, wants and likes of different groups in the potential readership. Transactions become more complex. Misunderstanding of how early paywalls might work was based on an assumption carried over from mass media. All customers could be treated and served in the same general way without needing to be understood in detail. A writer at Gawker, whose income rests on advertising, put it brutally by saying that a paywall won't work for any content (or its near equivalent) that can be found for free. 'The fact that readers *like* you is not enough to support an online paywall: readers must *need* you.'[33]

- The number of mainstream newspapers trying paywalls is increasing, particularly in the United States. This reflects both a spreading awareness that digital advertising rates are never likely to replace the equivalent income in print, and a greater sophistication in avoiding making a digital offer that readers can easily refuse. No survey can completely keep up with news paywalls, but in 2012 there were thought to be between 150 and 300 in the United States.[34] Another estimate at the same time gauged that 20 per cent of the 1,400 dailies in the United States would be operating some kind of paywall by the end of that year. That total includes the four largest circulations: the *Wall Street Journal, USA Today*, the *Los Angeles Times* and the *New York Times*. The numbers were boosted by the decisions of several chains, Gannett among them, to charge across many of their titles. Fairfax, the second largest newspaper group in Australia, simultaneously announced the firing of almost 2,000 editorial staff and the setting-up of paywalls at their newspapers. Four Canadian newspapers followed suit; more than half of the country's top 20 have paywalls. Similar experiments were being operated or planned at up to 12 German newspapers (including at the giant Axel Springer group), at Singapore's largest newspaper group and at Finland's market leader, the Sanoma Corporation. News Corporation had already put paywalls in place at some newspapers, including *The Australian, The Times* and the *Sunday Times*.

- Online subscription prices have begun to edge upwards. A survey by one subscription platform for publishers showed a 40 per cent increase in average monthly subscriptions in the United States between 2011 and 2013. But that was from a low base: $6.66 to $9.26. The average 'meter setting' (the number of clicks for free before charges kick in) is dropping.[35]

- This swing towards paywalls at large institutions emphatically does not mean that it will work. What little hard evidence any of these companies have disclosed (generally very little) suggests that 'porous' or 'metered' paywalls do better than enclosures that force payment for all or any of what is inside. Incomplete paywalls drive away fewer potential readers. But they may also have the effect of weakening engagement with the newspapers using them if large numbers of readers stop reading just before they hit the paywall. (What might work or not at the *New York Times* may not apply anywhere else; the newspaper is very unusual in several respects.) One expert has suggested that a 'reverse meter' might work better: take an upfront subscription sum from your loyal reader and then give 'credits' for intensive use, interactive participation or energetic linking.[36]

- As reading online has become more and more normal, public attitudes have shifted towards being more willing to consider paying for online news. *The Economist* operates a 'metered' paywall that charges the heaviest users and allows frictionless sharing on networks. One survey at the end of 2012 claimed that 86 per cent of its respondents thought it 'fair' to pay 'something' for newspaper content. It also found that 42 per cent spend at least £8 a month on digital news.[37] This is a large change from the 2–4 per cent proportions of web users in the 1990s who declared that they would be prepared to pay for news content. Much of this change seems to be driven by tablets and their ease of use.

- The wisest media companies treat payment as an experiment and are prepared to react to whatever it tells them. The largest ones can afford to run an array of experiments. Rupert Murdoch's News Corporation, whose grasp of the implications of the internet has been uneven, was widely described as having decided in favour of paywalls when *The Times* and the *Sunday Times* installed them. Fewer analysts remarked on the fact that the company is in effect conducting a series of tests in parallel. The two London papers adopted what might be called 'radical' paywalls, shutting users out of all content unless they pay, allowing no sharing, and blocking search engines. *The Sun* originally decided against such a paywall but did charge for particular services, such as online bingo. Sky News, whose site has received heavy investment, is free. The *Wall Street Journal* uses a partial, porous paywall that does not cover all its content and allows content to be found by search engines.

- One experiment that News Corporation did not launch was a system that would broker the interests of a network consisting of both publishers and subscribers. Although the company considered forming such a system, disagreements among publishers seems to have scuppered it. These systems are commoner in continental Europe than elsewhere and vary from country to country but usually collect payments on behalf of a group of publishers; customers can subscribe to single publications or packages of several. A wide group of Belgian media, for example, announced a collective system for registering as readers.[38] French publishers have set up Le Kiosk to do the same thing. A US firm, Press+, has attempted to do the same thing but had only 400 affiliates by early 2013. Google launched a scheme called One Pass, which attracted few publishers, even though Google's charge was only 10 per cent against Apple's 30 per cent in iTunes. One Pass closed after just over a year. Piano Media collects subscriptions for a portfolio of online publications in Slovakia and Poland.

- There were regular suggestions that if consumers of news wanted to access only single articles then 'micropayment' systems, which allow instant small payments from a mobile phone, might be the answer. Some much-vaunted technologies arrive just after being announced; others are slowed down for years by technical or regulatory snags. Micropayment systems have for years been just around the corner.[39] While they may contribute an extra revenue stream to some news organizations, small one-off sums will not solve the basic problem. Willingness to pay for content has increased – but not to the point where it can yet replace the hole left in traditional businesses made by the departure of advertising. Media are learning to manage abundance – and abundance is keeping prices down.

- There are now experiments under way with paywalls for individual writers and bloggers. Internet news readers can go straight to a reporter or commentator they like; they no longer have need for the other contributors to the bundle. This opens new possibilities for a new kind of star power: a solo business model. Andrew Sullivan, who has a claim to be the leading serious blogger in the United States, has had a home at the *Atlantic* magazine site, *Time*, the *New Republic* and the Daily Beast. In 2013 he announced that he and his small team were going independent and would charge $19.99 per year for the blog, which comments on American politics, media and culture.

Sullivan sees little logic left in writers grouping themselves into teams to make printed magazines. Until 2011 he had read printed newspapers and magazines, but switched to reading them on a tablet:

> Part of me has come to see physical magazines and newspapers as, at this point, absurd. They are like Wile E Coyote suspended three feet over a cliff for a few seconds. They're still there; but there's nothing underneath; and the plunge is vast and steep.[40]

The former editor of a Dutch paper *De Pers*, closed for lack of advertising in 2012, has created an app which allows users to subscribe to individual journalists rather than to a whole organization.[41]

- Paywalls don't seem to make much difference, positive or negative, to digital advertising income. Papers with subscribers should be able to work towards creating a 'members' club' for the highest-paying readers. This is one of the ideas that lies behind the paywall at *The Times*, whose subscribers get discount offers for events, holidays and books. In theory, better data on readers' tastes should allow targeted, higher-premium advertising, but little evidence of this has been seen. Advertising to a readership inside a paywall can be sold at a higher rate 'per view' or 'per click', but to a smaller audience, and the net effect seems to be broadly neutral. The laboratory here must be the United States, because so many more experiments are going on there. Between the third quarter of 2006 and the third quarter of 2012, the US digital ad market grew from $4 billion to $9 billion. Over the same period, newspaper digital ad sales rose barely at all, going from $640 million to $760 million. Advertisers are no longer attracted to these platforms.

- Many of the dilemmas and choices listed above can be seen in the struggles that British national papers have with charging:
  - *Daily Telegraph*: 300,000 digital subscribers on iPad and mobile and a metered paywall for foreign users, extended to low (£1.99) charge for web access in 2013.
  - *The Times* and the *Sunday Times*: 132,000 and 126,000 paying subscribers at July 2012. That year, the wall was relaxed to allow Google to show some content. Revenue is likely to be disappointing.
  - *Financial Times*: 300,000 paying subscribers, 15 per cent of new arrivals on mobile. The paper has struggled to arrange a hierarchy

of content that both collects money but allows blogs to be shared. FT blogs now require registration to read, but not payment.[42]

- *Daily Mail*: no paywall and £31 million of advertising revenue online in the year to 2012, a 72 per cent year-on-year increase.

- *The Guardian*: no paywall (won't rule one out) but charges for iPad app. Digital revenues to 2012 up 16.3 per cent to £45 million.

- *The Sun* announced a paywall in 2013.

This set of fragile, empirical experiments will not remain stable. There are no striking successes here, given the losses from print advertising. The unwillingness to break out detailed figures is the clue.

The demand for news

The economics of mass media obscured for years the value of news as seen by consumers. Has demand for news fallen? Despite all the information in circulation, are people using news less overall? If the performance of established media and the failing grip on readers and audiences is any guide, the consumption of news must have declined. But does online make up the difference?

Any estimate must be as much art as science, given the fragmenting of news sources. The only academic study of this intimidating arithmetic found that the growth of online news reading has roughly offset the fall in the use of traditional media. Markus Prior of Princeton also found that the small group in the population that follow the news carefully are, thanks to a greater choice of sources, much better informed than the same group in the past. He also concluded that news junkies are fairly typical of the population as a whole in substituting online consumption for print or broadcast.[43]

This suggests that what people will look for from news organizations has not changed at a basic level; what has changed is how they acquire information and pass it on. That may change journalism in many ways but it should not change its position in a democracy. As an economist might put it, the producers have to reform what they do, but the demand side has not changed. In societies where people may choose their media, there has never been a mass audience for serious news. A fraction of an electorate fit the ideal template of the engaged citizen comparing political manifestos at election time and reading about policy choices between opportunities to vote. This has led political scientists to describe modern democracies as 'monitorial'. A combination of an active media interested in the account-ability of those with power and a small segment of the population who read and debate such information may be enough to ensure that politicians generally behave well. The majority of a population will remain content to be 'rationally ignorant' of details of policy and politics over which they have little influence except a vote at intervals.

Research suggests that this pattern has not been broken or changed by the disruption of news and its provision on the internet. A study of readers of the *Sydney Morning Herald* website found that readers of serious news websites tell researchers that they are going on to these sites to read about politics and the economy but in fact spend time surfing the crime and celeb-rity news.[44] James T Hamilton looked at data for people searching for different kinds of news on the web and found that curiosity about political information ranked well behind seeking information related to purchases, work or entertainment. The web had broadened the range of news sources and varieties of news. The highest scoring types of stories would have been instantly recognizable to any editor of 50 or 100 years before. Aside from local community news, everyone from news junkies to occasional snackers on news wanted human interest and crime.[45]

Hamilton also pointed out the importance of deregulation and econom-ics on the balance between impartiality and opinion in news. Large national or network news organizations seeking big audiences have an incentive to present themselves as objective and impartial in order to maximize their appeal. This was an influential idea both to the BBC and ITV in Britain and the three big US networks in the first phase of mass television audiences. But when the terrestrial television markets were deregulated in the 1980s, the market was split into smaller fragments. The economics of making smaller fragments profitable are different and had a gradual effect on editorial philosophy. A loyal audience of 1 million viewers can be defined and kept loyal by strong, controversial political opinion; the same partisanship will not build an audience of 5–10 million.[46] The division of television viewers into a 'long tail' of smaller audiences drove television journalism towards appealing to polemic and argument. Besides, talking heads are cheaper and deregulation made profits harder to find. That drove down what was spent on news, particularly by cable and satellite companies in markets such as the United States or India. Online news tends anyway towards quick commentary on news and a more informal and personal style: it is not a coincidence that the Drudge Report and Huffington Post are named after people.

What we don't know about online news

Providers of digital information of any kind can gather vast amounts of information about the users who interact with them, simply by using automatic software that tracks and aggregates visits, preferences, searches, purchases and more. Online news organizations are, among many other things, giant repositories of detailed customer data.

But in several other important senses, there is a lot we don't yet know about the users of online news and how their tastes and preferences might evolve. From the start, the outlines of how many people used a site was easy to track. Yet there are arguments over methodology between the rival firms that track usage. But the issue that has yet to be fully solved is more behavioural than mathematical. Fewer people spend time with newspapers, but when they do, they spend more time with them than looking at news on websites. Online visits are also much more occasional. Only a tiny fraction of visitors to websites are loyal and habitual in the sense that many newspaper readers once were. Newspapers have found in the last 20 years that they have a lower proportion of readers who read them every day, but they still retain a core of regulars. And if a website visitor clicks on an individual story and then leaves, they count as a reader but in quite a different sense to someone browsing the content of a site as they would a paper or magazine.

Surprising as it may seem given the quantities of data available to be crunched, news organizations, the measurement specialists and the advertising business are still grappling to locate and agree the best measures. Once, websites tried to quantify and compare 'stickiness' – roughly, the amount of time that a user spent on the site and how often they returned. This has gradually morphed into a preoccupation with 'engagement', but has yet to produce any consistently adopted measure.

Part of the difficulty lies in recognizing the large change in the way that people have been allowed to use information. Because peoples' choice of platforms is now so flexible, it can be hard to estimate how many people actually get news from the internet. A stable number of just under 1 person in 10 in Britain gets news from the internet alone. But if people are asked whether the internet is their 'primary' means of access, the number jumps to 40 per cent for national news (39 per cent for world news and 30 per cent for local).[47] People can flip through dozens of choices about what to read, sampling or not as they choose. They need never repeat a pattern if they don't want to. They can arrange for news on topics of their choice to be pushed to them; they can be confident that news of any importance will find a way to their attention somehow. Once alerted, they can find out the details quickly if they're curious. Social networks such as Facebook have set up a new criterion for judging all kinds of information, including news: how many times is it shared? Does sharing indicate a higher value or not? News organizations, many still trapped by the habits of the past, are still trying to find ways of connecting what they do with the moving target of what people actually value in their activity and output.

Different cultures deal with information saturation in varied ways. Societies with high levels of social confidence and trust are likely to take more easily to internet use because they already consume a lot of public information. Scandinavian countries – small, high-trust societies – have some of the highest levels of newspaper readership per head and they also have high internet use and adoption rates. The website of the Norwegian tabloid paper *VG* has been profitable since 2003 and its users are loyal (in 2010 only 3 per cent of its traffic came through Google). When the Asian tsunami struck in 2004, the Norwegian government released a list of 8,000 Norwegians who were thought to be in the area and might be affected. The pool of possible names was too large to be useful. *VG*, asking its readers for help, rapidly whittled the list down to 85 people unaccounted for. When the government issued its own list, it had 84 names, mostly the same. VG Nett reaches 1.6 million Norwegians, 32 per cent of the population.[48] Outside of Scandinavia, there are no other countries with as close-knit a digital public sphere.

Notes

1   Andrew Sullivan, the *Sunday Times*, 16 December 2012.

2   Fabien Curto Millet, Google presentation at City University London, 2011.

3   *International Herald Tribune*, 1 July 1998.

4   Leurdijk, A, Slot, M and Nieuwenhuis, O (2012) 'Statistical ecosystems and competitiveness analysis of media and content industries', European Commission, Brussels.

5   Shafer, J (2008) 'Michael Crichton, Vindicated', 29 May, available at **http://www.slate.com/articles/news_and_politics/press_box/2008/05/michael_crichton_vindicated.html** (accessed 20.5.13).

6   See for example **http://www.nytimes.com/1999/04/19/business/media-intel-s-chairman-tells-newspaper-publishers-supply-more-insight-but-who-s.html** (accessed 31.1.2013).

7   Claire Enders, Enders Analysis presentation, Competitive pressure on the press, to the Leveson Inquiry, 6 October 2011.

8 National Readership Survey (UK) via *The Economist*, 8 March 2003.

9 Sternvik, J, Wadbring, I, and Weibull, L (eds) (2008) *Newspaper in a Changing Media World: Swedish Trends*, University of Gothenberg.

10 Enders Analysis to Leveson.

11 Family Expenditure Survey, Office for National Statistics, 2012.

12 Figures from Alliance for Audited Media **http://newsosaur.blogspot.de/2013/05/print-circ-fell-42-at-top-papers-since.html** (accessed 3.5.13).

13 OECD working party on the information economy, The evolution of news and the internet (2010), Paris.

14 Wan-Ifra world press trends **http://www.wan-ifra.org/wpt** (accessed 20.5.13).

15 **http://www.themediabriefing.com/article/2013-02-11/datawatch-circulation-decline-developing-economies** (accessed 11.3.13).

16 Meeker, M, Kleiner Perkins Caufield, 'Internet Trends', presentation to D10 conference (30 May 2012) **www.kpcb.com/insights/2012-internet-trends** (accessed 20.5.13).

17 Meeker, 'Internet Trends'.

18 **http://yourstory.in/2011/10/rural-news-bulletin-gaon-ki-awaaz/** (accessed 31.1.13).

19 Meeker, 'Internet Trends'.

20 **http://econsultancy.com/uk/blog/9569-china-the-world-s-largest-online-population-infographic?utm_medium=feeds&utm_source=blog** (accessed 31.1.13).

21 Quoted by Jonathan Mirsky in *New York Review of Books* blog (NYR blog), 8 January 2013. **http://www.nybooks.com/blogs/nyrblog/2013/jan/08/old-fears-chinas-new-leaders/** (accessed 31.1.13).

22 **http://www.nytimes.com/2013/01/31/technology/chinese-hackers-infiltrate-new-york-times-computers.html?_r=0** (accessed 31.1.13).

23 *The Economist*, 12 June 2012.

24 **http://www.guardian.co.uk/media/greenslade/2012/oct/16/london-evening-standard-evgeny-lebedev** (accessed 1.2.13).

25 Pecquerie, Bertrand (2008) *Médias*, winter, Paris.

26 Auletta, K, *New Yorker*, 8.10.2012.

27 Picard, R G (2010) *Value Creation and the Future of News Organizations*, Media XXI, Lisbon.

28 For example the daily *New Orleans Times–Picayune* switched to printing three days per week in 2012.

29 **http://www.guardian.co.uk/media/greenslade+fairfax-media** (accessed 11.5.13).

30　http://www.niemanlab.org/2013/01/guardian-ceo-andrew-miller-on-paywalls-mobile-and-going-global/ (accessed 20.5.13).

31　http://moreintelligentlife.co.uk/con10t/ideas/tim-de-lisle/can-guardian-survive?page=0 per cent2C1 (accessed 2.2.13).

32　In common with some weeklies with distinctive character and content, *Die Zeit's* circulation has held steady, and even occasionally risen, in recent years.

33　http://gawker.com/5966560/online-paywalls-and-the-future-of-media-a-few-hard-truths (accessed 3.2.13).

34　http://www.niemanlab.org/2012/04/wait-so-how-many-newspapers-have-paywalls/ (accessed 3.2.13).

35　http://www.adweek.com/news/press/press-study-finds-digital-subscription-prices-rising-meters-dropping (accessed 11.3.13).

36　http://buzzmachine.com/2011/12/19/why-not-a-reverse-meter/ (accessed 3.2.13).

37　http://www.inpublishing.co.uk/kb/articles/mythology_versus_reality_of_uk_digital_broadsheet_pricing.aspx (accessed 4.2.13).

38　http://paidcontent.org/2013/01/02/belgian-media-planning-shared-digital-content-passport/ (accessed 4.2.13).

39　See for example http://www.slideshare.net/newsworks/journalism-media-and-technology-predictions-2013-final (accessed 3.2.13).

40　http://dish.andrewsullivan.com/threads/towards-tablets-and-paying-for-content/ (accessed 6.1.13)

41　http://www.journalism.co.uk/news/news-app-launches-which-lets-readers-subscribe-to-journalists/s2/a552079/ (accessed 15.2.13).

42　http://blogs.reuters.com/felix-salmon/2012/11/13/the-ft-backs-down-on-paywalled-blogs/ (accessed 3.2.13).

43　Prior, M (2013) *Conditions for Political Accountability in a High-Choice Media Environment*, Oxford Handbook of Political Communications, ed Kenski and Hall Jamieson, Oxford University Press, Oxford.

44　Van Heekeren, Margaret (2005) 'What the web news readers want: an analysis of smh.com.au readership story preference, ANZCA conference.

45　Hamilton, J T (2004) *All the News That's Fit to Sell: How the Market Transforms Information into News*, Princeton University Press, New Jersey.

46　Hamilton, *All the News That's Fit to Sell*.

47　Ofcom, via Millet.

48　http://georgebrock.net/zeitung-online-2010-postscript-from-vg/ (accessed 3.2.13).

07

Credibility crumbles

> Liz: You won't lose your job.
> Greg: Liz, the PCC...
> Liz: Oh, fuck the PCC...
> Greg: I'm on the PCC!
>
> **JOE PENHALL,** *DUMB SHOW*, **2004**

In the first years of the 21st century, three forces collided and traumatized journalism. A long decline in the economic fortunes of the mainstream print media was made worse by a technology-driven revolution that widened choice but fragmented public knowledge. The strains caused by these changes were among the causes of a handful of spectacular failures in journalism. A legislative and policy crisis occurred in several countries. The dramatic humiliation of Rupert Murdoch and his company in Britain at the Leveson Inquiry into phone-hacking was only the most high-profile drama of its kind; it was not the only one.

To see the downward trajectory through which the news media travelled, compare a movie and a television series, 32 years apart. In the film *All the President's Men* made in 1976 about the *Washington Post* stories that triggered the Watergate scandal, reporters are unblemished heroes. Bob Woodward and Carl Bernstein, played by Robert Redford and Dustin Hoffman, doggedly winkle out enough of the truth of what has been happening in the White House to start the process that unseats a US president. They are not delayed by any ethical dilemmas. Fast forward to 2008 and the fifth season of the television drama set in Baltimore, *The Wire*. One of the plot strands of that series is set in the local city paper, a newsroom battered and soured by falling circulation and profits. A reporter starts inventing things with which to embroider his stories; he moves on to bigger and bigger lies. His colleagues begin to suspect him.

So mythical and influential has the Watergate story become that the issues it raises are rarely looked at. One writer who did so, noticed that on Woodward and Bernstein's own published account, they broke at least one law and several rules that would be upheld in today's newsrooms.[1] Bernstein conspired with a local prosecutor to investigate a political opponent of the prosecutor. He also obtained phone and credit records illegally; today that is a federal offence in the United States punishable by up to 10 years in prison. They deceived sources and outed one of their FBI sources – who they thought had misled them – to his boss. At the time of Nixon's fall and the *Washington Post*'s triumph, there wasn't much reflection on how much bad behaviour can be justified in the pursuit of good journalism. That debate came later.

Newsroom culture

The commercial pressures on printed media that we have seen in earlier chapters bore down hardest on popular newspapers. Quality papers are rarely profit generators and thus came under less pressure. Mainstream television news in Britain, with the BBC continuing to set the benchmark for trust, did not dumb down and its viewing figures stabilized after a long period of decline that began in the 1980s. As the longest study showed, 'evening news bulletins on mainstream terrestrial channels remain by far the most important and trusted source of news'.[2] Twenty-four-hour news channels did not change the style of news. The presentation of news bulletins varied over time, but the content of the news remained unusually stable.

Popular newspapers faced a relentless and demanding market. As internet use gathered pace, it became steadily harder for daily and Sunday 'redtops' to find enough material of distinctive value that their readers wanted. Profits remained high at *The Sun* and the *Daily Mail* at the turn of the century, but cuts in newsroom costs were thinning the staff of their weaker competitors. The *Daily Mail* prospered relatively well by mixing judicious quantities of political reporting, empathetic lifestyle advice and celebrity coverage. But for papers such as *The Sun* or *The Mirror* or their Sunday sisters, the opportunities to stand out were shrinking. The breezy, swaggering arrogance of the 1960s gradually gave way to something more besieged and conspiratorial. The culture of these newsrooms turned inward.

Despite the Leveson Inquiry, much is yet to be revealed about how law-breaking on an allegedly wide scale was carried out at *The Sun* and the *News of the World*. The Leveson Inquiry in its first phase avoided all detailed questions of individual action and responsibility that could arise in criminal trials, which might last several years. But it is possible to say a few things about the characteristics of newsrooms that have bent once-fine ideas about journalism out of shape.

Reporting involves morally unattractive activities. At the least, most reporters are trying to persuade people to breach their obligations to someone or something by divulging confidences. Deception of sources is hardly rare. The overall scale of this is impossible to measure, but reporters on mass-readership papers routinely pay small sums for information. That much is obvious even to someone like this writer who has never worked in a popular newspaper's newsroom. Many journalists would recoil at this description, but reporters and editors live in a realm of frequent moral choice. The issue they face most often is: do the ends justify the means?

In some newsrooms, this question stopped being asked or never had been posed. What happened in some newsrooms where the hacking of phones and computers, and bribery, apparently became, if not well-known or normal, at least frequent? The deterioration had many dimensions and causes. They include:

- Misuse of the myths of journalism. Shortly before the *News of the World* was closed, three cricketers from the Pakistan national squad and a bookmaker were jailed for match-fixing and bribery. Their crime had been exposed by the newspaper in a classic investigative sting, impeccably executed. The potential audience was global and huge, the matter was serious, the detail legally sound and the style of presentation characteristically loud. The deception involved using undercover reporters and covert video, which had been used to get information that could not have been obtained by overt means. Popular journalism, the newspaper could rightly claim, at its best. The problem was that this strand of the paper's good investigative work was used to justify almost-routine journalism that did not share its qualities or defence. In this respect, executives at the *News of the World* spun a misleading story, which they came to believe themselves but which in the end failed to convince the rest of the world. The clearest put-down was delivered at the Leveson Inquiry by Deputy Assistant Commissioner Sue Akers of the Metropolitan Police, who led the three-pronged investigation into phone hacking, computer interception and bribery. In an interim report to the inquiry, she acknowledged that judgements about possible public interest defences for journalism would be made by prosecutors and the courts. She added:

> What I can indicate, however, is that the vast majority of the disclosures that have been made and which have led to the stories we are currently investigating can best be described as salacious gossip.
>
> They often involve... an invasion into the privacy of the subject(s) of the newspaper article.[3]

- A developing privacy law in Britain, developing from the Human Rights Act of 1998, was having some effect on popular newspaper reporting. But the effect was slow, the judgements were hard to predict because the law was broadly drawn, and only rich complainants could afford to use it. The self-regulation system operated by the Press Complaints Commission (PCC) had little or no effect in these newsrooms. In the early 1990s, the major press groups had defeated an earlier proposal for a privacy law. They had done this by apparently toughening the industry's own regulator: one of these measures had been the inclusion of the code of conduct into journalists' contracts of employment. This sounds like a practical step, but of course depends completely on the employer's attitude to journalists who break the rules. The affable Conservative peer then chairing the PCC, Lord Wakeham, told the Leveson Inquiry that this reform had meant that the PCC could refer breaches of the code by journalists to their employer. He mentioned as an example a severe judgement passed on a newspaper that had photographed a celebrity aristocrat in the grounds of a private clinic where she was receiving treatment.

    The paper was the *News of the World* and its editor then was Piers Morgan, who had indeed been publicly reprimanded by its owner Rupert Murdoch. Morgan's diary, published years later, gives his side of the story. Leveson juxtaposes an extract from Morgan's book with Wakeham's claim that the new sanction had worked. Leveson observes drily in his report that the two versions are 'somewhat different'. According to Morgan, his 'reprimand' had taken the form of Murdoch saying 'I'm sorry about all that press complaining thingamajig.' In case anyone misunderstood, Morgan later explained to Leveson that Murdoch 'did not give a toss' about the PCC. Murdoch, in his own evidence, said he did not recall speaking that way. Leveson prefers Morgan's version over Wakeham's: that section of the report is headed 'The sanctions did not bite'.[4]

- Over a long period of time, reporting a 'story' became a closed and not open process. A tip given or a disclosure sold to a newspaper was not the starting point for an open look at what had happened. News editors, short of both time and reporters, came to instruct writers to go out and 'make this story work'. This was by no means confined to popular newsrooms. This kind of instruction can have a benign meaning: if this story turns out to be true, let's tell it convincingly. But the ambiguity of the requirement to 'make a story work' can easily go wrong and become: justify this claim any way you can and irrespective of what or how much you know. Well before worse things occurred, many news editors had lost sight of the distinction between testing the evidence for a claim and justifying a headline they could already see in their heads.

- Private information about celebrities became a tradeable commodity with a market setting prices and brokers emerging to negotiate between people with information to sell, most often 'kiss-and-tell', and newspapers. In a pre-internet era in which celebrity in sports and entertainment was mesmerizing ever-larger numbers of people, this was the information that came closest to being distinctive for popular newspapers. Television was too heavily regulated to compete. Reporters and editors were so dependent on demolishing the idea of privacy that they became specialists in extracting legally safe publishable revelations that the famous did not want revealed. They extended this technique to people who weren't famous at all or who had no choice about their temporary fame.

- All newsrooms limit debate and discussion to a degree. The daily operational requirements of news make that a practical necessity. In popular newsrooms this went much further. A reporter, usually starting as a casual reporter on what amounts to a long audition without any security of tenure, will not try to offend a newsdesk. Renegade *Daily Star* reporter Richard Peppiatt says:

  > In my years spent in tabloid newsrooms I strain to remember a single instance in which discussion over content included empathetic consideration on the subject of the coverage, be it celebrity or simply someone in the public eye.[5]

- This indifference gradually became industrial. Smaller-scale invasions of privacy became normal. An anonymous red-top executive who said that 'lots' of journalists were hacking phones described the climate:

It was quite normal practice. When you have your editor shouting at you to get a story, you lose your morality. If you need to get a story and everyone else is doing it, you think that's normal.[6]

- Competitors drifted from what was legally ambiguous towards dark arts that were clearly against the law. If private detectives could 'blag' ex-directory phone numbers, they could use their professional skills and contacts to do more. Sunday newspaper newsrooms in particular are secretive places: scoops must be preserved from rivals till publication day at the end of the week. Sections of these newsrooms became secret societies operating in a world where lack of regulation and vague legal boundaries gave plenty of freedom to manoeuvre. Politicians even got used to living with it. Kenneth Clarke, on becoming Chancellor of the Exchequer in 1993, said:

    ... I had to move my bank account because my bank complained to me that journalists were trying to bribe the staff of the village branch where I had my bank account. It would have been regarded as perfectly customary in those days.[7]

With the advantage of hindsight and with the advantage of the evidence given to the Leveson Inquiry, it seems extraordinary that people could defend the aspects they could not conceal and could expect to keep secret what they could not justify. One of the noisy figures of post-war popular journalism, Hugh Cudlipp of the *Daily Mirror*, thought that something basic had changed in the 1980s. 'It was the dawn of the dark ages of tabloid journalism,' Cudlipp said, 'when the proprietors and editors – not all, but most – decided that playing a continuing role in public enlightenment was no longer the business of the popular press... when investigative journalism in the public interest shed its integrity and became intrusive journalism for the prurient.'[8]

Journalists at *The Sun*, the *Mirror's* nemesis, would probably have replied that what Cudlipp minded about was being beaten at his own game. But Cudlipp was right: something important had changed.

Operation Motorman

The two decades that preceded the phone-hacking scandal in Britain were marked by frequent tensions over privacy, regulation and the concentration of media ownership. But throughout that period both Conservative and Labour governments avoided outright confrontation with the major press groups. A Conservative government appointed a judge, Sir David Calcutt, to examine privacy issues. Calcutt reported in 1990 that the self-regulation system should be strengthened and that if it did not work to better protect individual privacy, then a privacy law should be passed. Calcutt duly reported three years later that the press's own regulation system was not working well enough and that privacy legislation was needed. Government ministers, already struggling with a very small majority in Parliament and facing minatory lobbying from media owners, shied away and shelved the issue.

Concern and resentment among victims of press misbehaviour grew slowly but were not easily voiced or heard, given that in the 1990s few newspapers wanted to take up the issue and there were few alternative ways to ventilate complaints. The PCC, heavily influenced by editors and paid for by the big press groups, issued criticisms in measured terms but had no sanctions for those who were prepared to suffer measured criticism and then carry on as before. Some newspapers were slow and reluctant to correct mistakes or issue apologies, which were often obscurely placed on inside pages of the paper. Providing that these issues did not come to a head and politicians continued to avoid confrontation, nothing was likely to change. Public pressure to address the issues did not exist. People continued to tell researchers who asked them that they did not trust what they read in mass-circulation newspapers. But they continued to buy them, albeit in gently falling numbers.

On two occasions before the phone-hacking scandal brought this to a head, scandal was so effectively muffled that no explosion occurred. In 2003 investigators working for the new Information Commissioner's Office (ICO), set up under new law to protect the privacy of computerized data, raided the office of a private detective, Steve Whittamore. The raid followed wider police investigations into what was growing into a thriving underground trade in personal information held on large databases. Whittamore was a meticulous record-keeper and his notebooks contained between 13,000 and 17,000 requests for information from newspapers, mostly in the period 2000–03. Almost every national newspaper had used Whittamore or his associates at least once. Ninety-one journalists from the *Daily Mail* and *Mail on Sunday* had requested 1,218 pieces of information.[9] The kind of information they were after included private addresses, ex-directory phone numbers, phone numbers of families and friends and criminal record checks. Whittamore operated a sliding scale of prices ranging from £17.50 charged for finding an address from the electoral roll to £750 for the details of a mobile phone account. Not all his research was against the law, but most was.

In 2006, the Information Commissioner Richard Thomas published two reports on what had been found:

> At a time when senior members of the press were publicly congratulating themselves for having raised journalistic standards across the industry, many newspapers were continuing to subscribe to an undercover economy devoted to obtaining a wealth of personal information forbidden to them by law.[10]

The prosecution of Whittamore fizzled out. The ICO managed to persuade itself that it did not have the clout to prosecute journalists, despite being clearly advised that they had broken the law and that few had any possible public interest defence. The ICO passed the problem to the PCC, which said little. It did say, however, that it could not actually do anything. Powerful newspapers, led by News International and the *Daily Mail*, lobbied Prime Minister Gordon Brown hard and successfully to ensure that the law was not stiffened to include prison sentences for the misuse of private data. Lord Leveson later concluded that prosecutions might have been a 'turning point for the good' and that if they had happened, phone hacking might not have been attempted on the same scale.

Phone hacking

Operation Motorman illustrated the extent to which some newspapers were now routinely dependent on low-level law breaking for everyday reporting. But that was not the full extent of the trouble. In 2006, Scotland Yard officers investigated a complaint from Buckingham Palace after a mysteriously sourced story about a knee injury suffered by Prince William. They swiftly arrested the royal correspondent of the *News of the World*, Clive Goodman, and a private detective, Glen Mulcaire. They also seized Mulcaire's notebooks. Mulcaire, who was paid as much as £100,000 per year for his services, had suspected that the newspaper might try to avoid paying the full fees for all his work and so he had recorded every assignment he was given. These events lit the fuse for a detonation that did not occur until five years later.

Goodman and Mulcaire were convicted of hacking voicemail messages. There was confusion among both police officers and journalists about exactly what the law prohibited. All we have learnt since tells us that, at least then, it was extraordinarily easy to hack voicemail messages and many reporters did it. Detectives investigating Goodman and Mulcaire discovered that the mobile phone companies were unaware of how easy it was to hack voicemails and how widespread the practice probably was. In newsrooms where there were few or no rules, technology offered a new opportunity to proof stories against complaint and to pick up tips. The full extent of voicemail hacking probably won't ever be established, but it clearly went very well beyond Goodman, Mulcaire and other journalists at the *News of the World*. Piers Morgan joked about it in front of outside guests at a boardroom lunch at the *Mirror*. It was a secret in plain view to many.

News International insisted that Goodman was a 'rogue' reporter and went to expensive lengths to settle with claimants who began to suspect that their voicemails had been hacked. A parliamentary inquiry suggested that the full truth had not emerged. The PCC stood on the sidelines. In 2009, *The Guardian* reported the details of some of the larger settlements, which suggested that the company had been prepared to pay hundreds of thousands of pounds to ensure that the claimants didn't talk about what had happened, and that the police held a few thousand names of people whose phones might have been hacked. The *New York Times* followed soon after with a lengthy investigation, which added more detail suggesting that the full truth was still hidden. The rest of the media were reluctant to touch the story. The police looked back at their material and said that they would not revisit their decision to stop their inquiries. The PCC criticized *The Guardian* for its reporting. Sympathy for the hacking victims was limited by the fact that they all seemed to be people who had chosen to be in the public eye.

'Quality' and 'seriousness'

Phone hacking was the public drama, but carelessness over privacy was not the only charge laid at the door of the national press. Many of these arguments reflected a paradox: the media in general and national newspapers in particular remained influential – at least on politicians – but editors and journalists continued to see themselves in 19th-century terms as the likely victims of attempts to suppress their liberties. By the time that the Leveson Inquiry began in 2011, editors of national newspapers were also painfully conscious that the economic foundation of their influence was fading.

Serious newspapers faced recurrent charges – as they have throughout their history – that they were 'dumbing down'. As circulations and the value of advertising declined, editors had to do more with less. Readership in the fiercely competitive national market could not be taken for granted. Readers could not only read more specialized material from all over the world on the web but could choose from a range of magazines expanding in almost every developed market in the world. Newspapers changed, lost some expertise and poise, but they were in many respects better than ever. But the changes in wider information were increasing the competition at a faster rate than any improvements. When *The Guardian* measured the content in various parts of *The Times* and compared 1968 with 2000, it found that the extent of the coverage was the same or larger in every department in 2000, save for a small decline in political coverage.[11] The largest increases were in features, womens' pages and arts. These proportions would probably have been the same for any quality newspaper across the same period.

The never-resolved debate about dumbing down was fuelled by the increase in public media literacy. The media, in the broad definition of news, entertainment, music and advertising, was becoming a sizeable segment of the British economy and advertisers could be attracted to more detailed coverage of journalism and entertainment. Media studies courses multiplied in schools and universities. Owners such as Rupert Murdoch, Robert Maxwell and Conrad Black, although wielding less power over politicians than the Rothermeres and Beaverbrooks of an earlier era, were rich and powerful enough to supply many column inches of tycoon watching. With the expansion of universities in the 1990s, media studies courses grew fast and likewise the academic study of journalism. All media businesses were adjusting to greater transparency, generated both by greater curiosity and more ways to gratify it. Journalism had once been something done in private and unveiled once a day or once a week. Media businesses were no different to any other large organizations that were getting used to being more visible, more commented on and more closely inspected by a digital audience that was more fragmented and harder to influence. Not all the unedifying discoveries thus made about the media were about bad or criminal behaviour on popular papers.

Phone hacking distressed its victims, but did not put children at risk of serious illness or even death. The reporting of the measles, mumps and rubella (MMR) vaccine did exactly that. As a scandal, however, it lacks the drama and villains of the tabloid press. The villain is something called 'false equivalency'.

Andrew Wakefield, a doctor later exposed as an inept researcher and fraud, claimed in 1998 that there might be a link between autism and the triple vaccine given to most British children and widely used in the rest of the world. It took 10 years for the *British Medical Journal* formally to retract its original publication of the claim. By that time the claim had been demolished by extensive studies, which showed no causal link at all. But by that time, vaccination rates had fallen dangerously. They had fallen because the media treatment of the subject had given credence to Wakefield's claims. Journalists were reluctant to go into reverse and admit that the claims might be implausible. Both Wakefield and his critics were given equivalent standing on a 'level playing field'. The romantic idea of a brave dissident doctor standing up to a stuffy medical establishment was too good to resist.

At the height of the crisis, a poll showed that 60 per cent of the British public thought – wrongly – that doctors were divided about MMR. Vaccination rates stayed above 90 per cent in the United States, where Wakefield's claims received much less press coverage. In Britain as a whole, vaccination uptake fell from 92 per cent to 80 per cent. Measles cases rose from 56 in 1998 to 1,370 in 2008. Almost 15 years after Wakefield's claims made in 1998, the numbers of children in Britain taking the jab had recovered, returning to above 90 per cent in 2012. Remarkably, there was no rise in death rates.[12]

Measles outbreaks occurred in South Wales in 2009 and 2013. In the latter outbreak one adult died. In 1997, the *South Wales Evening Post* had run a particularly vocal campaign giving full voice to parents who believed that the vaccine had damaged their children. Local vaccination rates fell further than in most of England or the rest of Wales. By 2013, the newspaper was treading very carefully. The good intention of impartiality had gone horribly wrong – and it had gone wrong in publications of quality just as much as in others. Even *Private Eye*, in a rare, extended *mea culpa*, admitted that it had given Wakefield the benefit of the doubt for far too long.[13]

In a world with crowded, competing media, the bigger the story, the greater the premium on having something different. Once competition reached a certain point, the need to have something different would, for some newspapers, trump any other consideration.

The full story of the disappearance of three-year-old Madeleine McCann from a holiday resort in Portugal in the spring of 2007 cannot yet be written – either as a crime or as a media morality tale. Madeleine's fate remains unknown. But the reporting of her disappearance did cause an unusually large number of journalists to wonder why a collective hysteria – which went well beyond red-top papers – had taken hold with the strength that it did. The appeal of the story is not hard to explain: Madeleine was a photogenic toddler and her parents were skilful at generating a global campaign to have her found. The BBC presented its main evening bulletin from Portugal at the height of the story. Some of the coverage, probably a minority of the vast total, was libellous, cruel, xenophobic and dishonest. Lord

Leveson's inquiry report analyses the McCann coverage in some detail and he came to two conclusions: 'If ever there were an example of a story which ran totally out of control, this is one... Not merely was the rigorous search for the truth the first principle to be sacrificed but also was any respect for the dignity, privacy and wellbeing of the McCanns.'[14] Leveson quotes with approval a judgement from the parliamentary committee on the media, which said that there had been a 'collective breakdown': 'The industry's words and actions suggest a desire to bury the affair without confronting its serious implications – a kind of avoidance which newspapers would criticise mercilessly, and rightly, if it occurred in any other part of society.'[15]

The *Daily Star* and *Daily Express* were eventually and successfully sued by the McCanns for suggesting, among other things, that the McCanns had killed their own daughter, that they had sold Madeleine into slavery and hidden her body in a freezer. Express Newspapers offered no defence when the case reached court and paid damages of £500,000 to the McCanns. Giving evidence to Leveson, the newspapers' proprietor Richard Desmond, who had withdrawn his newspapers from the PCC, admitted that 'we did do wrong'. But he saw no reason to strengthen regulation: '... I mean what are we trying to do in this country? Are we trying to kill the whole country with every bit of legislation and every bit of nonsense?'[16] Desmond's evidence to Leveson, a truly extraordinary moment in the hearings, made clear that not only did the *Express* proprietor not take the inquiry seriously but that he was quite uninterested in any discussion of whether newspapers ought to be truthful.

The McCann coverage was a study in innuendo. A British resident in Portugal, Robert Murat, won £600,000 from several newspapers over claims that suggested he had something to do with Madeleine's disappearance. His mother, partner, daughter and ex-wife had all been under siege. The experience, Murat said afterwards, came close to 'destroying' his life. Reporters never openly accused Murat of being involved in the crime but variously described him as an oddball with one eye (he has a detached retina) who had been pining for his daughter since his divorce and who had mysterious friends and an underfloor chamber at his house. *The Times* columnist Matthew Parris, laissez-faire in his outlook on media matters, listed the innuendo in detail and summed up:

> Though 'innocent until proved guilty' is a counsel of perfection, and though it is sometimes impossible to write useful reports without fingering guilty and innocent alike, there are still limits – cloudy though they must necessarily be. Reporting in this case has smashed right through them.

The whole disgusting business, the whole media-driven infatuation with this little girl and her parents, the whole sick, morbid, sentimental campaign of news generation and news manipulation, has been a disgrace to the British media.[17]

Looking back, the desperation of news media fearful of losing their hold on readers and viewers becomes clearer. The story was so big that it held the promise, at least for popular newspapers, of suspending decline. Driving the McCann story for all it was worth allowed editors to forget that the ground was moving under their feet. Competition, the sheer quantity of information and proliferating sources and opportunities to sample it demolished assumptions that had lasted for decades about how journalism should be done. There was no longer a small oligarchy of media outlets, a small cluster of national newspapers and a handful of TV channels, which overlapped to produce an agenda of public information.

The proliferation of new sources of news, new routes down which discussions of news could travel, more ways of comparing news were all creating a more sceptical body of readers and particularly of younger readers. A small guerrilla army of people armed with the means to puncture press claims came into existence. The documentary *Starsuckers* (2009) duped several newspapers into running – and embellishing – wholly fictional stories. At the time of the Leveson hearings, one of these stories was still on *The Sun*'s website. Full Fact, a small organization dedicated to pointing out reporting errors, faked a Facebook page, which claimed that the prime minister's new cat had been stolen from a London housing estate. The *Daily Mail*, told that the story they had printed was a hoax, refused to correct it.[18]

Online innovations posed particularly acute dilemmas at the BBC, where rules about how news should be done had to adapt. Leading correspondents started to give commentary on the facts of news, reflecting anxieties about the limited usefulness of only balanced facts (particularly if they must be illustrated with pictures) and a need to provide interpretation through large quantities of information available. That innovation extended to allowing senior correspondents to write blogs and to microblog on Twitter, which were limited to the style of commentary opinion on air. But these channels for opinion required strict supervision and self-discipline if they were not to breach the BBC's rules. The broadcast in 2003 on BBC Radio 4's *Today* programme, which began the chain of events leading to the death of Dr David Kelly and the subsequent Hutton Inquiry, revealed what could happen when this delicate balancing act – between attracting attention in a changed system of communications and holding trust – failed.

Andrew Gilligan, the reporter who made the first claim that the government had 'sexed up' a published dossier warning about the development of weapons of mass destruction in Iraq, embellished the information he'd had from Dr Kelly. Gilligan had been brought to the programme particularly to provide attention-getting scoops. Gilligan later claimed that subsequent discoveries had vindicated his claim of deception by the Blair government, but the claim could not be substantiated at the time of the government's attack on the BBC just after the broadcast. After the Hutton Inquiry, the BBC apologized and its chairman, director-general and Gilligan all resigned.

The BBC's difficulties over Kelly, and later over their failure to report on the entertainer and charity worker Jimmy Savile, illustrate that new conditions make trust harder to establish. Savile, openly accused only after his death of the sexual abuse of children over many years, had been a powerful star in his day. The cost of protecting his reputation as an audience-getter by ignoring rumours about his behaviour came in a later crisis of trust. In a survey in 2011, the BBC was rated as the most trusted news provider and the top four places were all taken by television news.[19] But even given that high level of trust, the prevailing scepticism about media has involved the corporation in multiple internal inquiries, all of which are designed to demonstrate to a public – more sceptical and more inclined to demand transparency – that it can be trusted to be accountable.

Trust and authority

Greater acquaintance with, and curiosity about, the news media can be called 'media literacy'. But what this really means is an increase in ways of seeing the news, a proliferating number of angles from which to judge it, and filters through which it can be seen. The big institutions of the media can influence how their output is seen, but they can no longer control that message. Consumers of news have too many points of comparison (just visit Google News for a few seconds); the media don't control what is taught in media studies and they cannot suppress comedians making fun of the mannerisms of news. Where there was once only *Private Eye* mocking Fleet Street's mannerisms and foibles, there are now a hundred bloggers, not all so forgiving or indulgent. Tens of thousands of people follow a blog called Fleet Street Fox, written for some years anonymously from inside a tabloid newsroom by reporter Susie Boniface. Scandals of invention, plagiarism and unethical behaviour have not been confined to the popular press. In the past decade, embarrassments have been revealed at CBS News, *Le Monde*, *The Independent*, the *New York Times* and *USA Today*. Many newspapers suffered in a more diffuse way either for believing too easily in government claims about weapons of mass destruction in Iraq or being reluctant to accept the scientific consensus on global warming.

Comedians such as John Stewart of the *The Daily Show* in the United States and Rory Bremner or Charlie Brooker in Britain are no longer marginal to how people see 'news'. Stewart has made it his business to parody and tease the argumentative talking heads of the cable news industry, which he calls the country's '24-hour, politico-pundit perpetual panic "conflict-inator".' In the 2004 US presidential election, 21 per cent of 18–29 year olds cited television comedy as a means by which they 'regularly learned' about the campaign.[20] A 2002 survey in the UK found that almost 40 per cent of respondents named comedy shows (such as Bremner or *Have I Got News For You*) as a way they learnt about news. The most frequently named source – ahead of TV news – was 'word of mouth'.[21]

Above all, people looking at news tend to swap and shift between platforms and outlets. The number of people who get news only from the internet has never risen above 10 per cent in Britain. But when asked their 'primary' source of news, respondents give a picture that suggests they have already shifted some distance from print-centred allegiances. In Britain 40 per cent call the internet their first source of national news; in France, 32 per cent, Germany 31 per cent and the United States 46 per cent.[22] Many of these users are, of course, visiting the websites of traditional news organizations, such as BBC Online. But given the infrequency of most visits to news sites and the prevalence of visits via search engines, people are now quite used to multiple perspectives on news – and to sharing news on social networks. We have left the stage when it was possible for a small number of dominant news organizations to set the agenda and the template of what is news, as they did in the past. There are too many new routes for news to travel and more people generating opinions on it.

Many surveys show that trust in news media and journalists is falling. These surveys almost all also show that respect and trust in public institutions such as universities, the church, Parliament and politicians is also falling, while trust in friends, family and work colleagues holds steady.[23] It would be more useful in this age to ask what outlets for news information people feel they can rely on and what value they think they get. There are two aspects of these surveys worth noting: suspicion of the press is markedly worse than any expressed about broadcast news, and young people are more likely to think media sources to be biased. One survey found that the belief that all media sources are biased had grown among the 18–34 age group in the UK between 2006 and 2011.[24] Research in the United States among the same age group compared the images of different news sources such as newspapers, cable, network, local TV news and internet. Newspapers came last when judged on trustworthiness, being up to date, offering 'news I can use', being a useful way to learn or being entertaining.[25]

Falls in trust levels can be healthy: they mean that people are not blindly trusting a single newspaper, magazine or channel but are taking in information about the media from multiple sources.[26] They no longer see the news media as a closed club of professionals playing a game with the political world, a game whose rules are understood by the players but not by the audience. It is impossible to underestimate, over time, the importance to news media consumers of the extension of choice. A 2009 study of trust found that few users of news any longer stuck to a single medium or outlet but swung between 'useful' (often local) news and 'amusing' news. They did not so much mistrust what they were told was happening as much as feel that journalists were indifferent to what they wanted and needed to know. Journalists were described as 'too close to power, preoccupied by a narrow range of interests and somehow frightened of letting the public set its own agenda'. As the study found:

> When distrust in the news was expressed... it was because people felt that
> their expectations of news were not shared by news producers; that they were
> being told stories that were not adequately explained; that their lives were
> being reported in ways that were not adequately researched; or that new
> communications spaces were opening up in which useful, reliable or amusing
> information could be accessed without having to subscribe to the authority of
> the mainstream media.[27]

A spell is broken

Criticism of some parts of the written press grew slowly but steadily. Dependence on printed papers as a sources of news reduced. The cumulative result was disengagement with newspapers. Commentators, think tanks and a small number of politicians had complained for years about the undue concentration of newspaper ownership in the hands of Rupert Murdoch, the behaviour of some newspapers and the feebleness of the PCC. Voices were raised to say that the worst effect of a poor press was to corrode faith in public life and civic virtue.

Tony Blair, stepping down as prime minister in 2007, appealed to the news media to consider the long-term effects of their relentless pressure on politics, describing media hunting packs as 'feral beasts'. This was criticism that Blair, one of the most successful and persuasive politicians of his era, had not dared to put in such terms until he was no longer running for office. The paparazzi chase in Paris on the night of Princess Diana's death in 1997 imprinted in the public mind an image of mobile, ruthless predators. An infant privacy law had only a modest effect in Britain, which was not the only country to debate this. In the 1990s, Australian judges developed a tort of unjustified invasion of privacy. The European Court of Human Rights also handed down increasingly restrictive judgements on the scope of reporting and photography of the famous.

Scholars such as Onora O'Neill in Britain and James Carey in the United States were quietly pointing out that most laws and policies based on the idea of 'press freedom' had been forged in an age of small-scale community or political printed media. A television age that concentrated media power into fewer hands, and an internet age that distributed the power to publish to thousands, might require these principles to be rethought or adapted to new realities. Large-scale corporate media (or bloggers with agendas) were not designed to ensure that the contest between truth and falsehood envisaged by John Milton or John Stuart Mill would always be won by truth. Readers and audiences, they argued, needed ways of assessing the accuracy of what they read and watched – and better guarantees of plural ownership. The marketplace of ideas and the economic marketplace for communications power are no longer the same thing.

One writer talked about the 'illimitable prurience of British newspapers, and their ruthless, sanctimonious targeting of public figures' and the intention of their journalists 'to deny or nullify any authority other than their own: to discredit specialised expertise, disinterested professionalism, educational superiority, technical precision...'[28] Journalism, wrote the columnist Polly Toynbee in 2003, has become incurious about any problem that cannot be blamed on a hapless minister: 'The trouble is that a generation of young journalists know nothing else, bred on the idea that attack is the only sign of journalistic integrity – all politicians are villains, all journalists their natural predators, or else toadies or lackeys.'[29] Others claimed that the British political system had been handed over to the manipulation of the Murdoch family.[30] The counter-arguments defending the popular newspapers against these charges said that to accuse tabloid journalists of lacking a sense of responsibility was missing the point. A robust, vigorous (and, alright, occasionally inaccurate and unpleasant) press was essential to shine light in dark places and to keep politicians and the powerful frightened of exposure. This unresolved and timeless quarrel was transformed by a piece of journalism that broke on the world on 5 July 2011.

On that day, two *Guardian* reporters revealed that one of the phones hacked by Glen Mulcaire on behalf of the *News of the World* had been the one owned by Milly Dowler, a 13-year-old schoolgirl who had disappeared in 2002 and was later found murdered. The story also claimed, wrongly as it later turned out, that Mulcaire had deleted voicemail messages on the phone, giving Milly's parents false hope that their daughter was alive.

This disclosure turned the media world upside down. The police claims that they had no need to reinvestigate phone hacking were rendered absurd: a massive, eventually three-pronged inquiry into phone hacking, computer hacking and bribery began. The Leveson Inquiry, with very broad terms of reference, was set up. News Corporation, besides going through one of the worst public disgraces to ever hit a major public company, was forced to withdraw its bid to buy the remaining shares (it already owned 39 per cent) in Sky TV. Rupert Murdoch and his son, James, made unprecedented appearances before both Leveson and a parliamentary inquiry. The *News of the World* was abruptly shut.

Until that point, newspaper buyers did not necessarily trust what they read and they were more sceptical of popular papers. But they gave cautious credence to the idea that tabloid newspapers, for all their obvious defects, kept powerful people under inspection. The Dowler revelations, and the inquiry that followed, lifted the lid and revealed the cost of the public's tolerance – and changed the game.

Notes

1   http://gawker.com/5918519/the-de+watergating-of-american-journalism (accessed 7.2.13).

2   Barnett, S, Ramsay, G and Gaber, I (2012) 'From Callaghan to Credit Crunch; Changing trends in British television news 1975–2009', Universities of Westminster and Bedfordshire.

3   DAC Akers, second statement to Leveson Inquiry, February 2012, www.levesoninquiry.org.

4   Leveson Report, p. 1556, section 6.55–56.

5   http://www.guardian.co.uk/media/greenslade/2012/mar/09/phone-hacking-richard-peppiatt (accessed 9.213).

6   Interviewed by Dominic Ponsford of *UK Press Gazette* and quoted in Brock, G (2010) 'Road to regaining the high ground', *British Journalism Review*, vol 21, no 4.

7 Leveson Report, p. 1423, 5.2.

8 Address at the funeral of Sydney Jacobson, 1988.

9 Transactions and clients are summarized in table E3.1, p. 267, Leveson Report.

10 Information Commissioner's Office (2006) *What price privacy?*, London.

11 Alan Rusbridger, *The Guardian*, 4 November 2000.

12 **www.parliament.uk/briefing-papers/sn02581.pdf.**

13 *Private Eye*, 5 February 2010.

14 Leveson Report, p. 550, 3.12.

15 Leveson Report, p. 555, 3.34.

16 Leveson Inquiry hearings transcripts, 12 January 2012.

17 *The Times*, 25 August 2007.

18 Leveson Report, p. 678, 9.18–21 and p. 713, 12.20.

19 Ipsos MORI survey, November 2011, 963 UK adults 16+. Reported in *The Times*, 6 January 2012.

20 Peters, C (2013) in Peters, C and Broersma, M J (eds) (2013) *Rethinking Journalism: Trust and Participation in a Transformed News Landscape*, Routledge, Abingdon.

21 Hargreaves, I and Thomas, J (2002) *New news, old news*, Independent Television Commission/Broadcasting Standards Commission, London.

22 Fabio Curtin Millet (2011) Google presentation at City University, London.

23 See for example 'Sources of Influence' in *The Changing Face of News, Future Foundation* (2001) or Barnett (2008) 'On the road to self-destruction', *British Journalism Review*, vol 19, no 2.

24 Natterman, P (2011) *Deadlines or Dead Ends? The Future of News in the Digital Age*, McKinsey & Co, New York.

25 Brown, M (2005) *Abandoning the News*, Carnegie Corporation, New York.

26 See Schudson in Peters and Broersma, *Rethinking Journalism*.

27 Coleman, Stephen, Scott, Anthony and Morrison, David (2009) *Public Trust in the News*, RISJ, Oxford.

28 Davenport-Hines, Richard, *Times Literary Supplement*, 28 October 2005.

29 *The Guardian*, 5 September 2003.

30 See Anthony Barnett, 'Murdoch and the Big Lie', OpenDemocracy, 4.5.12. **www.opendemocracy.net** (accessed 20.5.13).

The Leveson judgement

08

> *Nothing is more common with printers, especially of newspapers, than the continual cry of Liberty of the Press, as if because they are printers they are to have more privileges than other people.*
>
> **TOM PAINE,** *LIBERTY OF THE PRESS,* **1806**

> *I cannot, and will not, recommend another last chance saloon for the press.*
>
> **LORD LEVESON,** *REPORT OF THE INQUIRY INTO THE CULTURE, PRACTICE AND ETHICS OF THE PRESS,* **2012**

Public inquiries achieve a great deal before they ever report and recommend. They act as valves, receptacles and platforms for a wide range of information, denunciation, defence and argument that has not had wide exposure or examination. It was not a coincidence that around the time of the Leveson Inquiry in Britain there were major inquiries into the news media, law and accountability in Australia, New Zealand and South Africa. Each had a different starting point but all overlapped in their essential themes.

From the beginning, Leveson saw his job in clear historical terms: he would not repeat the mistakes of the past. He described himself, in the opening pages of his report, as standing at the end of a long 60-year-old tradition of inquiries – three royal commissions and two others into privacy – none of which had quite managed to tackle the real issues. Leveson knew that his prescription for press regulation in the future would be controversial and its implementation in the hands of politicians. He analyses in his report the reasons why the government of the day in 1993 had never acted on the advice of the second inquiry by Sir David Calcutt to enact a privacy law.[1]

So Leveson deliberately wrote a different kind of report. Previous inquiries had produced distilled judgements written in the impersonal style of judges and of the civil servants who help them. Leveson seems to have wanted to leave his mark on the issues in the form of a very detailed history. He sat for 97 days over eight months and heard 474 witnesses and took written evidence from many more. His report runs to 1,780 pages in four printed volumes and weighs 10 kilograms.[2] It amounts to a historical record of some importance. Leveson was angry about what he found and, despite the careful legal language in his report, he wanted readers to see why.

Diagnosis

Leveson described the events that had led to the inquiry as 'the greatest crisis in public confidence in information privacy since the creation of the data protection regime'.[3] He linked that crisis to a long and successful lobbying campaign by several press groups, which had weakened attempts to make journalism accountable to regulation and law. He saw it as his task to show that decisive action had to be taken and that it had to be designed to be proof against the sabotage or undermining that had taken place in the past. Slaying what Leveson saw as the monstrous power of the major press companies was the theme that overshadowed everything else.

Most news media in democracies operate under restraints of some kind. The amount of restraint differs according to the position chosen between two different philosophies. At one end of the spectrum lies the ideas drawn from the First Amendment to the American constitution: not only in favour of freedom of expression but explicitly prohibiting legislators from making law that could interfere with that freedom. At the other are broadly European ideas that aim to balance rights and obligations. Leveson placed himself firmly in the rights-and-obligations camp. His report quotes with approval academics who say or imply that First Amendment freedoms, written more than two centuries ago and in the specific conditions of a newly independent country with a vociferous printed press, may not be the ideal guide to journalism standards now. He wanted to strike a blow against what he thought was a warped and self-serving misuse of the idea of 'press freedom'. His report as a whole argues that press freedom is not the same as editors and journalists justifying their conduct to each other with no external inspection or check on the ethics of those decisions. He was sure, and said repeatedly, that some newspapers have acted as if they had no ethical or moral obligations at all, despite having proclaimed them in codes of conduct, which are ignored in practice. The theme of hypocrisy over proclaiming high standards and carrying out low practices recurs throughout his report.

Leveson placed the responsibility for this on the culture in certain newsrooms. His technique was granular: he accumulated evidence, drew a quick conclusion and moved on to pile up another example. His running commentary has several themes. He found that when intrusive papers are caught or criticized, no reflection and no consequences follow. A court case involving the *News of the World* revealed a reporter from the newspaper doing something that was 'tantamount to blackmail'. Nothing happened afterwards. Leveson was astonished to hear that Clive Goodman expected to continue to work at the *News of the World* after he had served his prison sentence for phone hacking.[4] Goodman was, in fact, sacked but Leveson underlined that even the assumption that work might be found for him is striking.

The long denial by *News of the World* and News International executives that anyone other than Goodman and Mulcaire knew about the hacking was maintained until 2011 when three members of the newspaper's staff were arrested. By the end of the Leveson Inquiry, the police had identified 6,349 potential victims of hacking, including 54 former or current MPs. The activity inside the newsroom, Leveson recorded, was all about containing legal risks and damage limitation. Internal 'inquiries' were not conducted to discover what had happened. Leveson recorded his bewilderment that neither the editor of the *Daily Express* or the *Daily Mail* were at all repentant about the coverage of the McCanns.[5] In short, the only power that the press (mostly) fails to hold to account is the power it holds itself:

> There is no organized profession, trade or industry in which the serious failings
> of the few are overlooked because of the good done by the many... That is
> indeed the function of the press: to hold those with power to account. It is,
> in fact, what *The Guardian* did in relation to the *News of the World*, and what
> first ITV and then *Panorama* did in relation to the BBC.[6]

Several papers had business models that depended on intrusion. In a long and revealing dissection of Operation Motorman,[7] Leveson recorded the then head of the ICO as grasping not only that many newspapers were 'blagging' information (up to and including medical records) but that their executives believed that their survival depended on it. The then head of the ICO, Richard Thomas, described to Leveson the angry newspaper reaction to the ICO's campaign against blagging:

> Although they rested their case... on the threats to investigative journalism,
> I was surprised by how hard they were fighting, and it really left me with a
> message that we were challenging something which went to the heart of much

of the – certainly tabloid-press activity. Someone once said to me: 'You do realize that you are challenging their whole business model?'[8]

The report profiles, by slow accumulation, the complete disconnection between the way people at the *News of the World*, the *Mirror*, the *Daily Express* or the *Daily Mail* thought things had to be done and the PCC rules that they had signed up to. The editors who appeared before Leveson were stuck: they could not admit openly that the rules were regarded as empty and with no force, because their company had solemnly promised to abide by them. The honest gadflys had an easier time. The editor of *Private Eye* and the blogger Paul Staines (who writes as Guido Fawkes) cheerfully admitted to Leveson that they had no higher purpose than mischief making and no truck with regulators of any kind. Staines uses foreign servers to host his blog in order to lower the risk of legal action disabling it.

Leveson rationed his sympathy for the celebrities who appeared before him, including Steve Coogan, Hugh Grant and Charlotte Church. He extended more concern to their relatives who were affected by intrusions, and to ordinary people, such as Milly Dowler's parents, who were propelled into the public eye by events beyond their control. Given the harm to ordinary people and to the relations of celebrities, Leveson did not buy the defence of intrusion, which said that any degree of celebrity or publicity-seeking justifies any form of intrusion. A single page of the report lists inaccurate or intrusive reporting as contributing to four attempts at, or deaths by, suicide.[9]

The sections of the report dealing with the relationship between the press and the police largely exonerate Scotland Yard detectives from the charge that they did not follow up the first phone-hacking arrests because some senior officers had over-cosy relationships with the *News of the World*. (Leveson did make clear that the police handling of the data gathered from Glen Mulcaire was extraordinarily inept.) He said that relationships between politicians and editors and proprietors have been too close and too secret, but acknowledged that news media have a right to lobby and pressurize. It is up to politicians to deal with this and in the report he quotes BBC chairman and ex-minister Lord Patten sympathetically:

> I think major political parties, and particularly their leaders over the last 20 or 25 years have demeaned themselves by the extent to which they've paid court on proprietors and editors… I think that politicians have allowed themselves to be kidded… that editors and proprietors determined the fate of politicians.[10]

Anyone reading Leveson's report is left with the indelible impression that the judge wanted to focus on the legal and regulatory solution to press misconduct and did not want to enter wider speculation about the future of news. But this self-imposed focus on regulation for 'the press' leaves a hole where the report's context should be and begs the questions as to whether there is any longer such a thing as 'the press'. Leveson observes late in the report that 'the development of online media content, as well as methods of delivery, has brought the regulation of print media into a whole new context'. But the questions that arise stay unexamined.

Leveson, who took little evidence from online news media, was preoccupied with the impact and size of mass media, which are large enough to intimidate or evade regulators. He made no allowance for the fact that the newspapers on which he focused are in long-term decline and that a few online news sites are maturing into journalism businesses with staff, newsroom cultures and internal rules of conduct. Britain has a relatively new privacy law that is having some trouble keeping up with Twitter, offshore servers, privacy settings in social networks and digital technology in general. Experts are already debating the journalistic ethics of sending pilotless drones to photograph what earthbound reporters cannot reach. It seems unlikely that anyone flying a drone over a celebrity's garden or beach house will think of themselves as 'the press'.

Leveson, on the rare occasions when he considered online news, wrote off its reach and influence as much weaker than that of printed papers. But precisely because online media is much more agile, important information can be dug out and disclosed by small online publishers or bloggers. Online journalism creates new and potentially powerful media institutions even as it takes down old ones. Leveson said of the gossip site Popbitch that its small size 'understandably' means that its reporting standards are lower. But Popbitch had 350,000 subscribers when Leveson was hearing evidence from its editor – and that is well on the way to being large. Leveson's descriptions of online make it sound like a distinct zone with no overlap with mainstream publishers, and as if readers do not often swap between platforms.

Leveson assumed that a new regulator for 'the press' will deal with questions raised by online. Those are likely to be very large questions to be dealt with by a regulator. Leveson's prescription for press regulation relies on mainstream journalism retaining its present shape and being dominated by established newspapers that also have websites. This is a fragile assumption. The problems posed for the accountability of journalism are not insoluble but they are new and complex. What we think of as a 'story' in any medium is now, with endless updating and many more sources, becoming an iterative and long process. That change alone poses some challenges for law and regulation. The internet splits readerships once bundled by newspapers. Instead of large publishing organizations that gather, process and distribute news, are we going to see the work of millions of small specialists aggregated, sorted and shared by a separate layer of online aggregators or search engines? The power to shape how we learn about the world will shift to new locations even as it also stays in some established news organizations that have successfully adapted. Leveson was unprepared to even admit that it can nowadays be hard – and even contentious – to locate 'journalism' in the torrent of information. He recommended that 'significant' news publishers should be regulated, but did not define how that potentially contentious distinction should be operated. The political parties in Parliament did no better when trying to frame a new law after Leveson's report.[11]

Prescription

The editors who had reason to fear what Leveson might say at the end of his deliberations gave their backing to a revamp of the PCC, which announced early in the inquiry that it would take a new shape. The proposed reorganization became known as 'Hunt/Black' after Lords Hunt and Black, two Conservative peers involved in the debate. Lord Hunt, an ex-minister, chaired what was left of the PCC, and Lord Black represented the *Daily* and *Sunday Telegraph*, having once been director of the PCC.

From the start, Leveson was preoccupied with the issue of how the quality of a press regulator can be checked and, if necessary, improved. He saw the absence of this verification mechanism as the fault that had allowed press groups to set their own rules and choose whether or not to obey them. He had asked at the opening of the inquiry 'Who guards the guardians?' and answered his own question in the report. 'The answer to the question of who guards the guardians should not be "no one".' He encouraged the newspapers to reinvent regulation so as to provide real accountability.

Lords Hunt and Black pulled together an unfinished scheme that would certainly have improved on the weak powers of the previous PCC but which lacked any verifying or 'recognition' body and did not ensure its survival by putting that guarantee into statute. This was exactly what Leveson did not wish to hear. When told by Lord Black that statute-backed regulation might face legal challenge, Leveson snapped back:

> This is not the attitude of an industry committed to raising standards and acting in the public interest and must be seen as what it is likely to be: an attempt to use the economic and political power of the press to defend their own interests.[12]

Leveson's suggestions on what a 'genuinely independent and effective' regulator might actually do provoked relatively little debate when they were published. It should hear, judge and provide redress for complaints, take an active role in promoting standards, impose sanctions and offer an arbitration service. Its members should be selected by a process independent of the press and editors should not have decisive power on any code (of conduct) committee. It should formulate guidance on public interest and encourage transparency about sources in news media as much as possible. To provide an incentive for publishers to join the system, he proposed that the civil law rules should be amended to allow courts to impose heavy costs and damages on those who did not subscribe to the regulator's rules or use the arbitration service.[13]

The keystone of this set of proposals commanded support in Parliament, as it had long been obvious that it would, but divided the media. Public opinion appeared to have lost interest in the details. Leveson recommended that legislation would be needed to give effect to the incentives to join regulation but most of all 'to recognize the new self-regulatory body and reassure the public that the basic requirements were met and continue to be met'. While fully expecting to be contradicted, Leveson made clear that this was not statutory regulation of the press. One issue that Leveson barely touched is the degree to which any national law or regulation can now cover media headquartered outside Britain. While the inquiry was sitting, a senior executive of the *Daily Mail* speculated openly that if the inquiry restricted the newspaper unduly, the online operation would move its headquarters to New York. That may have been bluff, but the Daily Mail & General Trust generates one-third of its £2 billion annual income in North America, mainly from newly acquired business-to-business publishing companies.

Prime Minister David Cameron, facing a split among his ministers if he planned to implement Leveson in full, said that the government had 'serious concerns and misgivings' over legislation. To pass a press law would cross a 'Rubicon'. After a few days of angry recriminations, politicians, officials and editors disappeared into closed consultations to see if they could negotiate a compromise in private. The late-night deal over a 'Royal Charter' to set up a new system did not look as if it had settled the issue. A spectacular humiliation for the most powerful private-sector media company in Britain had by then become an intricate technical wrangle hidden inside the corridors of Parliament, which may well later be fought out in the law courts.[14]

A third way

Law is the foundation for any accountability of news media, whatever form it may take. Regulation coexists with law and must work in relation to it. Leveson's failure to look more broadly at the wider context in which journalism is now being done meant that he concentrated on regulation and not on how law and regulation interact. And as he anticipated, most of the debate on his proposals has turned on the issue of whether legislation should be introduced to give them effect. There might have been, and might still be, a better way.[15]

To listen to a few of the opponents of Leveson's plans for statutory backing for regulation, one might imagine that Britain's press had never before been threatened with legal restraint of any kind. Free speech is never absolute. Clashes of rights, such as the collision between press freedom and individual privacy, cannot be 'settled'. They can only be managed by the best balance. Editors and journalists face a battery of laws, new and old, which shape the actions and processes of a newsroom every day. Law has been a stronger influence on the behaviour of journalists than regulation and it is likely to remain so even under strengthened rules. Besides the best-known examples of libel or privacy law, journalists can be affected by laws on contempt of court, bribery, data protection, corruption, official secrets and employment. As the Leveson report recognized, one of the principal discouragements stopping anyone taking legal action against a publisher or broadcaster has been the slow speed and cost of the law. The Leveson Inquiry was a rare, but missed, opportunity to look at the whole field of law as it affects the relationship between media and society. Developing digital technology requires a fresh look at laws such as privacy and data protection.

A 'law-first' approach would have given a larger role to an idea that makes only occasional appearances in Leveson's prescriptions: public interest. Leveson showed that some newspapers had, much of the time, lost touch with any defensible version of acting in the public interest. Essentially a test of public value, public interest is an elusive and contested idea. Some journalistic disclosures can be defended as being in the public interest even if they amount to a breach of the law. Lawyers, Leveson included, tend to dislike the idea of public interest because it is so slippery and uncertain. Leveson gave himself the task of outlawing bad conduct while not 'chilling' legitimate reporting, particularly investigative journalism. But it is hard to see how this balance can be struck without some better means of the law being able to judge what deserves protection and what doesn't. Such a balance would have risks and problems, but would be a more solid foundation than encouraging the entire 'industry' of 'the press' to try to write a working definition into a new code of conduct. The differences of approach to an idea like 'public interest' make a nonsense of the idea that there is any longer a coherent 'press' with common interests.

There are a few public interest defences in some of the laws affecting journalism, but they are scattered and inconsistent.[16] Journalism's history has shown that important journalism often works near the edge of the rules; occasionally it breaks them. But no society – and certainly not one that has just learnt what happens when journalists leave decency behind – is going to cut that journalism any slack at all if the newspaper can't show that what it was doing has a public value. When the *Daily Telegraph* bought a (possibly stolen) disc with details of MPs expenses, when a *Guardian* journalist faked a signature, when the *Sunday Times* bought a key document in the Thalidomide scandal – these infractions can only be justified by the overriding public interest in the disclosure thus made possible.

There is a philosophical objection to the use of a public interest test: that to write such a test into law is to allow the state to determine what good journalism is. But if journalists claim to help society by informing it, they cannot at the same time insist that society can have no opinion on the quality of that contribution. Battered, abused and misused as the idea of public interest may be, it is the foundation for deciding the balance of freedom and restraint, which press freedom in an open society requires.

Leveson could and should have urged consistent public interest defences in laws, both civil and criminal, where they would be useful to journalism that could make use of these defences. In the case of privacy law he might have extended this to clarify the Human Rights Act, which opposes the right of free expression to the right to privacy and leaves the courts to decide on the circumstances of each case. Leaving aside the cost and delay of a privacy action, conscientious interpretation of the law has produced something that is almost impossible for journalists or anyone else (save lawyers) to understand or navigate.[17] The introduction of a more explicit public interest test into privacy law is long overdue and would anticipate many of the difficulties that will besiege the law in its present state as technology makes intrusion and publication much easier.[18] It would be more valuable to have a public debate over the exact scope of a public interest test in a revised privacy law than to waste energy on debates about the legal mechanics of regulation.

A definition of public interest needs to meet three broad requirements:

1 the interests of a collective entity, a community small or large, beyond a single individual;

2 the advancing of some benefit or the prevention of harm;

3 a presumption in favour of disclosure and free flow of information and a reluctance to limit communication.

It might add either or both of the following statements of principle:

> Lord Denning (on fair comment): 'Whenever a matter is such as to affect people at large, so that they may be legitimately interested in, or concerned at, what is going on; or what may happen to them or others; then it is a matter of public interest.'[19]
>
> Lord Nicholls: '(The press discharges vital functions as a bloodhound as well as a watchdog.) The court should be slow to conclude that a publication was not in the public interest and, therefore, that the public had no right to know, especially when the information is in the field of political discussion.'[20]

If those elements are in place, more specific indications of disclosures with public value are possible, but the list will always be non-exhaustive. Those that are useful are:

1 Disclosing information that allows significantly better-informed decisions to be made.

2 Preventing people being misled by statements or actions.

3 Informing public debate.

4 Promoting accountability and transparency.

5 Exposing or detecting crime, significant anti-social behaviour, fraud or corruption.

In 2001, two academics, David Morrison and Michael Svennevig, did some opinion research on attitudes to the public interest, the media and privacy. Media professionals did not want legal intervention in deciding the public interest. The opinion of the public, however, was a quite different matter. As the authors put it, 'the majority of the public approve of quite firm parameters being set on what the media can do in the name of serving "the public interest"'.[21]

If Leveson had begun strengthening and clarifying public interest defences in law, he would have been in a position to create a powerful incentive to join a new regulatory organization. Leveson's suggestion for an 'arbitral arm' of a regulator, effectively building a bridge between the regulator and the court system to give swift, lower-cost access to decisions, makes good sense. Many of his suggestions for a more effective system of regulation are likewise an improvement on what has gone before. He has tried to build in an incentive to force publishers to join a regulation system. A more effective incentive might have been to allow courts to take editorial standards and integrity into account when faced with a public interest defence. Guidelines would make clear what this might mean. A newsroom wanting to establish its credentials would need to follow a code of conduct supervised and enforced independently and would need to allow a high degree of transparency. If court cases depended on this, the incentive to adopt regulatory rules and to keep them would be strong. Most publications face legal challenge sooner or later. This would be self-regulation, but in a framework that would prevent capture by the news media. Now put these interlocking elements together and rerun the recent history of the defunct *News of the World*, a newspaper that was frequently in court. Many of its stories might not have passed a public interest test, but some did. If the newspaper's editor could only make a public interest defence stand up in court, by being seen to treat standards and accountability seriously, that editor would have ensured that rules (not to mention law) were not broken. An editor is in the best position of all to enforce codes of conduct. Under these proposals, keeping the rules would be the key to winning more cases in court.

This package of interlocking proposals found no favour with the Leveson Inquiry. The report finds current privacy law usefully 'flexible' and makes no suggestions for adjusting it. It takes much the same view of any statutory definition of public interest, arguing that the idea is so changeable that it is better incorporated in a regulatory code, which is easier to change than a law.[22]

Regulation's future

Leveson proposed that Britain's media continue to be regulated in a mixture of systems. The regulation of newspapers, and perhaps some online sites, would still be lighter and on a different basis to the rules governing broadcasters. With the barriers between what were once distinct media platforms disappearing, how long could this varied system last?

The British mixed system assumes that broadcast is a uniquely powerful medium whose regulated standards are necessary as a benchmark for other media. Newspapers may generate more new stories and original reporting, and have agenda-setting influence on other media out of proportion to their circulation. They can do all this because they are less constricted by rules. (The US system works the other way round. At least until the recent rise of US online sites with big audiences and popular agendas, newspapers acted as the benchmark for quality and impartiality).

The use of video on news sites in the UK is already subject to confusing and overlapping sets of rules. Both the BBC and the broadcast and telecoms regulator Ofcom argued during the Leveson Inquiry that the mixed system should remain. However inconsistent it might seem in the converged internet age, its variety helped to guarantee a good balance of partial curiosity and impartial reporting. Leveson hinted obliquely that he could foresee a future moment when Ofcom might regulate fully converged media. If a new regulator and a 'verification body' to control the quality of the regulator could not be agreed by the press, he wrote, a last resort would have to be the new system overseen and checked by Ofcom. This suggestion, even as a last resort, was rightly criticized for allowing a political element into arrangements from which Leveson had claimed to want to exclude it. The head of Ofcom is a political appointment.

Plurality

The Leveson Report says little about the issue that some of its witnesses argued lay at the root of the trouble. If the *News of the World* had not been part of a group owning 34 per cent of national press circulation, its journalists would not have felt so entitled to break the law. The question of concentration of ownership lay within Leveson's terms of reference, but he confined himself to some technical observations about how plurality should best be measured.

It is impossible to say whether the powerful market position of Rupert Murdoch's newspapers instilled a (false) sense of immunity among the employees. The criminal trials involving journalists from the *News of the World* and *The Sun* may disclose more. But it seems probable. The evidence presented to Leveson made clear that journalists on the *News of the World* were in little danger of internal disciplinary action of any kind if they were caught breaking the law in pursuit of a story.

The convergence of common platforms, technological innovation and pervasive, recurrent concerns about the misuse of over-concentrated media ownership make plurality rules a concern across the developed world. The European Commission published the results of a two-year inquiry into plurality in 2013. Britain's Ofcom reported in 2012, its review prompted by public arguments over News Corporation's attempts, later withdrawn, to buy BSkyB. Canada passed new media ownership rules in 2008. Australia reviewed its rules in 2001 and updated them four times in the following six years. Convergence and regulation were the subject of separate Australian inquiries in 2011–12. Plurality is reviewed regularly by official bodies in both the United States and Germany.[23]

Plurality in the provision of news is essential precisely because no one provider has a monopoly on editorial excellence or truth. The problem lies in working out how to ensure adequate plurality fairly, while ensuring that investment is not discouraged. Much of the passion devoted to plurality – aside from the newer issues connected to phone hacking – rests on the questionable belief that a newspaper's formal political allegiance affects the way votes are cast. *The Sun* made a large contribution to embedding this idea in the minds of politicians by claiming to have won the 1992 general election for the Conservatives led by John Major. Subsequent research showed that *Sun* readers had not changed their opinions any more than the readers of any other newspaper; the polls had simply been wrong-footed by a late swing to Major. Just under one-third of *Daily Mail* readers vote Labour, despite the paper having never recommended a Labour vote in its history.

It is not hard to frame an argument that says that no one publisher should be able to own more than than a certain maximum in a market.[24] But the frequency with which these questions are reopened should give a clue to the depth of the problems involved. The two most recent reviews likely to affect Britain, by Ofcom and the European Commission, did not recommend fixed, quantitative limits to the media holdings of single companies. A flat limit, Ofcom told the secretary of state for culture, media and sport in 2012, makes it hard to take into account issues of 'commercial sustainability and innovation'.[25]

This is not the only issue. Others are:

- What do the regulators count? Available measures include:
  - circulation or audience;
  - 'reach';
  - availability of content;
  - impact;
  - 'share of reference' (the number of people referring to a news source in a market survey)

All these have been used somewhere. A European Commission report in 2009 listed 75 possible threats to pluralism, 45 risks and offered 166 indices for measuring them.[26]

- Is online news consumption to be measured by page views, 'unique visitors' or some other measure of engagement?
- Should media be counted platform by platform or as one single marketplace for news?
- Is the BBC taken into account in the calculations or not? By almost any measure, the BBC dominates the field for news. In Ofcom's measurement of reach in 2010, the BBC had 81 per cent. News Corporation and Sky combined 51 per cent, with ITN next at 40 per cent. Other than the News International newspapers counted into the total above, only two newspaper groups have reach over 10 per cent: the Daily Mail & General Trust (18 per cent) and Trinity Mirror (12 per cent).

In 2012, the government began reviewing the Communications Act, then almost 10 years old. The act makes no mention of the internet. Governments that find they have to legislate on media and communications find that there is never a perfect moment to freeze the various competing organizations and ask them to stop moving while the rules of the game are rewritten. If they stack the rules one way, they will be accused of destroying media properties that are already in decline. Stack the rules the other way, in favour of established incumbents, and those in power will be accused of failing to create the right conditions in which the strong competitors of tomorrow can grow.

Recent history does not suggest that politicians are keen to face this. During the phone-hacking scandal it was often suggested that News International's close relations with politicians of both major parties ensured that the issue of concentration of ownership posed no danger to the company. But Leveson found that when the current rules were written into the Communications and Enterprise Acts (2002 and 2003), ministers in the Blair government were genuinely divided over how to hit the right balance between deregulation and control. Blair had made it clear that he wanted a legislative framework that would be loose and attractive enough to tempt the world's largest media players to develop businesses in Britain. Leveson's only suggestion was for a more transparent justification for political decisions in mergers, takeovers or the results of plurality reviews. Several months after the Leveson Inquiry reported, the deputy leader of the Labour Party, Harriet Harman, suggested new legislation to limit any single owner from having titles accounting for more than 30 per cent of the market. The odd thing about the proposal, which the party never made when in office between 1997 and 2010, was that it made no mention of whether the limit would count only print circulation or print and online. It was a solution to the problem posed by the previous era.[27]

But the issue is not likely to go away. The gradual failure of the business model for print has encouraged further consolidation of newspaper holdings in countries all over the world, very similar to the elimination of competition that went on when television became a mass medium in the 1960s. This has left a number of countries in a worse position than Britain. The Finkelstein report in Australia reproduces a table (see Figure 8.1) that ranks 26 countries according to the market share of the largest single media owner. When the table was compiled, Britain ranked ninth with 34 per cent held by News International. Above Britain were Switzerland, Israel, Ireland, Portugal, France, Turkey and South Africa. Australia was in top place with 58 per cent of daily circulation, held by Rupert Murdoch's News Ltd.

TABLE 8.1   International newspaper ownership concentration, share of total daily newspaper circulation (per cent) held by top companies

Country	Top 1	Top 2	Top 4
Australia	58	86	99
Switzerland	45	62	76
Israel	44	57	70
Portugal	41	77	94
France	41	61	82
Turkey	38	53	78
South Africa	36	64	96
UK	34	54	74
Taiwan	32	56	96
Netherlands	30	58	90

SOURCE: International Media Concentration Research Project, 2011

Notes

1   See Chapter 7.

2   The Leveson Inquiry was designed to be done in two parts; the report published in November 2012 covers only the first, thematic, phase. At the time of writing, there is doubt about whether the second part will take place at all.

3   The Data Protection Act was passed in 1998.

4   See Chapter 7.

5   In 2008, the McCanns started legal action against the *Daily Mail* and *Evening Standard* (then both owned by Associated Newspapers) over 67 articles. The action was settled.

6   Leveson report executive summary, paragraph 10. The reference to the BBC is to the coverage of allegations concerning Jimmy Savile.

7   See Chapter 7.

8   Leveson Report, p. 1106, 2.5.

9   Leveson Report, p. 485.

10 Leveson Report, p. 1440, 3.9.

11 http://georgebrock.net/this-blog-is-back-quick-leveson-dogs-breakfast-catchup/ (accessed 24.4.13).

12 Leveson Report p. 1674, 7.5.

13 Leveson executive summary, paras 47–76.

14 David Pannick QC, *The Times*, 11 April 2013.

15 These views are in detail at http://www.levesoninquiry.org.uk/witness/professor-george-brock/ (statement of 18.7.12).

16 http://www.guardian.co.uk/law/2011/nov/21/leveson-inquiry-investigative-journalism-law (accessed 9.2.13). An improved public interest defence is in the new defamation law passed by Parliament in 2013.

17 For a good example of the delicate balancing act involved, see www.judiciary.gov.uk/Resources/JCO/Documents/Judgments/ferdinand-v-mgn-ltd.pdf (accessed 9.2.13).

18 George Brock, 'What interests people isn't the public interest', *The Times*, 10 May 2011.

19 Denning in *London Artists v Littler*, 1969, 2 QB 375, 391.

20 House of Lords, Reynolds v Times Newspapers, 1999.

21 http://www.ofcom.org.uk/static/archive/bsc/pdfs/research/pidoc.pdf (accessed 19.2.13).

22 Leveson Report, p. 1508, 4.2–4.3.

23 Collins, R and Cave, M, 'Media pluralism and the overlapping instruments needed to achieve it', *Telecomms Policy*, forthcoming.

24 http://georgebrock.net/a-reply-to-alan-rusbridger-on-convergence-plurality-and-regulation/ (accessed 10.2.13).

25 http://stakeholders.ofcom.org.uk/consultations/measuring-plurality/statement (accessed 10.2.13).

26 University of Leuven, 'Independent study on indicators for media pluralism in member states', 2009, http://ec.europa.en/information_society/media_taskforce/doc/pluralism/pfr_report.pdf.

27 http://www.guardian.co.uk/media/2013/may/12/communications-act-murdoch-internet (accessed 20.5.13).

09

Throwing spaghetti at the wall

> *It is the imagination, ultimately, and not mathematical calculation that creates media; it is the fresh perception of how to fit a potential machine into an actual way of life that really constitutes the act of 'invention'.*
>
> ANTHONY SMITH, *GOODBYE GUTENBERG*, 1980

Some of what you have read in earlier chapters is at risk of being overtaken by events, for we are looking at a fast-moving picture. Much of the detail I describe in this chapter will change. The business of establishing the truth of what matters to people is once again a work in progress. The single most powerful force driving people to rethink how to do journalism is the increase in the quantity of media available. The entrepreneur and engineer Peter Diamandis observes that a Kenyan with a smartphone has access to more information than Bill Clinton had as US president. One estimate reckoned that the average American in 1960 had about 82 minutes of media content available to choose from for every minute in the day, counting books, magazines, newspapers, radio and television. By 2005, the same average American had an estimated 884 minutes of media content to choose from for each minute in the day – and that is counting the entire internet as a single minute. So the true increase is very much higher.[1]

The richness of information made available by the internet revealed how little we knew. Take high estimates and assume that 40 per cent of 'information' on the internet is x-rated porn and the same proportion is spam. Even if you only value one-half of a per cent of the remaining 20 per cent you are still within reach of a great deal more knowledge than ever before. That radical extension of possible knowledge guarantees nothing about good or bad outcomes. We can only look, as this chapter does, at probabilities. All that technological change allows is the exploration of new possibilities. That exploration and experiment accelerates the working of the law of creative destruction. When creative destruction is happening, it is the destruction that dominates the foreground of the picture. Destruction is often dramatic and distressing. This chapter is devoted to the other half of the equation: the generation of creative energy to rebuild with new materials. These are the people who throw spaghetti at the wall to see what sticks.

Four core tasks

Journalism was once very easy to identify because it was, when transmitted in print or on terrestrial broadcast platforms, a visible industrial process. Now, however, amid the abundance of information flowing between people in all directions, journalists lose the easy identification that went with their industrial process and machinery. If anyone can publish what they choose to call news or journalism to readerships large or small, what defines a journalist? Journalists have justified and defended their activity by its value to society. Can we any longer see that distinct value?

If journalism is the systematic attempt to establish the truth of what matters to society in time for that information to be useful, the activities that define journalism still matter even if the context in which they are done has changed. There are four core tasks that journalism should perform, which can be better done by people trained and experienced in this work. They will usually be better done in groups or organizations that can produce output on which consumers and users can consistently rely. The four tasks are:

- *Verification:* the elimination of doubt about what has happened, especially about things that are, or are likely to be, disputed.

- *Sense making:* some facts are easier to establish than others but there are very few that are 'pure' in the sense that they can be divorced from context or values. There never was a golden age when newspapers 'of record' just stuck to the facts. Good journalism makes sense of facts that it selects and transmits. That involves the exercise of judgement, which involves risk. Sense making may go under the labels of reporting, analysis, comment or opinion.

- *Witness:* new technology has eliminated the need for the vast quantities of blanket, routine reporting that was needed in the past. But, irrespective of the hugely amplified power of digital recording, there remain situations best captured, with whatever technology is available, by an experienced eye-witness.

- *Investigation:* there remain facts of importance that are hidden. They require skill, experience, patience and resources to tell. It is a specialist skill.

News media contain a great deal and a great variety of material that do not fall into these categories. People who do not call themselves journalists may do some or all of these things. Journalists may perform these four functions well or badly. But these four tasks are the irreducible core of what can be distinguished as journalism and they are the basis of the trust on which it relies.

These tasks are also the foundation on which journalism in the 21st century is going to be rebuilt. Rebuilding by experiment, recombining old practices with news tools and circumstances is what journalists have done repeatedly through history. The single greatest difference today is the way in which the profusion of information affects trying to nail the truth.

This is more of an opportunity than a problem. As I sit here typing this text, a small black window pops up in the top right-hand corner of my screen every few seconds carrying a new 140-character Twitter message. Twitter can be used to both send and follow fragments of information, opinion, news and gossip in hundreds of different ways. I use it to follow what is happening in my speciality, journalism. I have flexible choices. I can switch it on and off: it is normally off if I am writing. I can extend or shorten the range of people whose tweets I follow. I send relatively few tweets outbound but I could send none at all and just savour those of other people. I can use it superficially, skimming only every so often and getting a fast impression of what subjects and news is being swapped. Or I can drill down and click on the links and go through to the material that these tweeters want to bring to the attention of their followers. I can adjust the quota of jokes and the style of the humour: I can choose shouty, reflective or a mixture. I can 'clip' what I want to keep and with just a few clicks store it in a personal database held under my name by the site Delicious. My Twitter feed is the closest thing I see to a 'Daily Me', although I happen to shape it to pick up only my professional interests. That is my choice of how to keep the information flow under control; many others will scoop up much more.

This morning I have glimpsed short messages noting that it is the first anniversary of the death of the *Sunday Times* reporter Marie Colvin in Syria;[2] advice about 'digital adventures in China'; the juicy bits from the transcripts of the BBC's internal inquiry into the failure to look into Jimmy

Savile's crimes; *Guardian* journalists planning a strike over job cuts; an ex-*News of the World* journalist, arrested months ago, discovering that he will not be charged, a link to something about Emile Durkheim (which I am unlikely to read); and moans about journeys to work in London and the price of a latte in Beijing. I have retweeted a message linking to a story about the reform of libel law and the Leveson Inquiry fallout, which in turn links to the full recording of a lecture I gave a few evenings ago. No one else will see exactly this tailored combination of messages, to that extent that I am in a 'filter bubble' of my own choosing. I would not choose this to be my only information: I have also read a newspaper, briefly listened to the radio; during the rest of the day e-mail bulletins will drop into my in-box summarizing news both specialized and general.

My selection of Twitter messages is completely typical for the start of a weekday. None of this fact, opinion, gossip and link consumption is in the slightest remarkable: hundreds of millions of people all over the world have roughly the same consumption choices. The exchange of scraps of information, opinion and gossip is not new. But because of that, it is easy to lose sight of what a sudden, recent increase in choice, ease and information this represents. The connections between me and those from whom I get information are what anthropologists call 'weak ties' and this description is right. I know some of the people I follow on Twitter personally but many I don't know at all and never will. There's a risk that I will be fooled by a fake Twitter account or believe something that is known or later proved to be wrong. But those are risks that, to some degree, come with all the information I consume: I adjust my wariness according to the source I'm looking at. So any ties to those I read or send on Twitter are weak, but they are also useful. They have measurable value because I could not get this much varied information so flexibly and quickly in any other way. The people whose news I follow and the few thousand who follow mine are one – only one – of the communities to which I belong.

In an open, media-rich society such as Britain this new value comes on top of plenty of other ways of finding out what's happening. In societies in which media are either held in very few hands, or the rebuilding of journalism is happening only slowly, social media networks build fresh information communities at extraordinary speed. They are built fastest where unmet demand meets the ease with which, say, a micro-blogging network like Twitter or (the Chinese) Weibo can spread messages that will not be carried in more established and centrally controlled media.

The use of micro-blogging services tends to expand in direct proportion to the rigidity of mainstream media, or social and political laws, or conventions that restrict discussion. Twitter is enormously popular in Saudi Arabia and especially popular among women. One day in Dammam, one of the kingdom's oil production centres, agents of the 'morality police' or Hayaa[3] marched into an exhibition of models of dinosaurs being held in a shopping mall and ordered it closed. Tweets began mocking this unexplained shutdown almost immediately. One suggested that the Hayaa was worried that people might start worshipping dinosaurs instead of God. Was the problem that male and female dinosaurs were not put in separate rooms, wondered another. Many tweets played on jokes and puns about the dinosaurs running the country. Many attacked the Hayaa: 'Hello Stone Age,' said one, 'we have some of your people – can you please come round and collect them?'[4]

This wasn't exactly journalism; looked at one way, it was just jokey gossip, conversation without speech. But it was also an unprecedented kind of political conversation, accelerated by smartphones, on a political subject, using mockery. It created an instant, perhaps transient, community. Many of the preconditions for journalism are there. The communication spreads knowledge of a significant event and invites people to understand it and to share their own understanding. What happens can now be turned into communicable and accessible information with an ease and at a speed unthinkable 10 years before. No editors or intermediaries were involved. Similar flows of information that are unlikely to make it down established routes have carried similarly subversive messages in countries such as Mexico, the Philippines and Russia. The odds are that these are the first stirrings of the next generation of journalism in those societies. Journalism grows and develops in unpredictable places and in odd ways. The opportunities afforded by new ways of connecting people to information creates a generative energy that renews journalism and has done so regularly in the past.

We were having journalistic moments!

This section looks at a number of case studies in Europe and the United States in which journalism is being developed from scratch – sometimes by deliberate design and sometimes as an accidental by-product of something else. Many of these examples are local or regional. There are two reasons for this. First, with the exceptions of Britain and Japan, densely populated countries with 'national' news markets, most of the world's news starts local. Many national and international news organizations grew from local origins. Second, the disappearance of printed media is arguably more serious at local level; experiments to address the disappearance of local media are more numerous than at national level. Ofcom surveys have noted that young readers are leading the take-up of local media online.[5]

Start small, scale with care

Far more people can now compete to provide news, so generating income to support a continuing news site is harder by definition in the digital age. Sites that launch with immediate heavy costs have a lower success rate than those that grow cautiously and slowly from a small base. The social geography of communities that share an interest in news has changed. Whether you are generating news for a global community of mountaineers or for a hyperlocal community in a few streets, demand for shared information needs to be the foundation.

Will Perrin, the founder of a hyperlocal site near the mainline railway station of King's Cross in London, captures this in his account of the origins of a site based around a handful of streets. Perrin lived in one of these streets and, like his neighbours, worried about refuse, crime and local planning. An embryonic neighbourhood association began meeting to coordinate efforts to put pressure on the local council and police to improve conditions. After a year or two, the increasingly active and vocal group was generating a good deal of information: complaints pursued or ignored, reports of meetings, new developments in the dialogue between residents and the authorities. Perrin, who is knowledgeable about information technology, offered to pool the information on a website they could all use to find out more easily what they needed to know. The site, then and now, is run by volunteers and they don't have the resources to do journalism. As the site puts it: 'We go on holiday, have lives and stuff so it isn't a 365 × 24 process.' Besides, Perrin has little time for journalists and their outdated, self-inflated 'belief system'. 'If we happen to do journalism,' he says, 'then fine; otherwise we just collect together what we know so people can use it.' But as time has gone on, information of this kind features in arguments, debates and collisions of interest; that puts a premium on it being defensibly accurate. So the site now says: 'We mainly write original material sourced from the streets, from readers emailing us or from news that we have picked up from various outlets. We research our material thoroughly before publishing and include relevant links to source material wherever possible.'[6]

There is no definitive count of local online sites in Britain. Ofcom reports found 432 local sites in May 2012 and that figure had grown to 633 nine months later. Ofcom's researchers calculated that one person in seven in

Britain uses a local news website at least once a month.[7] One map lists 700 sites. Perrin, who founded the coordinating and training group Talk About Local, reckons that the map records less than half of the local websites.[8] Some are started and run by activists with declared local political aims; some are digital noticeboards; some are whimsical blogs written by single individuals. Birmingham has a local investigative site, helpmeinvestigate.com, which has notched up impressive disclosures in health and education and relies heavily on 'crowdsourced' material and tips. The majority are put together by volunteers; few try to make money and even fewer actually do so. But making money from it is not impossible.

For many sites, the arrival of Google's Adsense was a turning point in making a site financially viable. That was the case for SE1, one of the oldest community sites in London operating on the south side of the Thames in the centre of the city. SE1 has been going for 15 years and its founder, James Hatts, describes the business side as 'fragile'. But the site owes no money and has survived with 166,000 monthly unique visitors and a core or regular user base estimated at 15,000. Hatts thinks that this readership is as high as it can go for the area, although the 'relatively transient central London population means you have to keep up your promotional efforts just to stay still'. The site's unique selling point has been its unrelenting focus on the politics and economics of the plans to regenerate the battered inner-city area known as Elephant and Castle. Hatts says that he has often been to meetings about the Elephant and Castle in order to record multimillion pound decisions, and he has been 'the only journalist present (and often the only person in the public gallery at all)'.[9]

One effect of all this new grass-roots activity has been to reinvigorate local newspapers. Sometimes they have allied with new sites; sometimes they have competed with online sites of their own; in many places they are careful not to compete too directly. In both Birmingham in Britain and Seattle in the United States, local newspapers have woven together networks of local bloggers. Dramatic events can propel small operations into the limelight. The riots in several British cities in the summer of 2011 gave prominence to Sangat TV, a Sikh station largely devoted to charitable and religious broadcasts – and viewers in Birmingham it had never dreamt of getting. The online sites suffer the disadvantage that they must build a loyal audience from scratch and struggle for income. But online has one clear edge: it can both generate and measure engagement far more easily than print. Engagement can be measured by the number of times people link to the stories and posts, by the number of comments overall or per story, and by the amount of information that people offer or contribute.

But engagement or scoops do not always trump legacy. In Grimsby, the daily circulation of the established newspaper, the *Grimsby Telegraph*, is less than half what it was 30 years ago. But the paper's own surveys suggest that multiple readership of each copy means that it is seen by 49 per cent of the town's population. A new newspaper, the *Cleethorpes Chronicle*, has opened nearby. The readership is much smaller but its founder claims that the *Chronicle* is financially secure. To complete the picture is a neighbourhood blog called Crazy Council, run by a dyslexic local businessman who suspects the council of being up to no good. His claim that the local authority was run by a bunch of monkeys – accompanied by a picture of three monkeys – brought objections from the council, which tried to have the post taken down. The blog simply published the letter of complaint.[10]

The sites that have succeeded have simply survived. To do so they need good local knowledge. But they also need to convey a sense of service to the community in which the site has a stake. Chains of local sites set up by large media companies have not prospered. The US media giant AOL runs 800–900 'Patch' local sites but admits that only 100 are profitable. In theory, they have economies of scale because advertising is sold on commission by a single person for several sites. But Patch sites, with only a few exceptions, lack the editorial personality or the authenticity of sites started by local people, because they could not find the news they wanted when they wanted from legacy media. According to a painful critique released in 2012 by a group of AOL investors, Patch lost $147 million in the previous year against $13 million in ad revenue. 'We do not believe Patch is a viable business,' the investors said in the report.[11] Chains and networks of local sites in the United States such as Backfence and Everyblock have failed and folded.

Similar problems have dogged British online local chains. The British government said in 2011 that the revival of local journalism should be led by 'existing media companies'. A study of four of the online Local People network[12] – out of more than 150 local sites launched in 2009 and owned by the Daily Mail & General Trust – found that the sites had low rates of use, very few comments on the stories or other evidence of engagement, and were hampered by relying too much on print templates for their journalism.[13] In 2012, three-quarters of the local freelance 'publishers' retained to fill the sites did not have their contracts renewed.

Local sites are a continuous experiment in connecting people to what they want or find they value. The development of many sites has been a zig-zag as they learn from local civic campaigns, train amateur writers who show willing and promise, and simply discover by trial and error what works and what does not. The better-established sites have now become destinations. 'Every councillor on the island reads *On the Wight*,'[14] a locally active politician said of the Isle of Wight site, 'they may not admit it but it's the first place they go.' *Sheffield Forum* has 161,000 members and a total of 6.5 million posts accumulated in a city of 450,000 inhabitants.[15] Even in small places, where the page-visit totals are small, the proportion of the community reached by sites that strike a chord can be very high. Richard Jones of *Saddleworth News* found it hard to sell online advertisements despite being able to claim 20,000 unique monthly users in an area of 24,000 people.[16] Alderleyedge.com, covering an affluent Cheshire commuter village with a population of under 5,000, gives away its own iPhone app. One London website and two in Wales are breaking into print editions.

Recombining old and new

Financing news start-ups has proved to be exhaustingly difficult in almost every country in the world except the United States. The relatively rapid decline of American newspapers and the size of the US economy and its advertising market have opened more opportunities than anywhere else – although the recession that began in 2008 did not spare fledgling sites in the United States any more than anywhere else. Aside from the problems of trying to generate advertising income, the two factors that seem to determine how far and how fast online start-ups can spread are levels of internet use and attitudes to mainstream media.

In 1997, Japan's extraordinarily successful and economically resilient newspapers had recorded a total circulation of 53.8 million copies. By 2011, this had fallen to 46.8 million. Most newspaper revenue in Japan is subscription income, which falls more slowly than advertising revenue. So these companies had avoided the sharp falls in advertising revenue seen in other parts of the world. But this left these newspapers relatively conservative. When contrasted with the innovatory speed of digital technology enthusiastically embraced by Japanese consumers (especially young ones) this rigidity has generated a backlash.

The 2011 tsunami created new opportunities for nimbler online media to show what they could do when the public badly wanted exact, reliable information about radiation dangers in real time. One survey that year found that in the 'value of media' category, people rated the internet as more important than newspapers, which came in second place next to television. Another found that trust in the internet and social media had increased sharply. The size of typefaces in Japanese newspapers has been increasing for some years in response to complaints from the increasing population of ageing readers who say they have trouble reading. Young people in Japan call print papers 'empty news sources' or 'mass-gomi'. The latter is a pun on 'mass communications' and 'gomi', meaning 'rubbish'.[17] Japan has huge bulletin-board sites that serve as neutral platforms, the largest known as 2-channel. They have now spawned curation sites that pick out and repackage debates of wider interest, and these have acquired some agenda-setting influence. In Japan, very few journalists have left mainstream newspapers for online start-ups, since few newspaper jobs have been lost.

In France, by contrast, many start-ups have been driven by journalists who are disillusioned or have been made redundant by established media due to financial crises. In France, as in several European countries, online news consumption is dominated by the sites of mainstream broadcasters, some of whom enjoy state support. Government support for established news organizations and a conservative advertising market have inhibited the growth of online start-ups. Aid in all forms to the French press amounts to between 12 and 14 per cent of its total revenue. A number of the most prominent start-ups, created in opposition to a mainstream media entangled too closely with the political class, have won large audiences but have also built in heavy costs. French business culture is not friendly to innovative methods: anyone registering a foundation must accept a representative of the state on the board.

A national site devoted to citizen journalism, Agora Vox, has struggled both to find enough citizen journalists and income; it is still financially protected inside a consultancy company. The site is worthy and serious, but has few individual voices and shows little interaction. In June 2011 Agora Vox had 650,000 unique users; France's largest online news site was then TF1, the country's main television channel, with 9.5 million users. Rue89, a site begun by reporters leaving the ailing newspaper *Libération*, likewise took on an ambitious agenda of national and international news, mixing professional reportage, aggregated content and contributions in approximately equal proportions. The '89' in the name is an oblique reference to three seminal events: the French Revolution of 1789, the fall of the Berlin wall in 1989 and the invention of the world wide web in 1989. But despite its wit, editorial talent and admired journalism, the site struggled to take revenue that could match annual costs of more than €2 million.[18] Rue89 was sold to the magazine *Nouvel Observateur* in 2011, four years after launch.

In France, online has provided a rich crop of fresh opportunities to tell stories that *liaisons dangereuses* with politicians have smothered; but no pure-play online sites at a national scale have yet shown that they can run a sustainable business model. Open blogging platforms such as *L'Observatoire des Medias* have started a more vigorous debate to open up discussion of French journalism's problems. French publishers won a €60 million settlement from Google in a copyright case, which will go towards the development of online media.

Subscription business models have fared a little better in France. Mediapart, founded by a former editor of *Le Monde*, Edwy Plenel, has an explicit mission to open up stories that the rest of the Parisian media won't touch. The site did just that with a series of revelations in 2010 about the occult funding of the president's election campaign in the scandal known as 'the Bettencourt affair'. Mediapart confirmed its leading position when its reporting forced the resignation of a Socialist minister who had lied about having a Swiss bank account. Plenel's mission statement for his site's agenda and style could have been framed by any editor determined to shake things up from the past 200 years:

> For too long there has been a tradition of 'journalism of government'. One that takes its legitimacy from those in power and which has forgotten that it is in the service of the people, of the law and citizens' right to know.[19]

Mediapart's site has 58,000 subscribers at €9 per month and claims to have made a profit for the first time in 2011. It too carries the substantial costs that go with investigative reporting.

Local online start-up businesses are thin on the ground in France, although there are numerous blogs. They dislike having to register with the government's publications and press agency commission and online businesses pay VAT at the full rate (19.6 per cent) while newspapers pay 2.1 per cent.[20] One local site that has overcome these problems to break even with a subscription model is Dijonscope. Its editor is an experienced journalist, Sabine Torres, who defends the importance of local reporting:

> Regional has too long been thought of as something trashy, devalued, sensationalized and that everything online has to be free. I fundamentally do not believe that to be true. Regional journalism is the backbone of liberty or political justice – and there is a wealth of good reporting to be done if it is done properly.[21]

Ms Galant's greenhouse

New Jersey is not a typical American state: its population is relatively well educated and, on the average, well off, since many of the state's inhabitants work in New York City. But the affluence is not evenly spread: the city of

Newark is the fourth poorest in the United States. In a small upstairs office in the university in the town of Montclair, Debbie Galant has a map of the state on her wall. The map has several dozen yellow flags with red pins marked with names such as Highland Park Mirror, Planet Princeton and Jersey Tomato Press. The flags mark online news sites that she knows of, but the impression given by the number of flags is misleading. As Galant says, not all the sites really do news or do it often enough to really count as news sites. Recession has knocked out several. She reckons that the state has 10 truly 'real functioning' independent hyperlocal news sites. For a state with nearly 9 million inhabitants, that total is discouragingly small.

New Jersey is a case study of how the an 'ecosystem' for news should be working in a country where local newspapers have found life tough and where people are ready to take their news on any platform. There is no shortage of goodwill and energy. But the regeneration of news is barely happening. This is hardly Debbie Galant's fault. She was one of the pioneers of a local news site in Montclair, Baristanet, and is now a one-person coach and mentor to news sites to encourage them to grow in a state where the main newspapers are gradually failing and television has never been very local anyway. She must operate like a gardener in a greenhouse, carefully watering small green shoots of journalism.

Hyperlocal is hardly the whole system. But all the parts of what might be a renewed local news system struggle to put down roots. The big local news-paper, the *Star-Ledger*, is in decline and has laid off journalists. Some of those went to *NJ Spotlight*, a site that covers the state government. Some of the loudest anxieties voiced when newspapers began to fail were about the regular and knowledgeable coverage of state capitals such as Trenton in New Jersey. But *NJ Spotlight*, mostly staffed by *Star-Ledger* refugees, is dependent on foundation grants and donations and they are barely holding on financially. There is a relatively new state politics site (politiker.nj) owned and started by the *New York Observer*; *Star-Ledger*, of course, has a digital presence (nj.com). There is local television, but in New Jersey it comes mostly from the edges of the state: Montclair State University produces an evening news programme; and there is New Jersey Public Radio. In the United States, local jurisdictions and powers are significant: in a state of 8.8 million people, there are 565 communities or jurisdictions that might need watching. That's before counting bodies such as the power and water utilities. The news coverage is uneven, there are gaps. But in the city of Hoboken, there is an AOL Patch site and three other rival sources.

Debbie Galant, supported by foundation grants, can encourage, train and support news sites that want help. If they are going to grow anywhere they should grow in New Jersey's college towns where the population is relatively well off and interested in arts, education and the life of their community. But no amount of advice or subsidy can forge the connection between writer and reader, between editor and audience. It either happens or it doesn't. It can happen accidentally or deliberately; in neither case can anyone be sure that it will follow the plan. Initial success in providing information that people want and can use does not ensure that the connection can be sustained over the long term.

Debbie is a veteran of one of the state's oldest online sites but she illustrates the accidental and unpredictable nature of new news growth with the example of *Jersey Shore Hurricane News*. The Jersey shore – 'the Shore' to those who live and holiday there – has a very distinct identity: it has given its name to a rock-music genre and a reality TV series on MTV. Every community on the Jersey Shore is affected by the hurricanes that hit north-east United States every so often.

Justin Auciello is an urban planning consultant who lives in South Seaside Park on the Shore and he is fascinated by weather. He is, of course, on Facebook. When Hurricane Irene looked like hitting the coast in the summer of 2011, Auciello began posting useful information: reliable sites to check the weather, emergency preparations and community services. He got 1,000 'likes' in one morning. He did very little 'original' reporting, at least at first: he simply linked to what looked useful and what he thought people might want to know. He made value by putting available information in one place.

Auciello got a lot of feedback, most of it friendly and complimentary, and he liked it. He kept going after the hurricane had passed. He takes pictures of sunsets and posts them: his pictures – and those taken by others of sunsets on the Shore – are now one of the most popular bits of the site. He started to become a clearing house for community information. He was a quick worker, and if he got something wrong he was quick to correct it. He covered disasters and emergencies. A helicopter would crash: Auciello would aggregate fragments of the story, filter what he got and fill it out as more information arrived. He fact-checked; he shared a lot. He aggregated information if he felt like it, such as listing places in Shore communities that would be open on Thanksgiving. He connected volunteers to organizations needing them and publicized charity appeals. By the time of Hurricane Sandy in 2012, Auciello was doing journalism without bothering to call himself a journalist. He could do this faster and more effectively than local newspapers because he has 200,000 fans on Facebook for *Hurricane News*. That, as Debbie Galant says, in a state the size of New Jersey is 'a big sample'. Galant is now trying to help Auciello turn the site into a business; thus far it has only sold T-shirts.

Galant knows more than most in New Jersey about how hard 'monetizing' a site can be. She founded 'Baristanet' in Montclair, starting in 2003 when she had been writing about the area for the local edition of the *New York Times*. At first it was a blog called 'Barista of Bloomfield Avenue', but she quickly acquired other helpers and a partner, Liz George, who worked as a journalist at the *Daily News* in New York. George found that she had plenty of time to work on the site when she was at her desk in the *Daily News*. 'You can work anywhere if you're in touch with your audience,' she says, 'but you need to speak the dialect of the area.'

Galant and George quickly discovered that existing local media had stopped speaking local dialect: they were reporting stories slowly (in an era in which people were swapping gossip and pictures constantly) and in a formal news language that seemed impersonal and increasingly odd. Baristanet found a voice that suited a well-educated and curious community: humorous but not snide, perky and informal but not contemptuous. They judged themselves by how much people were not only reading what they wrote (on subjects such as school book donations, local statistics, crime and restaurants) but also by how much they shared it with other people. To what extent was a new post something that people would talk about to other people? Did people bother to correct any mistakes they had spotted on the site?

'Barista is a coffeehouse that news people can talk about,' says George, who is now in sole charge. 'It's an elevated way of getting news: you get it in a caffeinated way, we up the tempo. People can count on the fact that if there's a murder on a Saturday night, it'll be in Barista on Sunday.' The site has stabilized at 90,000 unique visitors per month. Over nine years, the site learnt by trial and error. A children's sub-site worked well. Two attempts to move into areas vacated by the shrinkage of the *New York Times* news blogs did not work. Competition arrived or revived: there is an AOL Patch site for Montclair and the local paper's website has raised its game. The site makes its income from advertising; it currently employs George and pays regular weekly amounts to four other people. In the site's best year, 2007, it paid salaries in the $40–50,000 range to both George and Galant. Both recession and competition have made financial life tougher since.

Barista covers all the town meetings, all planning decisions and is thinking of a food and entertainment newsletter. They try, George says, to be open to random acts of journalism. 'If you're open, it's easy to adapt. You pick, choose, curate. We say: people like this, we'll do more of this. Our mix is great stories and a poll on the best place for lunch. If you start with a plan for ads and money, you do it differently.' Like most such sites that have grown organically, Barista is wary of over-trained journalists. Barista takes contributions from an economist who writes limericks – about economics. They had someone in the team who had worked at *Newsweek* and a journalism professor. They have trained one person from scratch. They have evolved conventions about linking and crediting. No rules are written down. Would they do investigative journalism? 'I don't know if we'll do that,' George says, explaining that the local paper does investigations and they tend to ask themselves what they can offer that other people aren't doing.

Barista is an emblematic example – and there are many more – of what can be done in an affluent college town where there is a pool of readers interested in events beyond their immediate knowledge. Even in that promising soil, growing such a site has not been easy. It's possible that societies like the United States are at the start of a long innovation 'adoption curve' that will see Barista-like experiments pop up in less easy environments. But the odds for that result are not good. A formula that assumes people will read what they think is good for them is not likely to work everywhere. Not all the plants in Ms Galant's greenhouse will survive in the harsh climate outside the glass. As printed news continues to weaken, there will be a role for more aggressive techniques of grabbing and holding peoples' attention.

Zero baggage and viral gold

The rebuilding of journalism brings the architects of new enterprises face to face with an inescapable dilemma: how to mix the need to attract and hold an audience with doing something worthwhile. This section looks at three examples of pure-play online journalism, all based in New York, and how they have experimented and worked out their answer to this dilemma.

American newspapers, at the start of this century mostly monopolies, were vulnerable to challengers. The sites that were the first generation to challenge the status quo and survive are still financially insecure but are reaching a stage at which they can lean back a little from the fight merely to survive. Much of the subversive energy derived from a strong feeling that the style and formulas of newspaper journalism were unsuited to a digitally connected world. Even if someone founding a site wanted to do something serious for an elite audience, they were not likely to want to do something in the manner of serious newspapers. Josh Marshall of Talking Points Memo (TPM), a hyperactive site for US politics addicts and wonks, was trained as a historian and then moved into website design and liked it. In the history of news media, he sees print monopolies as the anomaly. 'Economics forms the journalism,' he says: 'The old system was monopoly and anti-niche; you had to be bland. We're niche. What everyone sees as disruption is more a return to the norm.' The internet's disconnection from geography, and new advertising models like Craigslist, broke the monopolies.

But monopoly newspapers left a psychological imprint on journalists. TPM was different from websites started by newsapers in that it did not want or need to match print output on the web. Starting in 2000, TPM could build itself gradually with few resources; with a staff of 27 it still occupies a crowded single room near the Empire State Building, dominated by a constantly updating list of how many people are clicking on each of TPM's posts. Journalists and publishers, Marshall says, think that the aim of journalism is a story on the front page, but that only make sense, he says, in 'once-a-day economics'. It is more natural to break, recycle and comment on news as it happens: 'We were quicker, faster. We were allowed to do that for years; our competitors are closer (behind us) now.'

TPM has 3.5 million unique visitors per month with one-quarter of those visits on mobile devices; they would like to be three times bigger. Success so far has rested on understanding their niche and getting a handle on how to do stories in a way native to the medium. So stories were aggregated or written as soon as they appeared, sometimes just a few paragraphs. Elite readers, Marshall believes, need factual details at speed. His editorial philosophy could be described as a cross between the operational discipline of an old-fashioned news agency and the informal humour of the internet era.

These demands have provoked a recruitment crisis for Marshall:

> We're supposed to hire to grow. But there aren't that many good people; there are lots who are good at A1 (front page) journalism. We move as quick as possible to suit the format. Not everything gets jammed into a 700-word arc. Hire big names? Tried it; never works. They've been doing the same for 15–20 years. They want to spend a day, when we might need something every half hour. This stuff has a very short half-life.

Was he worried that TPM's writers might be doing the journalism too fast? 'In the civic concern sense? I don't have a lot of time to think about that,' he deadpans. More seriously, Marshall believes that all variations in taste can be catered for in a freer market for communication. 'The 8,000-word piece is not going to disappear. Words are very persistent and people want text. The last 20 years has seen a renaissance for text. Video is for entertainment. Details need words.'

Lockhart Steel, like so many others, began his accidental career as a blogger when he was also a journalist. He worked as a reporter for *Cottages & Gardens* covering high-end property in the Hamptons, the millionaires' playground east of New York. The job conferred two advantages: he had a boss who taught him about journalism and publishing, and his vantage point allowed him to see what was wrong with property reporting. To amuse his friends, in 2001 he began a blog about the Lower East Side of Manhattan, just then becoming a cool place to live. At the end of 2002, Gawker.com began changing the face of US journalism by doing internet gossip with a gloves-off meaness that New York had not seen for decades: scrappy, snarky and sarcastic. It wasn't that gossip was new, but the style and speed were startling.

Steel had started his blog, eventually calling it Curbed.com, while still working as a magazine reporter. Curbed made fun of presentations by property developers and exploited the passionate New York hunger for gossip about real estate prices. He did not imitate Gawker's tone but borrowed a little of its DNA, aiming to be funny but not nasty. Steel was clear that 'voice' was the key. 'You must empower writers. Too many layers and you strip the voice out of the writing.' On the web, he said, you had to feel you knew the person writing. Impersonal prose was not authority. Curbed clicked: people linked to it, sent in pictures of buildings being demolished, contributed to a series about burnt-out cars. It was niche with rich potential: in 2005, a two-year real estate boom began. Steel was hired as Managing Editor at Gawker and enjoyed a wild ride as the start-up went from 15 employees to a business now employing 150 people in a group of websites with a turnover estimated at well over $30 million per year. A friend took over Curbed, for which Steel still wrote, and developed the advertising income. By 2007, Curbed was taking $200,000 in a year.

They allowed two young graduates to start a Curbed in Los Angeles. On the West Coast they were allowed to depart from the original formula as long as they stuck to the main aim to be 'non-boring'. The Curbed team in New York looked at ideas for a restaurant site and impish foodie to handle it. Restaurant coverage, dominated by public-relations people, looked ripe for a shake-up. Above all, people were getting accustomed to wanting much, much more detail. They discovered that what Steel terms the 'PR-industrial complex' successfully discouraged magazines and papers from running pictures of new restaurants until the PRs wanted them seen. The moment they knew about new restaurants being built and fitted out they took pictures of them, calling it the 'Plywood Report'. They did feuds between chefs, and managers getting fired. Their target audience was people in the trade and food obsessives.

It worked and most recently has been replicated in Racked, a similarly cheeky take on fashion. Racked breaks even, whereas the two older sites make money. Steel says that 50 per cent of the three sites' content is original, the rest aggregated from other sources. His staff, who work in an eerily quiet room, are a mixture of journalists with experience and those with none. Until recently, writers were expected to produce a minimum of 12 posts per day, a quota now relaxed. They prefer to find people with a passion for the subject and let them find out what happens when they make a mistake: 'We have very demanding readers; people smell mistakes.' Steel claims that by drilling deeper on property, food and clothes they have occupied territory abandoned by the established newspapers that are under financial pressure:

> The city papers where we are[22] had stopped covering our verticals properly. We're the main sources now. We're not covering national defence or the cure for cancer, but we are the definitive source on what we do cover. We keep investing in better journalism. We now plan big-overarching projects for the year: health inspections, the nightlife industry.

Steel's climb towards journalism mixes traditional elements – comprehensiveness for obsessives and experts, an identifiable tone and voice, mischief making – with ruthless efficiency in holding down costs and holding the audience's attention while income grows. Many now-huge media businesses have formed from similar recipes.

Jake Dobkin, the founder of Gothamist.com, was once, like Josh Marshall, an information architect. His clients went bankrupt simultaneously in the dot.com crash of 2001 and he played with a blog about New York life when work was short. He got hold of the url 'gothamist' and discovered that his voice was creating a community of 'like-minded downtowners' who liked commenting and linking to it. For several years he did not do it full-time, as he was at business school. But he and his partner had built an audience in the low hundred thousands. 'We're trying to be the voice of the city, the hometown hero type,' Dobkin says. 'We're talking to New York in the voice of New York about things that New York cares about.'

They started taking advertising (the first ad was from Gawker), took a windowless back room and held parties every two months for contributors in lieu of payment. They invented the site's quirky, querulous voice as they went along, keeping a careful eye on the new tricks being invented at Gawker but without mimicking its tone. By 2008, Gothamist had a dozen imitators. Failure killed off the low performers and it now fights nine rivals. Someone left the loose collective in New York for a job in Chicago, took a little DNA with her and started Chicagoist.com.

Dobkin realized that they were edging towards journalism. They took a bigger office in Brooklyn and hired two senior editors. They got rid of free-lance writers who weren't dependable enough. They started to pay writers. The changes meant 'some ugliness'. Dobkin was firing people from jobs they didn't have.

> Rules didn't exist and now they do. Somewhere in the middle I must have invented it. I bought books: I read all of the Associated Press manual. We were bloggers having a good time. We were having journalistic moments! Then it was journalism.

Gothamist then had to fight to join the closed club of news organizations covering the city. They subscribed to the alerts from the fire and police service and put the alerts on a real-time online map. There was a row and they now appear on a map after a 45-minute delay. They applied for press passes issued by the police; the rules were changed to make that harder. It took several appeals for Gothamist reporters to get their passes. They had to threaten to sue the police in order to receive the regular press releases. 'If you had to start from scratch and invent journalism,' Dobkin said, 'it would take you some time. It took me 10 years.'

Dobkin's requirements for his staff are that news should be true, updated quickly and 'interesting and authentic'. They have hired a mixture of enthusiasts and one experienced reporter to 'class the place up'. The editorial team of eight or ten people look for 'viral gold' that will be shared by users. Dog-shows qualify: 'Nobody should be superior to pictures of dogs getting shampooed.' The tempo is fast. Gothamist, like Curbed, had a minimum 'post count' that each writer had to meet each day, also now relaxed. A writer is safe in their job if their 'unique clicks' are more than the site's median average for the past 12 months. In New York that will be around 500,000 clicks (the site had 2.7 million unique visitors in December 2012). They expect three or four pieces per day per person, of which two must be original. Dobkin describes the site as 'very porous': it gets up to 500 e-mails per day from readers and up to 1,500 comments on anywhere between 40 and 100 stories posted each day. 'If we get it wrong, we start again the next morning.' At the end of 2012 less than one-third of the site's content is original, with the rest culled and aggregated; he hopes to reach 50 per cent of original content.

Dobkin's real target is the Metro (city) section of the giant *New York Times*. If he could double his staff to 20, he claims, he could give the *Times* Metro staff of 60 a run for their money, 'because we're three times more efficient'. Whether or not Dobkin achieves this ambition, his plan is a neat illustration of what business economists call disruption theory. A new entrant to a market establishes a low-cost, low-margin foothold. From this position, they eat away at slower-moving competitors weighed down by high costs. As the insurgent competitor advances, the quality of its output rises. The incumbent often does not realize the full scale of the threat until it is too late.

The Gothamist of 2014, Dobkin says, will not be like the site of a year before. 'We have no attachments, zero baggage. We can be shaped and transformed by readers. If we're not doing that, what are we doing?' But this porousness, flexibility and economic efficiency leans against his social ambition: 'I want to make New York and other cities better. But there's a tension: I have to have enough money to pay my writers. I don't want to make money without purpose.'

Error is useful

As the last few examples have shown, American journalism has taken a turn not seen elsewhere in the world. The new journalism that has flourished in digital's new possibilities is gossipy, unashamedly popular and heedless of the fact that many journalists would call it 'downmarket'. This is hardly a new formula, although the classic era of American tabloid journalism was a century ago. Lockhart Steel quotes Nick Denton, the founder of Gawker, as saying: 'What we're doing is what journalism has done for years but with a different sensibility.' Gawker has run blogs in the past that included one called Defamer and another called Fleshbot, the latter described by the *New York Times* as 'the thinking person's diary of smut'. The editorial technique is stories and videos that young readers might want to share, delivered with a fast-paced, scathing panache. In 2005, Gawker's Fleshbot was one among several sites that posted a pornographic video of Fred Durst, frontman of the rap-rock group Limp Bizkit. Durst threatened to sue and most sites, including Fleshbot, took it down. Most sites, however, did not write the next post aimed at Durst in the style of that posted by Gawker editor Jessica Coen:

> Honestly, though, we don't know why you're so mad at us. The situation is really rather simple. Someone sent us a link to a video of your penis, we went into shock, and we shared it with the world for about two hours. Then we wept, found God, took a hot bath, and removed the video from our site.

This mix of disclosure with attitude is a technique as old as mass journalism and it works. Popular makes money, but it can also be used to build a platform on which more serious reporting can be done. People worrying about the future of journalism should be alert to popular sites moving, as economists say, 'up the value chain'. The clues revealing this movement tend to be less aggregation of others' material, a higher proportion of original reporting and hiring high-priced specialists. If successfully popular sites experiment with more serious content, they enjoy higher odds of success because they already have a record of high-quality experiment. They know how to do trial and error. Curbed is extending its reporting range as its reach and income grows. Gothamist is taking the rules of journalism more seriously as it sees off its rivals. The Huffington Post, its lack of original reporting once derided, has been bought by a major media company and won its first Pulitzer Prize. At the start of 2013, Gawker's sports site, Deadspin, broke a meticulously researched story about a football star inventing an apparently moving story about the death of a girlfriend. The story was read by 150,000 people in its first five minutes after publication and set the sports news agenda for days. The Gawker network, under the slogan 'Today's gossip is tomorrow's news', expects to start up sites in India and probably elsewhere in 2013. It is estimated to have been profitable on substantial advertising income since 2006.

The ruthless acquisition of an audience creates a platform for wider opportunities. Jonah Peretti of Buzzfeed is using the same technique. As it raises money to expand, the site is more buzz than feed: repeating video loops, stories about cute cats and the First Lady's hair – most of it solicited from readers and curated on the site. The site's sections may start with 'Politics' and 'Tech' but the verticals that count have names like 'LOL', 'omg', 'cute', 'geeky' and 'trashy'. The site uses technology that makes it very fast to download and particularly to mobiles; at the site's start, the technical development team grew faster than the editing team. The site could be described as a collective effort to discover by experiment what makes people click. Stories are told in a rush and the site is explicitly aimed at people who are bored at work and need gossip to swap. But Buzzfeed has invested in political coverage and, in a chilly economic climate, few established news outlets will now do that. Venture capitalists have put $46 million into Peretti's brainchild.

'We think of ourselves as a news organization,' Buzzfeed's managing editor said in 2012,[23] explaining that in the Facebook era people exchange baby pictures and talk about the 'fiscal cliff' without thinking the combination incongruous. Ben Smith, the site's well-known editor, was hired to bring original reporting to what had previously been curation and aggregation.

Buzzfeed expects to start a business reporting vertical. But its encouragement of what would once have been called 'advertorial', editorial devoted to an advertiser, is liable to compromise claims to editorial independence. Buzzfeed has produced editorial content on clean energy as part of an advertising campaign for General Electric. Its managing editor acknowledged that the site 'might not' run a story criticizing GE's clean energy 'unless it was really good'.[24] Buzzfeed's journalism is not going to carry conviction until it defines its own rule about advertising. That guideline might be: any legal way to keep expenses below income is fine so long as it doesn't touch or influence the site's ability to report on anything, contributors and advertisers included.

Buzzfeed is trying to leverage its traffic to expand the range of what it reports. But its editors also think that viral web traffic is changing the way that engagement with information is being measured. The period is ending in which search engines, and the manipulation of their software, dominated who saw what. Social networks point people to information and news, but in ways less easy to manipulate. Users might once have been persuaded to go to one site over another by search, but viral distribution can't be manipulated in the same way. 'You can't trick to click any more', as the Buzzfeed mantra has it. The other slogan heard a lot at Buzzfeed – and at many other similar start-ups – goes: error is useful. Sites harvest huge amounts of real-time information on what people like and don't like, what works and what doesn't. Errors can be dropped and corrected at speed. That way they discover which bits of spaghetti stick to the wall.

Notes

1 http://rasmuskleisnielsen.net/2012/12/11/english-version-of-the-best-media-in-the-world-and-why-they-are-about-to-change/ (accessed 4.2.13).

2 22 February 2013.

3 Formally called the Committee for the Promotion of Virtue and Prevention of Vice.

4 *The Economist*, 26 January 2013.

5 14 per cent of UK adults says they use local community news sites; the figure for the 25–34 age group is 22 per cent.

6 http://kingscrossenvironment.com/faq/ (accessed 22.2.13).

7 http://www.journalism.co.uk/news-commentary/-hyperlocal-media-is-coming-in-from-the-cold-/s6/a552844/ (accessed 20.5.13).

8   Will Perrin **http://talkaboutlocal.org.uk/res-publica-carnegie-uk-trust-event-future-of-the-press-hyperlocal-is-it-worth-the-hype-a-primer/#more-5809** (accessed 23.2.13).

9   E-mail from James Hatts, 23 February 2013.

10 Tim Rayment, 'Not the end of the story', *Sunday Times Magazine*, 15 April 2012.

11 **http://www.ibtimes.com/broken-promise-hyperlocal-news-797717** (accessed 23.2.13).

12 The four are Bideford, Dalston, Chippenham and Dorchester, at **www.localpeople.co.uk** (accessed 20.5.13).

13 Thurman, N, Pascal, J C & Bradshaw, P (2012). 'Can Big Media do "Big Society"?: A Critical Case Study of Commercial, Convergent Hyperlocal News, *International Journal of Media and Cultural Politics*, 8(2).

14 Until 2012 called VentnorBlog.

15 Perrin, **http://talkaboutlocal.org.uk/res-publica-carnegie-uk-trust-event-future-of-the-press-hyperlocal-is-it-worth-the-hype-a-primer/#more-5809** (accessed 23.2.13).

16 Jones, R, *What Do We Mean by Local?* (2012) ed Mair, J, Fowler, N and Reeves, I, Arima, Bury St Edmunds.

17 Mikihito Tanaka in eds Sirkkunen, Esa and Cook, Clare, *Chasing Sustainability on the Net* (2012) Comet, Finland.

18 From 2010 internal accounts quoted in Bruno, Nicola and Kleis Nielsen, Rasmus, *Survival is Success: Journalistic Online Start-ups in Western Europe* (2012) RISJ, Oxford.

19 **http://uk.mobile.reuters.com/article/idUKBRE9380XM20130409?irpc=932** (accessed 10.4.13).

20 In May 2013, the French government promised to look sympathetically at a proposal from advisers that this discrepancy should be removed.

21 Quoted in Sirkunnen and Cook, *Chasing Sustainability on the Net*.

22 Curbed now has sites in nine cities outside New York.

23 Scott Lamb, presentation to digital journalism conference, Sciences Po, Paris, December 2012.

24 Scott Lamb, presentation to digital journalism conference, Sciences Po, Paris, December 2012. See also **http://dish.andrewsullivan.com/2013/02/21/guess-which-buzzfeed-piece-is-an-ad/** (accessed 20.5.13).

Clues to
the future

10

... There's no silver bullet – it's just shrapnel... there isn't one stream (of revenue) that's going to be successful.

JIM BRADY, TBD.COM, 2010

The future business of journalism will resemble the past and will also be unlike it. Ideas about journalism and the business that supports it interact, but also develop separately. What never changes is the accidental nature of experiment. News media does not follow a master narrative or plan because it involves connecting two elements: the person or group with something to tell and the people who are interested enough to hear it. Chapter 9 concentrated on those who are succeeding, but today's journalism innovators have a high failure rate. Some discover journalism almost as an accidental by-product of trying something else. The difference from the recent past is that there is no sign of a simple, one-size-fits-all business model that will replace the cross-subsidy of journalism by advertising. It is more likely that journalism will be sustained or rebuilt by varied combinations of income and support.

The rush of energy produced by new technology and investment generates a pattern of activity that resembles a children's soccer game. Every player on the pitch chases the ball wherever it goes. Adult football players use experience and practice to position themselves in advance in places where they think the ball might go next. Their chance of scoring is better if they get that prediction right. In news media, most new entrants chase each new fad down the pitch. There are very few players who have the knowledge, insight and experience to anticipate how the game will go. But the number of players who are acquiring that knowledge is increasing. As knowledge improves, so do the chances of sustainable business models for news.

Business models

Not every editor or publisher has the chance to grow a publication and a business from seed in the way that the journalism entrepreneurs discussed in Chapter 9 are doing. It seems increasingly unlikely that a single powerful business model, such as the cross-subsidy of reporting by advertising, will provide the platform for digital news. Combinations of solutions will vary from place to place, from market to market and from culture to culture. What kind of solutions are open to established media?

1 Subscription or 'paywall'. Early experiments show that this will work where the value of the content is clearly visible and cannot be replicated. Sites carrying sports statistics began charging for access almost as soon as they went online. Those who enjoy the numbers for cricket, football or baseball cannot get them except from a reliable compiler. Databases of sports statistics are not easy to build up and their value is relatively simple to demonstrate – and people will pay. Content that cannot pass easy replication or evident value tests will struggle to raise the subscription price to a level at which it can compensate for the fall in printed advertising. Contrast the fate of *The Daily*, a news magazine tailored for iPads and backed by the resources of News Corporation and Apple: readers did not see value that attracted them on the right scale and, losing an estimated $30 million per year, *The Daily* was closed before its second birthday. In short, the key to asking people to pay directly is the measure of the value they perceive – usually known as 'engagement'. How long do people stay on the site or page? Do they share the information? Johnston Press, one of Britain's largest regional newspaper chains, tried charging a small fee (£5 for three months) for access to six of its papers but abandoned the trial after only a few months. A new chief executive at the company who took over not long afterwards said that if local papers make stories hard to share, they weaken their contribution to their communities.[1]

2 Engagement may be a lesser worry if advertising income is the aim. Online readerships are starting to be sifted into new categories. Big digital audiences are not always profitable if they don't deliver either repeat visits or attention to the advertisements. But the larger the total audience, the bigger the 'core' of users who may notice what's on the site. Different sites argue with advertisers about whether 'pass by' occasional users pay more heed to advertisements or less than

regular users. The aggregator site Newser had 2.5 million unique visitors in 2011. It calculated that 12,000 of those were 'addicted', 225,000 'avid' users and the remainder – more than 2.25 million – pass by with a click or two, never to return. Advertisers will also need to make sure that users retain something from ads and the advertisers will run their own research to check. That is why magazines that can carry the habit of leisurely time spent reading them to the web have an in-built advantage: the *Atlantic* magazine has been making money with more than half its advertising revenue being digital. Advertisers have learnt that users who look at a lot of pages are a small minority of the total number of visitors to a site. One medium-sized US newspaper site counted 'fans' and 'regulars' as 7.4 per cent of the visitors to their site but they accounted for over 60 per cent of the site's page views.[2]

3   Philanthropy, often promoted as a new way of protecting journalism, looks as if it will only be enough to protect specialized journalism – and then in societies where rich, disinterested donors are thick on the ground. A great deal of experimentation in journalism in the United States is funded by a single foundation, the John S and James L Knight Foundation, based in Miami. ProPublica, an independent investigative team of journalists, is funded by an initial donation estimated at $35 million from the Sandler family; its editorial costs run at $10 million per year. Several other US investigative 'non-profits' also live on lesser donations. The British equivalent, the Bureau of Investigative Journalism,[3] received a £2 million initial donation from the Potter Foundation. Philanthropic donors seem to have fared better funding specialized journalism rather than general news. Australian digital millionaire Graeme Wood funded the *Global Mail* in 2012 but it has had a slow and unhappy start. In 2009, Yale University's chief investment officer suggested that news media should turn themselves into endowed institutions like universities. But no solution to the problem of persuading owners to surrender their stakes in their businesses was offered and the author's credibility suffered when Yale's own funds shrank badly in the global financial crisis. But the arguments did help millionaire John Thornton (who was alarmed by the fall in the number of journalists covering Texas politics) to raise money to match his own start-up cash for the *Texas Tribune* (see point 7 below).[4] Media analyst Alan Mutter calculated that the US news business alone, in order to keep going, would need an endowment of at least $88 billion – almost one-third

of the annual total given to charity in the United States.[5] Some publications, from the *Tageszeitung* in Berlin,[6] to the new online *Port Talbot Magnet* in Wales, have appealed for small donations to keep them going. But any success has been small scale in local communities. Money has been raised more effectively for stories, projects or causes on sites such as Kickstarter.

4   Free newspapers enjoyed a vogue as publishers cast around for new models. Distributing a newspaper for free, abandoning the cover price income and relying on advertising, works in limited circumstances. For example, if large numbers of people can pick up newspapers quickly from self-service racks, such as railway stations in cities, then a free newspaper can be supported. London supports one in the morning (*Metro*, from Associated Newspapers) and one in the afternoon (the *Evening Standard*, from Alexander Lebedev's Evening Press Corporation). Both rely heavily on owning the right to distribute on the overground and underground rail networks. A Swedish company began an extensive empire of *Metro*s in cities in continental Europe in 1995. Their success varied, but at its peak there were 56 editions in 19 countries and 15 languages. By 2012, all but one had been sold (and a number closed) to allow the parent company to develop *Metro*s in Latin America, which it considered the last growth territory for free papers. With the exception of the *Evening Standard*, which has a long history, the journalism of these papers is not remarkable.

5   Sponsorship has only featured rarely in attempts to break out of cycles of decline. The boldest experiment has been made by *Atlantic* with a site, Quartz, dedicated to international business coverage, optimized for mobile and tablet reading and with very few advertisements. Quartz launched in 2012 with four major sponsors: Chevron, Boeing, Credit Suisse and Cadillac. The new site began offering what they called 'native advertising', which allowed smaller sponsors to generate articles marked as such. The test of this initiative in the end is whether consumers find the reporting trustworthy despite the presence of the sponsors – and whether they need it enough to keep coming back. The results of this test can emerge only over time. *The Age* of Melbourne had notched up some success with similar sponsorships for its weekend supplements and lifestyle reporting, but not to the extent that it could keep the newspaper from large-scale redundancies and, in 2012, a boardroom battle for control of the paper.

6 News has received public subsidy of some kind in most countries in the world. Given the impoverished condition of most governments in the developed world, increases in the future do not seem likely. Subsidies tend to be larger in Europe than elsewhere, but several European governments such as Italy have sharply curtailed aid to news media. Most governments (France has been a notable exception) tend to take the private, if not public, view that subsidies would be at risk of being misused to support established media whose business model could not be rescued because consumer behaviour has changed. In Britain, where the BBC represents a £4 billion per year intervention in the market and involves a specific tax to raise the money, it is hardly conceivable that any government would consider any further news media subsidy (see Figure 10.1).

TABLE 10.1 Press subsidies and public service media funding (2008)

	Direct press subsidies (euros per capita)	Public service media funding (euros per capita)
UK	0.00	68.20
US	0.00	2.60
Germany	0.00	88.50
France	7.00	48.60
Finland	0.10	71.70

SOURCE: Nielsen, R K (2011) Public Support for the Media, Reuters Institute, Oxford based on European Audiovisual Observatory and CPB YLE.

7 Digital news publishers stress multiple sources of revenue and one successful one calls it 'revenue promiscuity'. Oh Yeon-ho, founder of the Korean site OhmyNews, a veteran of the citizen-journalism movement, has started activities partly to engage its loyal contributors and partly to see if it will make money. The site runs a marathon, owns a school, publishes books and solicits donations from readers, promoting the idea that belonging to the site's club of donors confers social cachet. Evan Smith of the *Texas Tribune* (see point 3 above) reckons that 15 per cent of his income is from events and conferences run by the site.[7] Justin Smith of Atlantic Media, one of the most successful magazine-turned-websites, said:

> To say that the ad model is going to win over the pay model is foolish. I think that the solution will be multiple revenue streams, it will be experimental, how creative you are in seeking out those revenue streams... we must try everything. And we must not believe that one thing is going to work over the other until we actually experience it.[8]

8 News media are understandably wary of direct support from governments; but governments can give indirect support to news. Journalism that provides information and disclosure to strengthen the accountability of public bodies is gradually shifting towards what has come to be called 'data journalism'. The *Texas Tribune* believes that 60 per cent of its page views come from reporting of data from public bodies.[9] The movement to persuade governments to disclose data and to do so in a form that can be analysed and displayed for public consumption has barely begun and has a long way to go, even in countries where laws oblige a relatively open attitude to government information.[10] There is a small, but growing campaign to encourage the British government to adapt charity law to be more sympathetic to new news media who wish to raise money to support themselves. Current charity law only allows charity registration to applicants who can show work in community building, citizenship or education and who can show that they will not be politically partisan. The interpretation of the law in practice has prevented news organizations being recognized as charities – and many foundations will only give to registered charities. The sites, magazines and newspapers in greatest need of this change are at a local level. One report that supported a change to charity law also argued for a levy to be charged on the distribution of news by search engines and to be given to income-starved media.[11] Governments have shown no appetite for entering the minefield of decisions needed to share out such money. But governments can make oblique and indirect contributions that run no risk of either interfering with news or supporting expensive failures. They can help to ensure that internet communications are kept open and are fairly run. They can enforce the rules of transparency, such as making sure that we can know how search engines actually work in influencing users' choices and behaviour.

9 So varied are the circumstances and possible solutions that it is not possible to draw a picture of the journalism platform of the future. But a few of its desirable characteristics can be listed. News sites that have prospered online manage the alchemy of customer loyalty differently and often have some or all of these features:

- a clear and distinct promise of value;
- a lean organization that only scales up cautiously;
- diverse sources of income;
- niche target audience served by different sites or contributors.

Successful sites have three other basic strengths: high-calibre software, the proficient capture and use of customer data, and a willingness to experiment and not just to pay lip service to the idea. The last item in that list needs open minds, an allowance for failure and the ruthlessness to shut trials that fail. These strengths may not be sufficient for success, but they will help.

From the ashes of dead trees

Journalists should never confuse the platform with the content. As I have argued here, platforms influence how journalism is done and often profoundly; as platforms change, so will journalism. But platforms are interesting because they need to be understood to be fully exploited. Important discoveries are made at the junction between journalistic ambition and technical opportunity. But there is no law that holds that every change is progress. Journalism will survive if its 'reinvention' takes the best of the past into a new communications era. While I am pessimistic about the survival chances of some threatened daily newspapers, I am an optimist about journalism. There is a role for journalism even if some of its present institutions struggle to breathe. The global debate about the future of news media, while often agonized and gloomy, testifies to a wide understanding of the importance of reliable public information. Journalism has to make sure that it stays relevant to that need.

Journalists who think that optimism about online is irrational or overdone point to the inability of websites to generate the sort of income that supports original, expensive reporting in the public interest. There is no guarantee that this dilemma can be solved – and it is never solved permanently. But it is certain that there is no way back to the news media of the

20th century. There is no choice but to find ways of supporting journalism in new conditions.

Technological change offers opportunities by breaking habits, processes and – sometimes – organizations. Those breakages do damage, but also offer people new vantage points to create, to invent and to make connections and to supply content that did not previously exist. Digital electronics, in its widest definition, does journalism both good and harm by both opening opportunities and closing others down. But in the two decades since the internet was born, one benefit has been clear. The thirst to regenerate journalism without abandoning its values, to push it further and to make it better, has turned out to be powerful. This generative power to find better ways, to solve the problems of financial sustainability, is not something that can be precisely measured to provide proof. In phases of intensive experiment, failures are visible everywhere.

Creative destruction is no fun if it is your livelihood or beloved newspaper that is being destroyed. But my researches have convinced me that journalism is being adapted, rethought and reconstructed in thousands of ways in far more places than can easily be grasped. In short, there is enough experiment in train to be optimistic that economic sustainability will be found even if the experiments have a high failure rate. In open societies, this takes the form of new communities of interest, new market players, new suppliers of news. Even in some closed societies, information can often flow down different routes in informal, unpredictable ways. Some of those new flows are – or may become – journalism. New ways of dispersing information do not mean that 'everything changes'. Here are some examples of the variety of what does and does not change:

- Journalists worrying about 'paradigm shifts', 'network effects' and 'post counts' can often forget that, in many parts of the world, adapting journalism to disruption is not the big issue. Keeping reporters and cameramen alive and out of jail remains a priority for many news organizations. In 2012, 70 journalists were killed worldwide in direct relation to their work, making it one of the worst years since records began to be kept. The imprisonment of journalists reached a record high in the same year, with 232 individuals behind bars because of their work.[12] At a less dangerous level and in many places, journalists confront risks, obstruction and threats that are a feature of any society not accustomed to press freedom. The Russian deputy minister of communications Aleksei Volin recently told journalism teachers in Moscow:

Any journalist has to remember: he has no mission to change the world or make it better... You have to teach students that after graduation they will work for their big boss and this big boss will tell them what to write and what not to write and how to write; and the boss has the right to do so because he pays them.[13]

- Human beings like reading words from paper. For many, paper is both optically more attractive and carries greater authority. The internet creates potential business-model problems for newspapers, magazines and books since all of these rely on cumbersome and expensive distribution systems. But the impact has been felt first at daily newspapers, whose heavy reliance of immediacy once a day was most easily upset by the internet's ability to send information without a regular timetable. That in turn caused advertisers to be increasingly sceptical that daily newspapers were holding the attention of their readers, and particularly younger readers; the scepticism predated the internet. Magazines and books remain effective ways to send information that readers value.

- Newspapers are very reluctant to die. They may cut staff, hollow out their content, be a shadow of their former selves and change their readers – but actual extinction, taken as a whole across developed societies, still remains rare. Printed newspapers will be a lower and less important layer of the news system in many countries, but it is not likely that they will vanish entirely. It has happened at more rapid rates in some places in the past than it is happening in the second decade of the 21st century. News readers, particularly over the age of 40, are readers of habit; even if they use a tablet to read newspapers, they will adapt most easily to reading apps that mimic structures and layout in print. The readers of the *Daily Mail* on paper are among the most enthusiastic users of its site *MailOnline*. The DNA of printed journalism will alter over time, but at a slow and evolutionary pace. Any potential audience contains 'lean forward' readers – technologically adept, engaged, interactive – and 'lean back' readers who enjoy the journalism more passively for its writing quality, sense of humour or character. Some readers have both of these approaches at different times, on different subjects and in different moods. News publishers must adapt their strategies to the temperament of the audience they have or they want, because members of their audience can switch so easily.

- One key reason why newspapers will still retain a place in a more complex information system is the wide understanding that print has long been a main carrier of news not published elsewhere. Television is, and will remain for some time, the dominant news medium by 'reach' in almost all parts of the world. The internet will often carry the widest-ranging and quickest comment because that is what the web is often best at. Newspapers – printed or online – have specialized in trying to produce news that no one else has. The ability to see a story – to frame selected facts readably – produces bad results when it goes wrong. But at its best, it sharpens the attractions of information. Julian Assange paid tribute to this skill, despite his loathing of mainstream media, when explaining why WikiLeaks had partnered with several major newspapers: 'We see actually that the professional press has a nose for what a story will be – the general public becomes involved once there is a story.'

- There are pure-play online sites doing journalism, of which most usually consist of a mixture of aggregation and original reporting. But because of the investment and resources required for the reporting, it has taken effort, time, money and much trial and error to reach the point where these newsrooms can grow to the scale where they can challenge established print operations that are also on the web. (The established, legacy media suffers the reverse problem: plenty of allegiance from users derived from habit and tradition but unsustainable costs.)

- What may appear revolutionary is better labelled as evolutionary. The sites experimenting with different ways of producing sustainable journalism have significant quantities of journalism in their bloodstream. They may hire journalism experience when confident of an audience, they may train their own people, they may institute rules for editorial quality and integrity. A high proportion of founders of new journalism operations have been journalists themselves before striking out on their own. They are living proof that journalism is not being reinvented without any legacy from the past. The past is part of the mix.

- The hunger for video and the switch to mobile devices are the two major trends that business strategists must adapt for in the second decade of this century. But none of that sweeping change alters the fact that the internet is a universe of words. That means that writing – and the editing that inspires, sifts and improves it – will matter in what people choose to read. Since there is no space constraint on the web, long-form writing may flower. Much long-form will continue to appear in print, but there will also be sites specializing in writing of length and depth outside of academic journals. A few such sites for a general readership already exist.

- As digital communications become the quickest and simplest ways of getting and sending information, the conventions of 20th-century print will fade in importance. The rules and conventions of fairness, impartiality, objectivity and accuracy are relevant for news organizations anywhere and are imperatives for news outlets such as news agencies or public service broadcasters. But impartiality will be qualified by the importance of sense making – variously called analysis, opinion, commentary – and the increased importance of the individual voice. In a world in which most people have access to far more information than they had previously, the problem is not acquiring information but sifting the reliable from the dodgy. But the quantity of information also raises the premium on being able to sort it, illuminate its meaning and importance. That also boosts the importance of individual voice. The power of habit or subscription is weaker in a digital information economy where the consumer can rapidly switch source. Attention, a vital currency, is more easily secured and kept by an individual voice. There will be some publications whose claim on readers' attention will be based on their collective qualities, but they will remain a small minority.[14] Many sites in the 'new guard' in the United States, such as Vox Media, are alliances of dozens or hundreds of blogs done by individuals or small teams.

- That is only one adaptation that journalism will make. Editors and writers have adapted slowly to realizing that the future possibilities and shape of journalism will be explored by experts in software, code and information architecture. Many of the examples of success I have mentioned base their competitive edge on a well-designed 'back end', which no user ever sees but will experience as 'ease of do'. Most editors are adjusting equally slowly to the idea that the front page is no longer the front door, the route by which most users enter the bundle of content under a 'brand' title. Only 12 per cent of visitors to the *Atlantic*'s website start at the front page. There is no agreement on what is the most effective way of telling stories on digital media: trial and error rules. That is partly because no one has hammered out what combination of words, sound and images wins more often than another. But it is also because operating systems and devices constantly change: there is no equivalent of the newspaper broadsheet page to focus the development of storytelling syntax.

● It has taken time but we are now seeing the emergence of multi-channel news outlets, which are competing against each other as global players. This group ranges from business-oriented sites such as the *Wall Street Journal*, *Financial Times* and Bloomberg to those with broader agendas such as the BBC, Al-Jazeera (in English), CNN and China's CCTV News. The BBC currently runs the world's largest news-gathering organization, employing 6,000 people worldwide. CCTV's global operation, when fully developed, is expected to overtake the BBC total. These organizations have the levy income (BBC), the state's resources (Al-Jazeera, CCTV) or subscription income (Bloomberg, *Financial Times*) to keep expanding well outside their original core market. Several newspaper websites such as the *New York Times* and *The Guardian* would like to count themselves as in this group, but it is not yet clear if either paper can overcome its financial weaknesses to expand to compete in the long term.

Journalism's platform is moving, in a literal sense. In Britain, print circulations have fallen at an average of 3.08 per cent every six months in the five years to 2012. If that rate of decline continued, the 10-year drop would be 45 per cent. Compare that with smartphone data. In 2012, the volume of data exchanged on the world's smartphones was estimated as 0.9 exabytes.[15] By 2017, that figure is expected to be 11.2 exabytes, a compound annual growth rate of 66 per cent.[16] Journalism does not have to abandon its original purpose or values; but it does have to adapt. If information flows like liquid in and out of devices 24 hours a day, journalism's value lies in something it has done before: sifting, distilling, taking the signal from the noise. A 2011 survey asked people to describe how they felt about the information flow from the internet. More than two-thirds (72 per cent) picked the description 'a roaring rover, a flood or massive tidal wave'.[17] Journalism's function has often been to organize information so that what is most important is available and accessible. The world's information flow creates a demand: it is up to journalism to supply it.

The evolutionary renewal of journalism has many precedents. The age of mass media will leave an imprint on the coming era of social, dispersed media. But the last century, when journalists were part of industrial oligopolies, may well have been historically unusual. Journalism cannot survive without adapting again. The determinants of success or failure are the quantity and quality of experiment. Journalism's recent history has shown that existing institutions have been slow and cautious to experiment radically and disruptively enough inside their own organizations. Experiments have not been numerous enough nor good enough. Agile challengers have done better. The size and stability of many legacy media companies have insulated their journalists and managers from having to consider precisely how to deliver a value that will be recognized in the new era. These newsrooms have precious expertise if journalists can come to see how the value of what they do can be adapted and refashioned.

*****

This book has pointed to a few of the directions that journalism may take. Because journalism lives on the frontier between democratic purposes and the commercial market, it is constantly being reorganized and renegotiated. But for all the fluctuations, something of enduring worth is captured by the term 'journalism'. That value now has to be made visible again by a new generation.

Notes

1 http://www.guardian.co.uk/media/2012/mar/21/johnston-press-ashley-highfield-paywall (accessed 25.2.13).

2 Grueskin, B, Seave, A and Graves, D (2011) *The Story So Far: What We Know About the Business of Digital Journalism*, Columbia Journalism School, New York. http://cjr.org/the_business_of_digital_journalism/

3 Disclosure: I am a trustee of the BIJ.

4 Michael Massing (2009) 'A new horizon for the news' in *New York Review of Books*, 24 September.

5 http://newsosaur.blogspot.co.uk/2010/03/non-profits-cant-possibly-save-news.html (accessed 24.2.13).

6 The newspaper is owned by a cooperative of 12,000 readers.

7 http://www.huffingtonpost.co.uk/gates-cambridge-scholars/were-drowning-rightaccoun_b_1609027.html (accessed 25.2.13).

8 PaidContent Live conference, New York, April 2013.

9 Andrew Gruen, presentation to digital journalism conference, Sciences Po, Paris, December 2012.

10 Brooke, H (2012) *The Revolution will be Digitized*, Windmill Books, London.

11 http://www.carnegieuktrust.org.uk/publications/2012/better-journalism-in-the-digital-age-%28full-report%29 (accessed 20.5.13).

12 Figures from Committee to Protect Journalists: **http://cpj.org/killed/2012/** and **http://cpj.org/imprisoned/2012.php** (accessed 27.2.13).

13 Annual conference of professors of journalism, Moscow State University, 10 February 2013.

14 *The Economist*, with very few individual by-lines, would be the best-known example.

15 An exabyte is one billion gigabytes.

16 http://www.mondaynote.com/2013/03/03/growing-forces-in-mobile.

17 Survey by Magnify.net. Quoted in **http://www.nieman.harvard.edu/reports/article/102798/Breaking-News.aspx** (accessed 8.3.13).

INDEX

NB page numbers in *italic* indicate figures or tables

DATE DUE

1 FEB 2020